MUSLIM NATIONHOOD IN INDIA

PERCEPTIONS OF SEVEN EMINENT THINKERS

MUSLIM NATIONHOOD IN INDIA

PERCEPTIONS OF SEVEN EMINENT THINKERS

SAFIA AMIR

Foreword by
Prof. Akhtar-ul-Wasey

KANISHKA PUBLISHERS, DISTRIBUTORS
NEW DELHI-110 002

KANISHKA PUBLISHERS, DISTRIBUTORS
4697/5-21A, Ansari Road, Daryaganj
New Delhi-110 002
Phones : 327 0497, 328 8285
Fax : 91-328 8285

First Published 2000

ISBN 81-7391-335-8

PRINTED IN INDIA

Published by Madan Sachdeva for Kanishka Publishers, Distributors, 4697/5-21A, Ansari Road, Daryaganj, New Delhi-110 002; Typeset by Vidhi Laser Point, Delhi, and Printed at Nice Printing Press, Delhi.

ACKNOWLEDGEMENTS

This book began as a doctoral dissertation, and I must thank Professor Akhtarul Wasey, who is largely responsible for its appearing before the public eye in its present form. The original work was made possible due to a research fellowship granted by the Hamdard National Foundation, and an opportunity to work in Jamia Hamdard.

Professor Anwar Moazzam deserves special thanks for showing me the direction, and guiding my first uncertain steps. My supervisor Dr. Baseer Aḥmad Khān was kind enough to see my work through despite his numerous preoccupations. I also wish to record my indebtedness to all the members of the Departments of Islamic Studies in both Jamia Hamdard and Jamia Millia Islamia for their ungrudging co-operation and valuable advice. I owe a special debt of gratitude to Professor Shees Mohammad Ismail Azmi for his generous help and fatherly solicitude. I also wish to thank the staff of the various libraries where I have had the pleasure to work, foremost being the Central Library at Jamia Hamdard, and the Zakir Husain Library at Jamia Millia Islamia.

Much of the credit for this work goes to my husband. But for his patient support and constant encouragement, it might never have seen the light of day. My two little daughters deserve no less credit for putting up with gross neglect. I have been constantly motivated by their innocent idealism and keen curiosity. All the members of my larger family too have contributed in their own way. Their blessings and support have meant more to me than words can say.

FOREWORD

The concept of nationhood has had a prominent place in Indian political discourse ever since the emergence of national consciousness in this part of the world. The discussion has acquired new dimension on account of the new developments both at the macro- and micro-levels in the last half century, impinging upon this consciousness. At the macro-level rapid advances in the field of information technology reducing the world to a global village has brought question marks on the validity and viability of nationalism. The trend of globalization in the economic and political thinking has pitted the idea of world-citizenship against citizenship of a particular nation. Nation-states are facing the challenge of abridgement of sovereignty. The fear is particularly strong in countries which have attained independence from colonial rule after the Second World War. They are struggling to safeguard their interests in the new world order in which not only economic and political but also cultural domination of the former colonizing nations, with strong economic and military power, is seen manifest.

Principles of democracy are evoked both in support of globalization as well as in defence of national sovereignty. Protection of national identities and interests are sought on the basis of equality and justice without which fraternational co-operation among nations, a pre-condition for peaceful development of human society, is considered hard to achieve. The same principles at the micro-level calls for protection of human rights which boils down to protection of individuals and communities incapable of defending themselves against the power of nation-state.

The concepts of nationalism, nationhood and nation-state are a comparatively new development in human history. Nationalism has been defined as "a state of mind in which the supreme loyalty of the individual is felt to be due to the nation-state."* Its emergence is traced to end of eighteenth century although because of its popularity some protagonists of nationalism tend to treat it as if it is as old as human civilization. Fact is that till the end of eighteenth century loyalties were attached variously to native soil, paternal tradition or established territorial authority in the form of city state or religion or ruler of a particular territory. They are now treated as religious, tribal, communal and regional loyalties which nationhood demands of individuals to supersede or rise above.

In Europe where this concept took shape first, the feeling of nationalism resulted from perceived competition of people living in one territory with those of another. The competitors were bound together with a sense of identity based on commonness of language, religion, culture and territory. In colonized countries like India the perception was due to a feeling of unjust treatment by colonizers or imperial powers who considered people of colonies as inferior requiring to be civilized. The European and American states where the idea became operational people formalized their national bonds on the basis of what have come to be known as the democratic principles like equality, fraternity and social justice. Oppressed people of colonies reacted to their situation by asserting that the democratic principles which governed what were called the mother countries should also be applied in their case too. Revolting against the sense of racial superiority displayed by the imperialists they invoked their own religio-cultural traditions to assert that they were no less civilized than their imperialist rulers. Nationalism therefore found expression in terms of demand for equality, freedom and right of self-determination. Exploiter-exploited relationship was sought to be replaced by equality and self-determination. Growth of nationalism or nationhood was therefore less problematic in those colonial countries where populations were religiously or ethnically homogeneous. Growth of Indian national consciousness had to be seen in this context and discussion on the subject has to be predicated on the fact that it is a country of vast ethno-cultural and religious diversity. National unity therefore will stand not only on perceived threat perception but also on the confidence that diversity would be respected and different segments accorded equal treatment by the nation-state.

This book, presenting the concepts of nationhood among seven selected Indian Muslim thinkers, is a contribution to the discussion on the role of Muslims in shaping Indian nationalism. Partition of British India simultaneously with the departure of the colonial power and the birth of a separate nation-state on the basis of claim to religion-based

---

* *Encyclopaedia Britannica,* Vol. 16, page 60, 1969, USA.

nationhood touched off a debate on which the Muslim community is alleged to harbour separatist tendencies. The seven thinkers discussed here represent the broad spectrum of Muslim response to Indian nationalism. Interestingly almost all of them are votaries of harmonious relations between the various religious communities. From the facts presented it should be possible to discuss what circumstances led some of them to think of Muslims as a separate nation and establishing a separate nation-state of Muslims. Proper objective understanding of the phenomenon will be of immense help in formulation of ideas on Hindu-Muslim relations, indeed about relations among all communities, and promote national integration which comes under severe strain from time to time. It will be helpful not only for India but also for other developing countries in similar situation. Experience has proved that neither religion nor ethnicity is strong enough binding force for well-integrated nationhood. Nor is it possible to completely obliterate what are called primordial loyalties and develop a single and uniform identity; multiplicity of loyalties and identities have to be recognized and respected as has been done in the formulation of the Constitution of free India. Strains appear when we deviate or seem to deviate from norms set therein.

Of the seven discussed here Sir Sayyad Aḥmad Khān is a typical case of misunderstanding arising from neglect of historical perspective. He has been pejoratively described as a loyalist because as the author says his political stance stemmed from his conviction that "British rule was here to stay for none else could govern India; it was folly to challenge its authority since it had proved itself invincible and its permanence would be beneficial for Indians, and particularly Muslims."

The allegation would be valid if the country as a whole were in a mood to and capable of severing the British connection. The revolt in 1856-57 had been roundly defeated and its remnants were only the Ulama who were desperately but unsuccessfully trying to recharge the spirit of revolt. The anarchy that had prevailed in the last days of the Moghul rule had made people welcome the British rule as a blessing. The British had succeeded in winning over bulk of the population and suppressing the opponents, the Muslims being the main target. The Hindus had adjusted themselves to the situation. Sir Sayyad only wanted them to follow the example of their brethren and take to modern education so that they were not left behind in affairs of governance.

Sir Sayyad's plea for extending co-operation to British rule came in this historical background and, as the author recognizes, it was not for the benefit of Muslims alone but for India as a whole. If the Muslim community is particularized it is because in the post-1858 period they were the worst hit. And non-co-operation till then was not the policy of any section except for a handful of Ulama whose advice could have kept the community educationally and economically backward.

It must also not be overlooked that national sovereignty in the modern sense had never existed in India till that time as throughout the known history till that time sovereignty was the attribute of the sovereign, the king, the ruler by inheritance or conquest and the people owed allegiance to whoever had sway over a particular territory. And the extent of the territory depended upon the military power that the ruler was able to muster. So far as territorial sovereignty was concerned no ruler yielded to another whatever the religious equation among them. The powerful Muslim rulers who preceded the British rule, the Pathans or Moghals, never accepted the Turkish Khilāfat even though they never denied or ignored the Muslim obligation to perform Haj.

The demands for right to participate in governance during the British rule was being raised at regional level platforms but it never took the form of even home rule under the crown. Even when the regional associations were brought together to set up a pan-Indian movement, the Indian National Congress, it was pleading the case on the plea that Indian participation would help the Crown administration to better attend to grievances of the subjects and consolidate the rule. The annual conferences of this new political formation always ended with reiterated allegiance to the Crown by singing 'Long Live the King.'

Significantly the demand was made not for extending democratic rights to all people but for the educated Indians most of whom were Hindus. Indeed most of the leaders of the Congress enjoyed patronage of the British and betrayed no intention to forego it. The Congress was also well aware of the reality that different communities needed to be welded together into a nation. It is pertinent to refer to the Presidential Address of W.C. Banerji, the President of the first session of the Congress which he described as "the first National Assembly ever yet convened in India." Elucidating the aims and objects of the Congress he placed them under the following heads:

(*a*) The promotion of personal intimacy and friendship amongst all the more earnest workers in our country's cause in the different parts of the Empire.

(*b*) The eradication by direct friendly personal intercourse, of all possible race, creed, or provincial prejudices amongst all lovers of our country, and the fuller development and consolidation of those sentiments of national unity that had their origin in their beloved Lord Ripon's ever memorable reign.

(c) The authoritative record, after this has been carefully elicited, by the fullest discussions of the matured opinions of the educated class in India on some of the more important and pressing of the social questions of the day.

(d) The determination of the lines upon, and methods by which, during the next twelve months, it is desirable for native politicians to labour in the public interests.

It is therefore less than fair to single out Sir Sayyad for accusation as a loyalist. He was only calling upon a community which had lagged behind in the race for equipping themselves for participation in any activity to serve the country in any form to equip themselves for serving both the country and the community. His plea in fact was for enablement before empowerment. And in this endeavour he never, by word or deed, promoted hatred or discrimination against Hindus or any other community. On the contrary he never deviated from the belief that Hindus and Muslims, the two major religious communities of India, were like two eyes of a beautiful bride and that damage to any one of them would disfigure the bride.

The use of the word 'nation' or its 'Hindustani' equivalent *qawm* had not yet acquired the definitive meaning that it has in contemporary discourse. It was used indeed more for communities whether religious, regional, caste or tribal. When Sir Sayyad talks of making Muslims a nation it has to be understood that he meant to unify them by developing harmonious relations among the various sects of Muslims and fostering a realization of the need to be in step with the march of civilisation. A confident Muslim community, free from a sense of insecurity would certainly be a positive factor in building a strong and united Indian nation.

What had created suspicion in the mind of Sir Sayyad was the treatment being meted out to Urdu and demand for enforcement of Hindi as sole official language. Urdu is not a foreign language; it is born in India and has grown in this country with the contribution of all communities. Its exclusion from the business of government meant denial of employment opportunities to a large number of Muslims. Besides it is a fact that most of the religious literature used by Indian Muslims is in Urdu and if they are divorced from this language their very identity would be endangered, Sir Sayyad was pleading in its behalf only to keep equal opportunities open to Muslims and to preserve their religio-cultural identity.

Without going into further details it can be said that had his pleas on the language question not been met with hostility he would have come to think of nationhood in the same way as others. Of course only when the consciousness of the entire country had reached that stage. From the discussion of other six thinkers presented here there should be no doubt left that none of them was an advocate of separate state of Muslims though all of them did dearly value and cherish the distinct Muslim religio-cultural identity. Even M.A. Jinnāh, the founder of Pakistan, was till mid-thirties an ardent advocate of common nationhood and by his conduct earned the description as "ambassador of Hindu-Muslim unity." Only when he despaired of getting justice at the hands of the majority community he changed course and campaigned for a separate state of Muslims. The solution to the problem he suggested and forced may not have proved to be the solution but his view of common nationhood survived even Partition.

By discussing this perspective my intention is neither to defend Sir Sayyad nor to endorse Partition. Separation has ill-served the entire subcontinent and all communities. History has proved that national unity and progress has not been assured by appeal to Islam or to any other religious sentiment. And development of common nationhood is impeded if justice and fair play are ignored. This book can help us identify our failures and weaknesses in the march towards nationhood and national integration.

Hony. Director
Zakir Husain Institute of Islamic Studies
Jamia Millia Islamia
New Delhi

Prof. Akhtar-ul-Wasey

CONTENTS

INTRODUCTION

This work attempts to explore the nature of Muslim existence in pre-independence India, as reflected in the thought of the following Indian Muslim personalities: Sayyad Aḥmad Khān, Shibli Nu'māni, Muḥammad Iqbāl, Muḥammad 'Ali Jinnāh, Abu'l Kalām Āzād, Sayyad Ḥusayn Aḥmad Madani, and Sayyad Abu'l A'la Mawdūdi. The question is whether or not we can detect in their ideas any concept of Muslims being distinct, as a community, from other segments of Indian society, and thus possessing a sense of nationhood. If so, an effort is made to examine what they regarded as the basis of this separateness: religion, culture, history, or language — the different constituents of nationhood.

This work focuses on the crucial period spanning the revolt of 1875 and independece in 1947, when the question of identity was being most hotly debated. Although the creation of Pakistan was a watershed in this respect, yet it has far from resolved the issue, and has indeed thrown up more questions than it has answered. Many of the issues raised herein regarding Muslim nationhood have refused to die out: they may have altered somewhat in the changed scenario, but their significance persists, and has even acquired a new urgency.

This work is being offered as an academic and critical interpretation of statements, developments and facts, aimed at furthering our understanding of the enigma of Muslim identity in India, as we stand on the threshold of a new millennium. Indeed the outgoing century has witnessed intense debate regarding the identity of various political, racial, religious, cultural and liguistic groups. Although Muslim behaviour in India has attracted the attention of scholars, no such study on the subject has been attempted in the past, which systematically analyses the factors constituting the Indian Muslim presence, *i.e.* its nationhood.

The personalities selected for this study are not only representative of significant trends, but have also made a lasting impact on Muslim thought and opinion in India. Yet, the limitations of any such work demand that even some important thinkers possessing a rare insight in the subject must perforce be excluded due to practical constraints. This study is for the most part based on primary sources. Although it does not claim to be exhaustive, an earnest attempt has been made to tap all the available material.

Chronological sequence has been kept in mind while arranging the chapters (each of which is devoted to a thinker rather than a theme), as well as the material within each. This helps to trace the evolution of the central ideas in the work over a period of time, as well as to follow the intellectual development of each thinker. Although points of interest, comparison and contrast are indicated as they arise, the different thematic threads are taken up for full discussion and analysis in the Conclusion. An analysis of the poetic works (where they exist) of the thinkers is not within the scope of this work, which limits itself to prose expressions of views.

It would do well to elucidate some of the key terms used in the work. The Urdu word *qawm* (which has been defined as "a people; tribe, race, family; sect or caste", and rarely as "group" [1]), has most often been translated as "nation": where otherwise, this has been duly indicated in the text. The fact that the single word *qawmiyyat* may be employed for "nationality", "nationhood" as well as "nationalism" [2], creates some complexity, and has been translated accordingly. *Millat* and *ummat* are Arabic words which mean "nation" and "followers (of a faith)", but in Urdu usage signify often "the Muslim nation." *Ummat* also connotes disciples, adherents, and brethren in faith.[3]

Whereas it is nearly universally agreed that a "nation" is a large "community" or "extensive aggrate of persons so closely associated with each other by common descent, language, or history, as to form a distinct race or people"; there is much difference of opinion as to how far unity of religion, territory and government constitute necessary criteria for its existence. (In case the last two conditions are fulfilled, the "nation" would become a "country" or "nation state"). A common consciousness of myth and shared experience, as also common institutions, traditions, customs, and a sense of social homogeneity and mutual interest have also been regarded as hallmarks of a nation.[4]

"Nationality" has often been equated with the "nation" itself. While it may signify "separate or complete existence as a nation", it also frequently denotes "a people potentially but not actually a nation"; or "a national group" which may or may not form part of one or more "politically independent" countries. Nationality also signifies distinctive national quality, characters or trait. It also connotes "nationhood" *i.e.* "the state or fact of being a nation."[5] Nationhood may also be described as national or group consciousness.

It is important to differentiate between "nationhood" and "nationalism", which implies a strong feeling of love, loyalty and pride in one's nation, leading to the advocacy of national interests and unity. Its goal is often "political" and "cultural self determination": the desire "to be separate, distinct, and independent from other nations, and equal to them."[6] It is a modern movement which became generally recognized only at the end of the eighteenth century. The American and French revolutions may be regarded as its first powerful manifestations. The nineteenth century, whose political thought was dominated by this concept, has been called the age of nationalism in Europe.

"Nationalistic" thus means "strongly favouring nationalism"; while a "nationalist" is one characterized by national sympathies, or a believer in nationalism. While "patriotism" also signifies loyal support, love and devotion for one's country, it may be differentiated from "nationalism" which turns this devotion into "principles or programmes", whereas mere patriotism can be "devoid of any project for political action."[7]

A few words regarding the scheme of transliteration. The letters of the Urdu-Arbic alphabet are transcribed as follows, in Urdu alphabetical order.

a b p t ṯ th j ch ḥ kh d ḏ dh r z s sh ṣ ḍ ṭ ẓ ' gh f q k g l m n ṇ w h y

Hamza is written as', *tā marbūtah* as *ah* and *alif maqsūrah* as *á*. The short vowels used are: *a i u ;* and *ā ī ū* for long. The Urdu vowels *e* and *o* are always long. *Ay* and *aw* denote the diphthongs. The Arabic article is transcribed as *al.*

Notes and References

1. *A Dictionary of Urdu, Classical Hindi and English* (1986) ; Dr. Mawlwi Abdul Haq, *Urdu English Dictionary* (J.S. Sant Singh and Sons, Delhi).
2. *Qawmi English/Urdu Dictionary* (Delhi).

3. *Standard Twentieth Century Dictionary*: *Urdu into English.*
4. *The Oxford English Dictionary* (1970); *Oxford Advanced Learner's Dictionary of Current English* (1996); *Webster's New Collegiate Dictionary* (1961); *The Random House Dictionary of the English Language* (1983); *The Concise Oxford Dictionary of Politics* (1996).
5. *Ibid., The Concise Oxford Dictionary of Current English*; *Cambridge International Dictionary of English* (1995), *Chambers English Dictionary* (1990).
6. *Ibid.*
7. *Ibid.*

Chapter 1

SAYYAD AḤMAD KHĀN (1817-1898)

What is *qawm*?

Before we begin to analyse Sir Sayyad's views regarding nationhood, it would be pertinent to first study his usage of the word *qawm* itself. We discover that he employed it rather loosely, to connote various shades of meaning.

Sometimes Sir Sayyad used the word to denote "class", "caste", or even merely a "social group". He thus described *kāyasths*, gypsies, tanners, *sayyads, shaykhs, nawābs, muftīs* and *qāḍīs* as *qawms.*[1] Elsewhere he asked candidates wishing to go abroad, to mention their *qawm* and *madhhab* in the application form, alongwith other particulars.[2]

Sir Sayyad most frequently employed the word in its common and loosely-defined sense of "people", "race", and "nation". He thus referred to the English, French, Germans, Greeks, Egyptians, Turks, Arabs, and Persians etc. as *qawms.* It is interesting to observe that he described both "the people of Hind" collectively, as well as Hindus, Muslims, Bengalis, and Parsis etc. individually, as *qawms.*[3] On one occasion he implied that every *qawm* has its own particular country and language.[4] *Qawm* may thus be used simultaneously for the world community of Muslims, as well as to signify their different "nationalities".[5] Similarly, in the same passage *qawm* may refer both to the Indian Muslim community, and to the social classes within it.[6]

It is therefore not surprising to see Sir Sayyad frequently using *qawm* for Indians generally, as well as the Muslim community particularly, in the same breath.[7] At times he clarified as to what specifically he meant by the term[8], but at others, his tendency to communicate on different planes simultaneously, and to continually shift the perspective, causes considerable ambiguity.[9]

Thus it is, that while Sir Sayyad was only too conscious of the multiplicity of religion and *qawms* in India[10] (often comparing it with Europe in this regard[11]), he tried repeatedly to reconcile this with the idea of India as a single *qawm*. He emphasized that a country had an organic relationship with the various *qawms* of which it was composed (see *infra* pp. 7-8). India's "national pride" was thus not the separate, but the cumulative honour of all its *qawms*, to be attained by their collective education, "irrespective of their religion, and country of origin."[12]

Sir Sayyad emphasized the similarities between the Indian *qawms*, and the fact that for a foreigner they were all equally and indistinguishably "Hindustani", in spite of their internal differences.[13] On the same grounds he repeatedly juxtaposed Indians and the British as two different *qawms*: the ruler, and the ruled, the native and the foreign.[14] On one occasion he credited British rule with uniting "under one sceptre, the various peoples of this vast continent."[15]

Hindu-Muslim Relations

It would now do well to study Sir Sayyad's perception of the relationship between the two major Indian communities, and its practical manifestation in his own life.

The Revolt and After

Writing the *Asbāb-i-Baghāwat-i Hind* in 1858, Sir Sayyad (he remained strictly loyal to the British during the revolt of 1857) referred to the Hindus and Muslims as "mutually antagonistic nations" (*qawms* in the original). However he felt that in the army, the constant intercourse caused by the intermingling of both groups in each regiment, had generated friendship and brotherhood, and obliterated former divisions. He shrewdly observed that this unity had proved disastrous for the revolt, which might have been averted had the regiments been ordered on an exclusively religious basis.[16]

It is however interesting to observe that while describing the fierce fighting in Bijnawr between Hindus and Muslims during the revolt, in another work of the same period *i.e. Tārīkh-i Sarkashī-i-Ḍila' Bijnawr*[17], Sir Sayyad hastened to make the point that before this there had never been any animosity or conflict between the two communities in Bijnawr. They had not only lived together amicably, but had also intermingled harmoniously. Nevertheless, irrespective of their condition before the revolt, he sensed clearly that the fighting during it had bred fierce religious hatred and animosity between them. He felt that the tree of Hindu-Muslim aversion planted during the revolt had become "very tall and too firmly rooted to be dug out." We thus get two very conflicting pictures of the revolt: both as a unifying and a divisive force; and of Hindus and Muslims too: as fundamentally hostile as well as basically friendly.

However, in spite of his perception of these differences, Sir Sayyad himself never exhibited the least prejudice, bigotry or ill-will. On the other hand, as a government servant (he had joined the Judicial Services of the East India Company in 1838-39, and was made a Munsif in 1841), he conducted himself with perfect fairness and justice. His reputation for impartiality was so well-known that the people trusted him completely, and even his superiors were impressed by it. When he was put in charge of Bijnawr, in spite of the deep ill-feeling there, the Hindus eagerly welcomed the decision.[18]

Rājā Jai Kishan Das, who was later to become a close friend and associate of Sir Sayyad describes how, on reading *The Loyal Muḥammadans* he had suspected Sir Sayyad to be "a prejudiced bigot who had no sympathy with the Hindus." However he realised how mistaken he had been when he first met Sir Sayyad during the famine in Muradabad in 1860, serving alike all the victims at the relief centre—sincerely and sympathetically, without regard to race and religion. Thenceforth a lasting friendship sprang up between the two men.[19]

Sir Sayyad's biographer Mawlāna Alṭāf Ḥusayn Ḥāli cites these and other incidents as evidence of Sir Sayyad's complete disregard for religious distinctions, and his desire to create national unity and social harmony. Far from excluding Hindus from national matters, his very purpose in setting up the Scientific Society at Ghazipur in 1863-64, was to further friendship and understanding between the British and Indians—Hindus and Muslims alike. The society also undertook the translation of English works on the physical sciences into Urdu. Its organ, the bi-lingual *Scientific Society Gazette* (published from 1866 onwards, and later to become the *Aligarh Institute Gazette*), remained impartial towards all communities, and neutral in the religious strife between Hindus and Muslims, urging both sides towards peace and reconciliation.[20]

In May 1866 Sir Sayyad formed the British Indian Association in order to enable Indians to set up connections with the British parliament, and thus secure greater rights from the government. Its members were again, both Hindus and Muslims.[21]

In keeping with this attitude, while speaking at a meeting of the Muḥammadan Literary Society in 1863, after defining "patriotism" as the sacred duty enjoined by the Prophet (Pbuh), to wish and work for the good of fellow-Muslims, Sir Sayyad did not hesitate to urge his audience to exert themselves to the utmost for the welfare of their fellow-countrymen as well, of whatever denomination or sect.[22]

Similarly, in *An Account of the Loyal Muḥammadans of India* (written in 1860), Sir Sayyad hastened to absolve himself of any charge of partisanship or bias although he was writing in praise of his co-religionists, for as he wrote, he was "a Muslim as well as a native of Hindustan."[23] In an incomplete and undated letter to an Englishman also, he described himself as "a Muslim, a native of Hindustan, and of Arab descent."[24] He apparently accepted such a multiple identity as a matter of fact.

Urdu Versus Hindi

The Urdu-Hindi controversy broke out in 1867, with the opponents of Urdu refusing to accept it as *the* vernacular of India, and striving to replace it as the official language, by Hindi written in the Devanāgri script.[25]

Sir Sayyad felt that the Hindus wished to wipe out Urdu which was in fact only an advanced form of Bhāsha, merely because its foundations were laid during Muslim rule.[26] It was this unjustified hostility and aggressiveness on their part which apparently pained him. For him Urdu was undeniably "our language" and "the vernacular of Hindustan." Irrespective of whether or not it was "the original language of the country", what mattered was that it was the only language which was universally used in India.[27]

According to Ḥāli, since Sir Sayyad was convinced that the Hindus were motivated purely by racial prejudice, therefore unruffled by the displeasure of his Hindu friends, he never kept silent in the face of attacks on Urdu. He had a lengthy correspondence with the secretary of the committee formed for the restoration of Hindi, which was even made public.[28] There is a great deal of verbal quibbling in these letters of 1868, as to which was the "current mixed language" and the "original language" of India: Hindi or Urdu. Sir Sayyad denied that the latter contained numerous Persian words, which he felt were employed only by those who were also well-versed in Persian.[29] At that time the demand of the Hindus was turned down, apparently due to the greater currency of Urdu.[30]

In 1882 when Sir Sayyad was a member of the Viceroy's Legislative Council (he had been appointed to it in 1878 by Lord Lytton), the Hindus of the North-West Province and Panjab again opposed Urdu, this time in the Education Commission. The Anjuman-i Ḥimāyat-i Urdu, formed by some friends of Sir Sayyad, also presented its counter-claims. It was widely believed that Sir Sayyad prevailed upon the Commission not to take a decision on a matter which according to him was a grave national and political, rather than an educational issue.[31]

During a speech in Patna on 27 January 1883 Sir Sayyad described Urdu as the language of neither Hindus nor Muslims, but a new creation—the product of their thorough interaction.[32] Urdu was thus for him a symbol of their composite culture, and any attack on it was a blow to their solidarity.

In March 1898 some Hindus again presented a memorandum to the Lieutenant Governor of the North-West Province. Although Sir Sayyad was then in great mental anguish and virtually on his deathbed, he wrote an article highlighting the popularity and currency of Urdu among both Hindus and Muslims. It was published in the *Institute Gazette* just nine days prior to his demise. At the same time he also proffered advice to the committee formed in support of Urdu, assuring it of his whole-hearted help.[33]

S. Abid Husain[34] blames Sir Sayyad for taking an "emotional" rather than a "realistic" view of this new trend of Hindu "renaissance"; the assertion by the Hindus of their "separate cultural entity"; and efforts to "safeguard their special interests." However the issue appeared significant to Sir Sayyad perhaps not so much because he saw in it the beginnings of Hindu revivalism and communal consciousness as suggested by Moin Shakir[35]; but since he perceived the anti-Muslim, hostile, and aggressive character of the movement. Ḥāli treats the eruption of the Urdu-Hindi controversy as a watershed in the life of Sir Sayyad, when for the first time he felt that Hindus and Muslims could not work together as a single nation (*qawm*) for the good of all. He would have us believe that Sir Sayyad now began to think in terms of the advancement of Muslims alone, whereas earlier he had always been concerned with the welfare of Indians as a whole. He is even reported to have predicted greater discord and hostility in the future, whereas earlier he had always believed in, and acted upon the principle of complete unity. The protests of Bengali newspapers against concessions made by the government to Muslims, and their writings against that community further compounded matters. However even Ḥāli acknowledges that in spite of these deterrents Sir Sayyad's desire for unity between the two communities remained unchanged, as is evident from his later public speeches.[36]

From the above account it is evident how strongly Sir Sayyad felt about the attempts to wipe out Urdu, and what a keen interest he took in foiling such bids. He was apparently quick to perceive the deep and far-reaching implications of the conflict, and that explains why he exerted himself so much in the matter. We however hold that although the outbreak of the controversy caused him great distress and heartburn, he did not allow himself to be embittered by it. This is evident from the fact that even after 1867 many of his plans for the education and upliftment of Muslims were specially moulded so as to include Hindus in their purview. Thus, in spite of the challenge posed by the controversy to Hindu-Muslim unity, he never abandoned his conviction that such a unity was possible, and continued to work towards it with characteristic determination.

We find a clue to Sir Sayyad's attitude in a letter that he wrote to Nawāb Moḥsin-al Mulk in April 1870, in which he again prophesied a parting of ways for the two communities as a result of the vexatious quarrel. On the face of it he feels that this would be in the interest of Muslims, but on second thoughts he is compelled to acknowledge that they were severely handicapped by their weaknesses, and would not in fact prove self-sufficient. Finally he confessed that by his very nature he desired the welfare of all Indians irrespective of their religious belief.[37]

The Post-1867 Phase

In 1868, *i.e.* only a year after the debate was sparked off, Sir Sayyad set up the Civil Service Fund to assist Indians—both Hindus and Muslims—to travel to Europe for their education. The scheme however did not prove successful due to the widespread superstitions against such a journey, which was also very difficult. About a decade later these problems had been more or less been surmounted, and Indians had begun to go abroad for study. Sir Sayyad then felt that it was more difficult for Muslims to travel to England in order to appear for the Civil Service Examination. He therefore founded the Muḥammadan Civil Service Fund Association in 1883.[38] During his visit to Panjab next year, some Hindus requested him to include them within the scope of the organization. Sir Sayyad reminded them that he had targeted both groups when he had first initiated the scheme. However, finding the circumstances unfavourable and complete success unattainable, he was forced to content himself with partial success by limiting its scope to Muslims. He made it clear that it would be a grave error to deduce on this basis that he did not sympathize with his Hindu brethren, or that he desired the welfare of his co-religionists only. In fact he vehemently denied that such a thought had occurred, or could ever occur to him.[39]

Again in 1877 Sir Sayyad initiated a scheme for building an orphanage that would house both Hindu and Muslim children (who would be brought up according to their own faith), and urged members of both communities to help towards the noble cause.[40] In August 1882 he himself donated a gold medal to be awarded to the Hindu student passing the B.A. exam of the M.A.O. College with first division.[41] (He had founded the College in 1875 with financial help from both communities. In 1876 he retired from government service to devote himself to his educational efforts.)

In a speech in February 1884 Sir Sayyad confessed his feeling of national (*qawmi*) sympathy and enthusiasm for the welfare of the country, and the education of *all* its children. This had compelled him to serve his "nation" (comprising both Hindus and Muslims), as an educationist and a member of the Legislative Council, and to strive to "make it a nation"[42] (*Cf. infra* pp. 15-16).

This idea of Hindus and Muslims jointly forming a single nation occurs frequently in his speeches of 1884 (see *infra* p.11 *ff.*), wherein Sir Sayyad also attempts to rationalize his method of working for the good of all. Highlighting the factor of interdependence, he likened a nation to an organism which could not thrive and prosper without the well-being of all its component parts. Those who desired its welfare should therefore work for the betterment of all its inhabitants, irrespective of religion and race.[43]

Sir Sayyad emphasized that Hindus and Muslims should co-operate for their joint progress, which was as inseparable as their decline.[44] Not only these two, but all the communities (*qawm*) of India should unite for its well-being, or else they would perish. Mutual friendship on the other hand would ensure their individual, and above all, collective well-being. He therefore denounced those who did not see the point and tried to sow discord between the two communities.[45]

Sir Sayyad's attitude endeared him to the Hindus, who held him in great esteem. While bearing testimony to his efforts to improve the lot of Muslims, in an address presented to him in February 1884, the Hindus of Panjab also took note of his liberal and large-hearted attitude towards other sections of the population, which was evident from the fact that the doors of the M.A.O. College were open to all. They absolved his public career of any stain of bias or bigotry, acknowledging his impartial care for all. Above all they appreciated his services as a member of the Legislative Council, and his faithful championing of national views and interests.[46] As Wilfred Cantwell Smith[47] has truly remarked, in his early days the problem of communalism "on an important scale did not exist, and to be interested in the welfare of one community, as Sayyad Aḥmad was, did not imply any antagonism to the others . . . his object was to help Muslims, but his methods were nothing exclusive."

Qawm and Watan

There is of course no denying that Sir Sayyad was fired by an ardent love for his community, which pervades his life and works. As he said in a speech on 26 January 1884, for him being from among the progeny of the Prophet (Pbuh) meant loving and serving his nation (*qawm*), as zealously as did his mentor. His self-avowed desire was to see it regain its lost glory, and to strive relentlessly towards this end.[48] His efforts for the education of Muslims were in keeping with his conviction that national (*qawmi*) education could be achieved in India only when every community (*qawm*) worked for its own instruction.[49]

Although these sentiments do not appear to conflict with Sir Sayyad's identity as an Indian, there does seem to be a certain tension between loyalty and service to the nation, and to the community; and what may be called an attempt at self-justification, even in the early period (see *supra* p. 4), which becomes more marked in the latter. Sir Sayyad was conscious of the dichotomy between country (*watan*) and community (*qawm*). In an article published in 1875 he admitted to being deeply moved by the motto of a Tunisian newspaper which equated love and striving for the motherland (*watan*) and country (*bilād*), with service of the faith. It is significant however, that when he adopted the motto for his newspaper, the *Tahdhīb-al Akhlāq* (published for about six years from December 1870 onwards), he substituted *qawm* for both *watan* and *bilād*,[50] thus altering the very meaning of the motto, and in effect transferring the sentiment of patriotism from the Indian nation to the Muslim community.

In two of his speeches in the Panjab in early 1884 Sir Sayyad separately thanked members of his community (*qawm*), and his fellow countrymen (*watani bhā'i*) of an alien race (*ghayr qawm*), for their hospitality and help in setting up the College in Aligarh,[51] thus highlighting the differences between the two groups even while he was trying to bring them closer.

In a speech on 26 January 1884, after urging Muslims to strive to secure high government posts, Sir Sayyad hastened to add that it would give him equal pleasure to see a Hindu occupying such a post, since the ultimate object was that Indians as a "nation" should attain equality with, and respect in the eyes of the alien ruling race.[52]

Justifying the setting up of the M.A.O. College specially for Muslims in the above speech and another on 3 February, Sir Sayyad made it clear that it had not been established to set them apart from Hindus, but only to remedy their utter deprivation of modern education, which necessitated making special arrangements for them. (He reassured his mixed audience that there was no discrimination within the College, both "brothers" receiving similar education, and enjoying equal rights including entitlement to scholarships etc.) He illustrated the situation by the analogy of one or more robust brothers, whose duty it was to help their sickly and weak sibling. He repeatedly thanked the Hindus who had donated generously in this spirit, towards the College.[53]

Sir Sayyad's attitude is best expressed in a letter to the editor of the *Pioneer* dated 22 September 1893, wherein he describes himself as "a true well-wisher of his fellow-countrymen generally, and his co-religionists specially."[54]

Hindu-Muslim Entente

In the speeches of 1883 and 1884 we find Sir Sayyad trying zealously to effect a rapproachement between the two major communities of India, whom he likened to the two chief organs of the body.[55] In fact he brings to bear upon the task all his eloquence and powers of reasoning.

In these speeches Sir Sayyad repeatedly made the point that the religious belief of Hindus and Muslims was immaterial. What mattered was the obvious fact that they lived on the same soil, under a single government, sharing joys and sorrows, and were indispensable to each other. Centuries of cohabitation in India had caused their blood to mingle, and they had become as one, exchanging numerous rites, customs and manners, and producing a new language Urdu, which was not the language of either. In the present too, they lived in great physical proximity and social intimacy. Any attempt to stay aloof was not only impossible, but would cause them to perish.[56]

It is interesting that Sir Sayyad repeated similar sentiments many years later in 1897—in spite of, and nearly a decade after his tirade against Hindus and the Congress. In this later article he added that while some Muslims could be said to be pure Aryans, others had mixed Aryan blood; and there could be no estrangement between them and Hindus since they had been living together, and sharing all aspects of life for centuries.[57]

Time and again Sir Sayyad likened the communities to the two eyes of a beautiful bride—India, and sometimes in his zeal for unity, even to a single eye.[58] He repeated the analogy in the article of 1897 also.[59]

In a speech on 27 January 1884, Sir Sayyad described God's intention in settling the two communities in India as being that "they should live and help each other as brothers."[60] Speaking at the Madrasah Islāmiyyah at Amritsar a day before, he had reminded the students that Islām encouraged its adherents to cultivate friendly relations with their companions. He congratulated the school because its students comprised both Hindus and Muslims, who were brothers not only by virtue of being compatriots, but also as "school-fellows." He hoped that this would help them to build up mutual love in their future public life, which was essential for the country's progress.[61]

In order to rationalize his plea for cordial relations between the two communities (in an undated article, and another published in 1874), Sir Sayyad differentiated between "religious" and "human" love. Although a Muslim was prohibited to nurture the first kind of love for a non-Muslim, there was no bar on the latter. He therefore advised Muslims to develop true friendship and love (of the second kind) for all, irrespective of religion, for this was the teaching of Islām.[62]

Another argument that Sir Sayyad employed in this connection in a speech at Patna on 27 January 1883, was that a man's relationship with God and with fellow humans belonged to two different realms. Therefore his faith which belonged to God alone, should not come in the way of his cultivating sympathy and friendship with other men irrespective of their religious beliefs.[63]

In a speech at Ludhiana on 23 January 1884, Sir Sayyad advised the two communities to co-operate on this basis in all human and worldly affairs, and to nurture true friendship and tolerance.[64] Interestingly enough, in another speech delivered on 29 January 1884, he used the same argument to appeal for a triangular unity between the three communities (*qawm*) then living in India, to whom according to him it now belonged *i.e.* Hindus, Muslims, and Christians.[65] In a speech on the 25th, he recounted the basic principles of Islām as the unity of God and the brotherhood of man.[66]

Indian Nationhood

One Nation

It is therefore not surprising to see Sir Sayyad repeatedly and explicitly defining Hindus and Muslims as jointly forming a single nation or *qawm i.e.* India, in the speeches of 1884, as on 3 February:

> "By the word *qawm* I mean Hindus and Muslims both. This is the sense in which I interpret the word 'nation' (*qawm*)."[67]

His deliberate use of the English word "nation" suggests that he was employing it very consciously, and had in mind its current Western usage and the implied political connotations.

Although there are numerous references by Sir Sayyad in these speeches to Muslims as "my nation" (*qawm*), at some points he clarified that by "nation" he did not mean only Muslims, but both communities.[68] He even said that if they overlooked their difference of faith, then by virtue of being compatriots in India, they were in reality one "nation."[69]

Sir Sayyad very deliberately and earnestly tried to undermine the argument that Indian Muslims were "aliens." He did so in his characteristically vigorous style, by proving that far from being strangers to India, they had become its natives, and were therefore no less "Hindu" than the Hindus themselves. For this he redefined the term "Hindu" not as the adherent of a particular faith, but as a native of Hindustan. As such, it would equally apply to both the communities (*qawm*) living in India. He regretted that Hindus regarded only themselves as Indians, and Muslims as foreigners.[70] In an article written many years later in 1897, he repeated that since Muslims had also been living in India for centuries, like the Aryan invaders before them, they too deserved to be called "Hindu" *i.e.* natives of Hindustan.[71]

Geographical Nationalism

As early as in September 1867 we find Sir Sayyad groping towards a geographical basis for nationhood. He regarded India as consisting of numerous but similar nations (*qawm*), and pleaded that Muslims be regarded not as foreigners, but as a part of this native population. He reasoned that since nature had differentiated "nations" according to their country (*mulk*)—of domicile rather than origin—prolonged settlement in any area turned even a migrant population into a native one. He recalled that like others before them, Muslims had come to India twelve centuries back as an alien race, and had settled here. Irrespective of their origins, due to their lengthy stay here, like their predecessors they were gradually transformed by nature, and came to acquire the traits of its native population, becoming one of them.[72]

About a decade and a half later, in the speech at Patna on 27 January 1883, he made the point that like Muslims the Hindus too were originally foreigners who had settled in India. They had alike forsaken all ties with their original homeland, making India their home, and hence it was now the native country (*watan*) of both these nations.[73]

Exactly a year later in January 1884, Sir Sayyad could confidently and unequivocally assert that the only basis of nationhood was in fact geographical. He tried to demonstrate that the word "nation" was used for the inhabitants of a particular country, who may possess certain distinguishing traits. Thus the people of Iran, Afghanistan and other countries were said to be one "nation", and known by their country *i.e.* "Irani", "Afghani" etc. It is worth observing that he now regards all Europeans as a single nation (*Cf. supra* p. 2 and note 11), "although they profess different faiths, and people of other countries have also settled among them."[74]

On this basis Sir Sayyad concluded that all Indians were also "one nation", and should therefore develop concord among themselves. Since the country belonged to them all, they should unite for its welfare. As mentioned earlier (*supra* p. 11), he would include Christians also (besides Hindus and Muslims) in this united Indian nationhood, since they had also been living here for the past many years.[75] As he said to a Hindu delegation during his visit to the Panjab in February that year:

> "Gone are the days when the people of a country were regarded as two nations merely on the basis of religion."[76]

This may be said to be the high-watermark of Sir Sayyad's belief in geographical nationalism.

Muslim Nationhood

Definition

In spite of these vehement professions, *qawm* for Sir Sayyad ultimately and invariably signified "Muslims", and more specifically, the Muslim population of India, for whom he worked all his life with unflagging zeal. It would be interesting to examine what exactly the Muslim "nation" signified for him.

In a dateless article apparently written in the early years after the setting up of the M.A.O. College, and in two speeches of 23 January 1884 and 30 December 1888, Sir Sayyad defined his nation (*qawm*) as the *ummat* of the Prophet (Pbuh), comprising those who had uttered the *kalimah*, which bound together all Muslims.[77]

In another speech on 25 January 1884, Sir Sayyad clarified that mere recitation of the *kalimah* was not sufficient: being a Muslim also entailed the performance of religious obligations. He reasoned that the Muslim "nation" could sustain its identity only by remaining firm on Islām, which was the very ground of its being. He warned his audience comprising young Muslim students that if they became lofty as the stars but were not true to their faith, they would sever the relationship which bound them to their co-religionists, and thus cease to be a part of the Muslim "nation." It was therefore their duty to progress even while remaining steadfast on Islām, for which they must be prepared to live and die.[78]

It was apparently unexpected and uncharacteristic of Sir Sayyad to express such sentiments, for the compiler of the *Safarnāmah*,

Mawlawi Sayyad Iqbāl 'Ali remarks that he was surprised to hear Sir Sayyad talk thus, until the reason for it dawned upon him: Sir Sayyad had learnt that the son of the Extra Asstt. Commissioner who had spoken before him, was studying in a mission school.[79] It is worth remarking that we do not indeed find any instance of Sir Sayyad expressing such thoughts before 1884. However it is significant that he repeated very similar sentiments only four years later, in the speech on 30 December 1888,[80] cited above (see *infra* p. 19).

In the speech on 23 January 1884 (also cited above), Sir Sayyad had emphasized that, obliterating all former worldly distinctions and national (*qawmi*) definitions and relationships based on race and country, Islām had established a new "national" relationship which was spiritual, and above these categories. All Muslims were therefore brothers in spite of minor differences of belief, and should try to achieve mutual concord, which was the only way to progress.[81]

It is interesting that far from developing this idea further on the lines of an exclusive Muslim brotherhood, Sir Sayyad used it as the first stage in his larger argument: that not only Muslims, but all Indians were brothers. Turning the argument in an altogether different direction, he told Muslims that besides the "spiritual" brotherhood which they shared with their co-religionists, their compatriots of a different faith were also as brothers—in social and cultural matters. He reminded them that Islām preached good-neighbourliness, which included love for fellow-countrymen.[82]

Thus at this point Sir Sayyad did not develop any further the idea of Muslim nationhood *per se*, but used it as a launching pad to enlarge upon his ideas of Hindu-Muslim co-operation (see *supra* pp. 10-11). Later however we shall find him becoming more and more preoccupied with the idea of Muslim nationhood—not so much with its definition, as its preservation.

Education and Identity

Writing in 1870 or 1871 (corresponding to 1287 A.H.), Sir Sayyad expressed the conviction that purely secular education could never be successful, and that mass education neither had, nor could ever be achieved in any nation (*qawm*) or country (*mulk*), without the inclusion of religious education.[83] Thus so far the last is viewed merely as a means of popularizing education and making it appealing to the Muslim masses, who he believed shied away from the government-sponsored education due to its secular character.

In an article published around 1873 or 1874 (1290 A.H.), Sir Sayyad regretfully noted the observation of the Government of Madras that there were very few Muslim students in government schools, which tended to cater to the needs of the majority community. He noted with satisfaction the government order that separate schools be set up in Muslim settlements, employing Muslim teachers and "Hindustani" as the medium of instruction. He also appreciated the recommendations of the Bombay Government, that in order to remedy the educational backwardness of Muslims, Persian classes should be commenced in government schools; the office of the *qāḍī* should be revived, and granted to scholars of Arabic and Persian; and mass education should be encouraged through books in these languages. He also expressed satisfaction at the proposal of the Government of Bengal, that not only should schools be set up for Muslims, but in those where they study in sufficient numbers, special teachers should be appointed for Arabic and Persian, and Muslim teachers should be permitted to take religious lessons at fixed times.[84]

This was in keeping with Sir Sayyad's own conviction that Muslims stayed aloof from education not only on account of their own prejudice, but also due to inherent flaws in the system itself; and it was reassuring to see the government intent on remedying these. He does not here seem concerned with preserving the cultural, religious, or linguistic identity of Muslims, but only with attracting them towards modern education. However he betrays a streak of chauvinism when he remarks that the most pleasing aspect of the report was its finding that in Eastern Bengal, the Muslim population was much greater than the Hindu.[85]

We have earlier noticed Sir Sayyad expressing satisfaction (in January 1884), at both communities being educated together in the same school, as a positive sign for developing mutual brotherhood (*supra* p. 10). A day earlier he had emphasized that although the College at Aligarh had been set up to improve the condition of Muslims, Hindus also studied in it as equals (*supra* p. 9). He emphasized that since for an outsider they were all alike "Indians", the degradation of one community implied that of the other too. He therefore believed that they could not earn honour and dignity unless these two "brothers" were not brought up and educated together, similar avenues of progress being made available to both. Here and elsewhere he described the College as a source of national progress and an ideal for the "nation", which for him comprised both Hindus and Muslims; and which he fervently desired to "make a nation."[86] We shall come across this phrase (*qawm banānā)* used frequently, (*albeit* differently) in his later speeches and writings.

We perceive a slight change in Sir Sayyad's attitude when in a dateless article he repeatedly uses this phrase exclusively for the Muslim community. He now evinced the belief that in order to make Muslims a nation (*qawm*), and honoured among the "nations" of the world, besides providing good breeding and instruction, it was necessary that as far as possible their children and youth should live, study, eat, sleep, and play together, with arrangements for their excellent upbringing.[87]

We have earlier seen Sir Sayyad supporting both religious education and the teaching of Arabic and Persian, but only as it were, to popularize modern education among Muslims. Now for the first time we find him advocating these for altogether different reasons. He now believed that at least elementary (if not advanced) religious education (comprising a knowledge of the basic beliefs and commandments) should be imparted to Muslim students in order to acquaint them with Islām, which had united different nations (*qawm*) into a single Muslim "nation",[88] and was therefore the very basis of their group-identity. (We recall that he had earlier, in 1884, used the same argument to plead for the faithful observance of religious obligations among Muslim youth (*supra* p. 13).

We now find Sir Sayyad recommending the teaching of Arabic and Persian, not only because these were "superior, modern, and scholarly languages, satisfying the needs of Muslims"; but also because Arabic was "the language of Muslims", and Persian was "closely related to them", besides being "a treasury of Muslim sciences and history."[89] Thus for the first time we sense a new, deliberate, and self-conscious urge to preserve the religious, cultural, and linguistic identity of the community through education, which becomes more marked with the passage of time. He repeated nearly identical sentiments regarding the need for residential and religious education, and the teaching of Arabic and Persian, in another speech in December 1893.[90]

Sir Sayyad had always believed that for the progress of education among Muslims, the community should take upon itself the responsibility of its propagation, while also reforming, and benefitting from governmental education[91] (see also *supra* pp. 14-15). However in a speech on 27 December 1887, for the first time we find him advocating the setting up of national (*qawmi*) educational institutions (with boarding and lodging facilities) by the community, not merely for the spread of education, but so that it could run these according to its own wishes. He now felt that the existing schools and colleges (owned by the government or missionaries) could not satisfy the educational needs of Muslims, since they had no say in their organization. Merely "education" was not now sufficient for the Muslim youth, nor was it the sole end in itself:

> "To breathe into them the spirit of nationality is even more essential than their education."

Without it, the Muslim nation (*qawm*) would remain dull and lifeless, and could not succeed in any field. He felt that this spirit could not be instilled into young Muslims unless they were educated collectively at one place. Their hearts would then be inspired by the thought of their "national college", and the enthusiasm of being educated in it.[92] We should not find these sentiments out-of-place when we recall that only a day later he was to denounce the Indian National Congress in his fiery and historic speech.

By 1888 Sir Sayyad had completely abandoned the view expressed in 1884 at Amritsar, that India could not progress unless Muslims and Hindus were educated together (*supra* pp. 15-16). Speaking at Meerut on 14 March 1888, he expressed the very opposite view: that a Muslim studying among non-Muslims, who were moreover "his superiors in knowledge", would face numerous problems. On the other hand he would enjoy his studies immensely were he to be educated among "students of his own nation, who are his equals in their attainments." He therefore believed that arrangements should be made for Muslim students to "study in communities."[93]

Sir Sayyad now believed that for their good education and training it was essential that Muslims study, live, and eat together, and "learn to love one another", as only this could produce the desirable "national feeling and sympathy" (*Cf. supra* p. 16). He claimed that nowhere in India did Muslim students have so much "national spirit" and brotherly feeling for each other as in the M.A.O. College. Although these qualities had not yet attained the desired ripeness, when they did, national (*qawmi*) honour would be achieved.[94]

Dwelling on the effects of being physically gathered together, Sir Sayyad believed that such an assembly greatly influenced the heart and mind, generating unity, and a feeling of the glory of the "nation", which however vanished on dispersion. Moreover he felt that "these thoughts will not arise in the minds of men unless they are forced upon their attention." This he believed, was the reason why the Prophet (Pbuh) had ordered Muslims to meet in daily, weekly, and bi-annual congregational prayers.[95]

Sir Sayyad summed up these points in two speeches in December 1894, in which his stance is more aggressive than ever before. We recall his almost apologetic tone in 1884 while justifying the setting up of a college specially for Muslims (*supra* p. 9). Having come a long way since then, he now assertively defended the need for a separate educational institution for Muslims. He reasoned that not only did the education of Muslims suffer by studying amidst other nations (*qawm*) due to their different needs and modes of life, but they could never thus "become a nation." Their mutual sympathy and "national feeling" which were born only by living together would be stifled, and would gradually become extinct by being educated in government colleges where they were very few as compared to other "nations."[96]

In order to keep alive Muslim nationality (*qawmiyyat*), a feeling of "national unity and sympathy" must be generated, which was possible only if students shared all aspects of life together. To illustrate this point he cited the example of the students of the M.A.O. College, who he believed experienced religious enthusiasm and a feeling of national (*qawmi*) pride, pleasure, and sympathy at the thought of studying in their "national college"; which he felt was lacking in Muslim students of other colleges. This, he asserted, was a sign of "national progress", and it was only by such education that Muslims would become a "nation."[97]

By now Sir Sayyad was convinced of the need for religious education hand-in-hand with modern knowledge, but for altogether different reasons—so that:

> "A feeling of nationality *i.e. qawmiyyat*, and national unity and national sympathy, which is the first step to national progress, should be inculcated among Muslims."

(We notice Sir Sayyad again using the English word "nationality", for which compare *supra* p. 11, where however it had connoted Indian rather than Muslim nationhood.) For this it was necessary to ensure that they remained Muslims, and the reality of Islām remained firm in their hearts—they should therefore be taught religious tenets, and as far as possible, made to observe religious obligations. As before (*supra* p. 16), he emphasized that this was necessary alongside elementary religious education since Muslim brotherhood, national unity, and in fact nationality itself was based solely on Islām.[98]

Besides this Sir Sayyad believed that Muslim students should be taught Islāmic history, and about the spread of Islām, and Islāmic brotherhood, which was stronger than familial bonds. In order to keep alive their nationality (*qawmiyyat*) which he felt was being threatened by English education, they must be taught Arabic (the language of their religion, and of their forefathers), or at least Persian.[99]

We thus notice a very marked change in Sir Sayyad's ideas regarding nationhood. We may not be mistaken in suggesting that this was a response to the perceived threat to Muslim identity posed by western education, and the overwhelming majority and dominance of the Hindu population. As we shall soon see, he became extremely wary of the latter after the formation of the Indian National Congress in 1885, and publicly gave vent to his feelings for the first time in December 1887, to which time also dates the change in his views regarding Muslim education and identity-consciousness (see *supra* pp. 16-17).

Modern education, for which Sir Sayyad had been campaigning for nearly three decades, had now become quite prevalent, and its ill-effects had also begun to surface. He had told Muslim students on 30 December 1888 that he wanted them to master western knowledge, but while holding on fast to the *kalimah*. Warning them against the undesirable consequences of modern education, and of studying in England, which often manifested itself in indulgence in illegitimate freedom, thoughtless imitation of the darker side of western culture, and the flouting of Muslim mores; he urged them to remain faithful to Islām, or else they would be excluded from the Muslim nation (*qawm*).[100] As we have just seen, in 1894 also he would speak of the threat to Muslim nationality, posed by modern education.

Correspondingly we find Sir Sayyad's delineation of the Muslim "nation" becoming more and more well-defined, closely-knit, exclusive, and even aggressive. However as we have tried to show, these new trends in his thought were not completely abrupt nor severed from his former views, rather at times we can see their seeds in past experiences.

Opposition to the Congress

Although it is not possible to pinpoint the reason for this change in Sir Sayyad's attitude, as mentioned earlier, it may partly be attributed to the emergence of the Indian National Congress in 1885, which may be viewed as a watershed in his life. We know on the authority of Ḥāli that although he did not approve of its formation and activities, for two years he did not make public his opposition for fear that it would sour relations between the two major communities. However he was deeply disturbed on learning in 1887 that the forthcoming session at Madras was to be presided over by a Muslim (Badruddin Tayyabji), and was expected to attract a large number of young Muslims. It was then that he decided to break his silence, and his future sustained opposition to it embittered educated Hindus and specially the Bengalis against him, and in fact against all Muslims who for the most part followed his lead. In 1888 he even set up the United Indian Patriotic Association, of which not only Hindu and Muslim nobles, but Englishmen were also members. Through it he intended to counteract the activities of the Congress, to inform the British Parliament of the steps being taken all over India towards this end, and to convince it that Muslims were not participating in the Congress.[101]

Representation

The chief ground of Sir Sayyad's opposition to the Congress was its advocacy of the representative principle, which he was convinced was not suited to Indian conditions; although he had always supported peoples' participation in government. Writing the *Asbāb-i-Baghāwat-i Hind* in 1858, he had traced the fundamental cause of the revolt to the fact that Indians had no share in the Legislative Council.[102] A few years later, in a speech in 1864 he welcomed "the appointment of natives to the Supreme Council", and looked forward to the time when it would be "composed of representatives from every division."[103]

Ḥāli tries to justify the apparent change in Sir Sayyad's views on the basis of his later perception of communal (*qawmi*) differences as a result of the Urdu-Hindi controversy, and later opposition from the Hindus (see *supra* pp. 5-6); until he was finally convinced that "representation" was not practicable in India.[104] However we feel that there is no real contradiction here, since what he advocated in the early period appears to be representation through nomination rather than election, which he opposed unequivocally from 1883 onwards, when the issue first arose. In the same year Sir Sayyad resigned from the Legislative Council, according to Aziz Aḥmad[105] in order to meet the challenge of Hindu dominance in representative institutions. However nothing has been found to substantiate this view.

India is Not a Single Nation

Speaking on the bill on local self-government in the Viceroy's Legislative Council on 12 January that year, Sir Sayyad warned that rather than blindly borrowing representative institutions from England, social and political differences between the two countries should be kept in mind. He felt that whereas different nations (*qawm*) had not intermingled in India; in England, due to the progress of education and tolerance, major national (*qawmi*), religious, and even political differences had subsided, and for all practical purposes the people had become "a single nation." He thus opposed the election of all the members of local bodies on the ground that India was "a continent" inhabited by people of different "nations" and religions, who had been kept apart by the rigidity of religious and caste rules. He emphasized that besides numerical differences, their levels of education, enlightenment, and political awareness were also varying.[106]

Sir Sayyad felt that in such circumstances, the introduction of the unalloyed principle of election was fraught with social and political dangers—the conflict of interests would surface, and aggravate mutual differences. For the first time we find him expressing the fear (which was later to become a constant refrain), that the stronger "nation" would completely gain the upper hand over the interests of the weaker. He conclusively stated that so long as distinctions of "nation", religion, and caste remained, and continued to influence Indians in political matters, the pure rule of election could not be enforced peacefully.[107]

Later, in his first speech against the Congress on 28 December 1887 at Lucknow, Sir Sayyad defended his stand, and the modification in the Bill made under his influence—one-third of the members were now to be appointed. According to him the wisdom of this change was borne out by later experience which proved that were it not for this clause, it would be impossible for any Muslim to participate in local government. He once again asserted that Muslims were not prepared to "walk along a road for which neither they, nor the country was prepared."[108]

Besides religious, racial, and caste divisions, Sir Sayyad was also very conscious of regional differences. In a speech of 1884, he differentiated between Indian groups ("*firqoṇ*" in the original), on the basis of their nation (*qawm*), caste (*dhāt*), and region (*jā'-e sukūnat*). In another speech of the same year, and in his second political speech in Meerut on 15 March 1888, he differentiated between "the Muslims of Panjab and those of Hindustan" the Hindus of the north, "the Bengalis of Bengal, and the Brahmans of Bombay, and the Hindu Madrasis of Madras."[109]

In two letters of early 1888 Sir Sayyad once more emphasized that the interests of the different "nations", castes, and creeds of which India was composed, were not only conflicting but mutually irreconcilable. On this basis he denied that they belonged to, or could become "one nation", with common aims and aspirations. He therefore wrote:

> "I object to every Congress . . . which regards India as one nation on account of its being based on wrong principles. . . ."

In fact he reasoned that there could be "no such thing as a National Congress", nor could it benefit all the people equally, for a congress could be called "national" only when "the ultimate aims and objects of the people of which it is composed are identical."[110]

In reply to Tayyabji's suggestion that Hindus and Muslims should work together on common questions, Sir Sayyad retorted that the points on which they happened to agree were few and insignificant.[111] This is in marked contrast to the advice he had offered to these communities on 29 January 1884 : that whereas complete agreement was impossible, they should unite in matters of common interest, and for the welfare of the country as a whole; examples of which were to be found in other countries too.[112]

In another letter dated 22 September 1893, Sir Sayyad reiterated that the first essential precondition for representative government based purely on the majority principle, was the need for homogeneity among the voters—in matters of nationality (*qawm*), religion, national historical traditions, and social customs and conditions. He therefore held that in a country like India where there was no homogeneity in any of these respects, the introduction of such a system would only adversely affect the peace and well-being of the country. India, unlike England, was not a small country but a continent inhabited by vastly different peoples, whose civilizational, ethical, and political circumstances varied widely. He felt that they had never united after the fall of the Muslim empire, and instead of establishing an alternate government, had quarrelled incessantly among themselves until the advent of the East India Company which united them into a single dominion. He therefore accused the Congress of overlooking former historical developments, and the differences between the various "nations", who they assumed could be treated as a single "nation."[113]

From December 1887 onwards Sir Sayyad repeatedly expressed the view that the majority principle would also work against Muslims due to their fewer numbers. He reasoned that if, as the Congress demanded, the Viceroy's Council was constituted through election, the power of legislation over the whole country would fall into the hands of the more numerous Hindus, and Muslims would be unable to guard their interests.[114]

Unequal Development

Sir Sayyad was also very conscious of the disparity in education and wealth among different groups, and cited this as another reason why democracy could not succeed in India. He regarded Muslims as being totally unfit to participate as equals with the more able and educated Hindus, in the political process.[115]

Sir Sayyad did not want his community "to run a race with persons with whom we have no chance of success." He believed that only those should join the agitation of the Congress who had the strength to oppose the government. Since Muslims were very backward in all respects and therefore weak in comparison to the Hindus, he advised them to keep aloof from the "political uproar", and to concentrate on trade and education as the means of acquiring wealth and high government posts.[116]

Sir Sayyad opposed the holding of the Civil Service Examination in India for the same reasons: its different peoples had not intermingled to form a single "nation"; and they were not equally matched. For him both democracy and the granting of all appointments by competition meant a monopoly of the Bengali Hindus who were educationally the most advanced.[117]

Struggle for Power

Hindu Domination

Sir Sayyad believed that the Bengalis had advocated in the Congress, schemes which would benefit them the most, and "next to them the Marāthas and Brahmans." Knowing full well that the Muslims stood to gain nothing from it, they were flattering them to join the Congress out of purely selfish motives. He moreover felt that the Hindus hoped, by uniting under its banner, to be able to annihilate the Muslims and their religious rites. He however reminded them that they could cherish their own rites only by friendship rather than force, for animosity between the two communities would be to their own loss.[118]

Sir Sayyad, at the same time, persistently and defiantly asserted the will of the Muslims (whom he likened to a burnt but smouldering rope), not to be subjected to "slavery" or being "trampled" underfoot, or "thrown into a ditch." He therefore concluded that:

> "All political questions which can be discussed by the Congress are dangerous and prejudicial to the interests of Muslims and they should not take part in any political Congress."[119]

Sir Sayyad did not trust the intentions of the promoters of the Congress, and believed that they wanted to capture power and authority, the government remaining English in name only. He reasoned that although they did not publicly admit this and spoke in the name of all Indians, they knew that due to the ineffectiveness of Muslims they would become the real masters. Due to this perceived power-struggle, he described the Congress as "a civil war without arms."[120] Adopting an uncharacteristically aggressive posture, he demanded on behalf of Muslims, "a civil war with arms": if the government wished to hand over power to Indians, it should allow the different nations (*qawm*) to test their strength by the sword, the victor emerging the ruler. He even asserted the military prowess of the Pathāns, who would "make rivers of blood to flow."[121]

Sir Sayyad thus saw the schemes and activities of the Congress as being not only disastrous for Muslims, but injurious to India at large, because they threatened the peace, law, and order of the country by stirring up hostility and discord between its two major communities. He believed that if these proposals were adopted, it would lead to violence and incessant civil war. He repeated similar sentiments in an undated article, which internal evidence reveals was written in 1897.[122]

The Impossibility of Sharing Power

Sir Sayyad was thus astute enough to realize very early that the Congress posed a serious threat to the continuance of British rule, whose permanence he believed was essential not only for Muslim interests but for India as a whole, which could not survive without its stabilizing influence. Even before the emergence of the Congress, in 1884 when he was enthusiastically preaching Hindu-Muslim concord, he could frankly say on 29 January:

> "I have said repeatedly that for India it is impossible that either Hindus or Muslims are the rulers, and are able to keep the peace. It is inevitable that a third nation rule over us."[123]

The same conviction is later expressed more aggressively in the face of the perceived threat of Hindu domination. It appears that even in the pre-Congress era, and in spite of his concerted efforts to effect a reconciliation, Sir Sayyad remained conscious of the undercurrents of distrust and disharmony between the two communities, which came to the fore in his vociferous opposition to the Congress. From this statement, and his opposition to representative government in 1883 (*supra* p. 21), it appears that even in this period when he was vociferously preaching social unity and equality, he was strictly opposed to, and had no faith in, political uniformity and co-operation.

Four years later in a speech at Meerut on 14 March 1888, Sir Sayyad again asserted that if the English and their army were to leave India, it was "impossible" and "inconceivable" that Muslims and Hindus could share power equally : one would necessarily subdue the other if there was to be peace in the land. He further predicted ominously that in the absence of the English some other European nation would attack India. Since all European governments were far worse than the British, it was necessary that :

> "For the peace of India and for the progress of everything in India, the English government should remain for many years—in fact for ever!"[124]

Loyalism as a Political Weapon

Since he felt that the Hindus were uniting against them (*supra* p. 24), Sir Sayyad advised Muslims to cultivate friendship with their English rulers, who were also People of the Book, and to help to make their rule permanent and firm. If they did not want to become subjects of the Hindus they should not join their political movement, which would only bring them loss and degradation.[125]

It is interesting that Sir Sayyad thought on similar lines as far back as in 1857. In his account of the Bijnawr rebellion we find him urging a local *nawāb* to become a "well-wisher" of the government, whom it would "favour and promote", rather than fighting against it:

> "Remove this thought from your mind. The authority of the English officers will never go . . . Except for the English authorities, no one else can rule Hindustan . . . ."[126]

Permanence of British Rule

In fact, Sir Sayyad's reaction to the Congress was to a large extent conditioned by his experiences of the holocaust of 1857 and its terrible aftermath. It had impressed upon him that the government was invincible : trying to fight it was therefore like beating one's head against a wall, for while it could not be harmed, he had seen how swiftly and mercilessly its punitive and retributive arm fell on its opponents. He therefore believed that the best course was to win the confidence of the rulers rather than arousing their suspicion and hostility.

Sir Sayyad therefore felt that even if all Indians participated in the agitation of the Congress, they could not harm the government which was strong enough to put it down, as it had the revolt. He felt that far from benefitting them by producing a revolution in the government, the activities of the Congress would only make it vindictive. He therefore advised Indians to win "high positions" not thus, but by making "themselves worthy of the confidence of the government", and winning its friendship. Rather than arousing fresh suspicions of disloyalty, they should try to win back the trust that was betrayed in 1857.[127]

Sir Sayyad felt moreover that Muslims would suffer more than the Hindus by participating in the current political agitation, which was causing ill-will against the government by publicly accusing it. He reasoned that in 1857 too, the Hindus who had initiated the revolt went scot-free, whereas the Muslims who had only followed them eagerly and foolishly, were completely ruined. He felt that this was because the government was more suspicious of Muslims who were the former, and now deprived rulers, and moreover a brave and martial race. A Muslim agitation therefore spelt greater danger for it, and it would take extreme and violent measures to suppress it. He therefore advised Muslims that since the government was more wary of them due to their past record, they should cleanse away such suspicions and ill-will, and "cultivate mutual affection."[128]

Political Differences No Bar to Social Unity

It is interesting that soon after his fiery speech at Lucknow in December 1887, Sir Sayyad clarified that his earlier desire for Hindu-Muslim friendship, unity, and brotherhood had not undergone a change. He reaffirmed his earlier belief that they were like the two eyes of a bride; his respect for Bengalis due to their progress in education; his desire for religious amity for which he was willing to stop cow-slaughter; and his conviction that both groups should respect each other's religious rites, and minimise religious quarrels. He felt that they should improve their social conditions and try to remove their ever-increasing animosity, so that peace could reign in the country. He was convinced that they could, and should unite, only on these purely "social questions"; and he would have had no objection to the Congress if these had been its aims.[129]

Sir Sayyad also made it clear that by opposing the Congress he had "not girt up his loins to fight the Bengalis." Whereas he desired peace and friendship between all Indian "nations" *(qawm),* this was possible only if one did not try to put the other in subjection. He felt that since the Hindus were trying this game, it was his duty to protect and warn his community.[130]

A decade later, in an article apparently written in 1897, Sir Sayyad once more reaffirmed his desire for social intimacy, co-operation, and friendship between the two communities who were doubtless compatriots and brothers, and his willingness to give up cow-sacrifice for the same. Admitting to the political differences between the two communities, he however felt that both these, and their religious differences need not impede social intimacy; and should be overlooked in order to breed love and sympathy in social matters.[131] (This article has been cited before too—see *supra* pp. 10 and 12).

Jihād and the Islāmic Caliphate

We recall that Shāh 'Abdul 'Azīz had issued the famous and highly significant *fatwá* in 1803, declaring that India had ceased to be a *dār-al Islām*, which amounted to a call to Muslims to mobilize themselves and rise in defiance of the foreign power.[132] Sir Sayyad however did not agree, his views being wholly conditioned by his staunch loyalism.

In the early years (*i.e.* 1858, 1860 and 1871), he took great pains to show that since Islām enjoins obedience to the ruling authority which provides security and religious freedom (irrespective of its religious beliefs), Muslims should remain loyal and obedient to the British government.[133]

In the same strain Sir Sayyad ruled out there being any grounds for Muslims to wage a *jihād* against the British government. In fact such an uprising by Muslim subjects was unlawful and unwarranted by Muslim law, which according to him recommended either forbearance or migration in the face of oppression by a non-Muslim government. *Jihād* could however be waged by Muslim subjects of a Muslim ruler, against an infidel country which oppressed its Muslim subjects—provided no worldly or political considerations were involved.[134]

Sir Sayyad clarified that since tumult and disorder are repellant to Islām, it is opposed to aggression and bloodshed for conquest and territorial aggrandizement, as well as for spreading Islām. In order to allay British suspicions regarding Muslim religious zeal and intentions, he clarified that the Qurānic injunctions to fight polytheists until there is no mischief, and religion is for God alone, did not mean that Muslims should continue to fight all unbelievers till such a time as Islām is established as the only religion on earth; since this was both impractical and impossible. He reasoned that rather than being of universal import, these verses refer to the idolaters of Makkah at the time of the Prophet (Pbuh). He believed that overlooking the context and purpose of such verses would only excite hostility and criticism against Muslims, and embitter their relations with their rulers.[135]

Sultān 'Abd-al Ḥamīd had acceded to the caliphate in 1876, by which time Indian Muslims were trying to influence the British government in the direction of a pro-Turkish policy. The Russo-Turkish war was sparked off the next year, and the agitation of the Muslims during it was reflected in the Urdu Press. Huge sums of money were contributed by them to be sent to Turkey.

Sir Sayyad however did not approve of the popular sentiment in favour of the Sultān. He wrote in an undated article that the Islāmic "caliphate" or (*khilāfat*) as such had ended thirty years after the demise of the Prophet (Pbuh), with the termination of the caliphate of Imām Ḥasan. The rulers that followed were merely Sultāns, although they may have adopted the title of "caliph" for grandeur, which was in reality applicable only to a ruler who had cultivated a complete likeness to the moral and spiritual attributes of the Prophet (Pbuh). He believed that in the present there was none worthy of this title, and even if there was, as a caliph his power was limited only to the territory under his sway.[136]

Sir Sayyad therefore held that even if the Sultān of Turkey was a caliph, it was only within his own country. Since Indian Muslims were not his subjects, he had no power over them, and was not their caliph in the legal or religious sense. He did not agree with those who advocated a single caliph for the whole Muslim world (and regarded the Sultān of Turkey as such); since he felt that there has never been, and is never likely to be, any individual whose political power extends over the whole world.[137]

Sir Sayyad explained the sympathy that Muslims felt for the Turkish Sultān on the basis of their feeling of Islāmic brotherhood. However he reminded them that they owed no obligation to the Sultān, their only religious and legal duty being to remain loyal and obedient well-wishers of their government. In the context of the Greco-Turkish war of 1897-98 (in which Britain supported the former), he wrote in the same year that this duty could not be shirked even if the government's political policy was against Turkey. At the most, they could pray for friendship between the British and all Muslim states. In fact he generalized that in the event of a war between a Muslim and non-Muslim government, the Muslim subjects of the latter were strictly forbidden by their religion to support or assist the former in any way.[138]

As we have already seen, Sir Sayyad did not hesitate to preach to Indian Muslims in the name of religion, to abstain from rebellion and remain loyal to the British government. However it is interesting that in order to counter their pro-Turkish sentiments during the war, he reasoned that religion and politics must be kept apart. He tried to convince them that it was wholly unjustified to give present day wars a religious colouring since they were undertaken not with religious, but purely political motives.[139]

Notes and References

All references in this chapter are to the works of Sir Sayyad Aḥmad Khān, unless otherwise stated.

1. Muḥammad Ismā'īl Panīpati, ed., *Maqālāt-i Sir Sayyad*, 16 vols. (Lahore, 1941-65) vol. V, pp. 36, 88-89 and 95.
2. *Maqālāt* VIII, p. 147.
3. Muḥd. Ismā'īl Panīpati, ed., *Khuṭbāt-i Sir Sayyad*, 2 vols. (Lahore, 1973) vol. I, p. 447; Maqālāt vol. V, pp. 36 and 42-43; vol. VIII, p. 32; vol. XII, pp. 22, 28 and 30-31.
4. *Maqālāt* XII, p. 30.
5. *Maqālāt* VIII, p. 162.
6. *Khuṭbāt* II, p. 154.
7. *Maqālāt* XII, p.120.
8. *Khuṭbāt* I, pp. 444-45.
9. *Maqālāt* VIII, p. 157.
10. *Ibid.*
11. *Maqālāt* XII, p. 20. It is interesting to note that in this speech which appeared in the form of an article on 20 September 1867, Sir Sayyad speaks of both India and Europe not as a single nation (*qawm*), but as comprising numerous (albeit similar) "nations." The evolution in his ideas can be gauged from the fact that by January 1884 he had no hesitation in describing both Europe and India as a single unified "nation". (see *supra,* pp. 12-13).
12. *Ibid.*, pp. 18 and 22.
13. *Ibid.*, p. 20; *Khuṭbāt* I, pp. 445-46; Muḥd. Ismā'īl Panīpati, ed., *Sayyad Aḥmad Khān kā Safarnāmah-i Panjab* (Delhi, 1979) p. 195.
14. *Khuṭbāt* I, pp. 446-47; *Maqālāt* V, p. 93; vol. VIII, pp. 36 and 143; vol. IX, pp. 44, 46 and 54; and vol. XIII, p. 585.
15. Shan Mohammad, ed., *Writings and Speeches of Sir Sayyad Aḥmad Khan* (Bombay, 1972) p. 125.
16. *Maqālāt* IX, p. 107. Wilfred Cantwell Smith calls this a "singular lapse" on Sir Sayyad's part, which "is by no means representative of him." [*Modern Islam in India* (Lahore, 1969) pp. 22-23]. We would

however like to show that far from being an aberration or even unusual, this observation can be reconciled with the fluctuating pattern of Sir Sayyad's thought.

17. Translation in Hafiz Malik, ed., *Political Profile of Sir Sayyad Aḥmad Khān* (Islamabad, 1982) pp. 50 and 58.
18. *Ibid.*, p. 67.
19. Alṭāf Ḥusayn Ḥāli, *Ḥayāt-i Jāwīd* (Kanpur, 1901) p. 70.
20. *Ibid.*, pp. 88 and 179.
21. *Ibid.*, p. 85.
22. Malik, *op. cit.*, p. 332.
23. *Ibid.*, p. 196.
24. Muḥd. Ismā'īl Panīpati, ed., *Maktūbāt-i Sir Sayyad*, 2 vols. (Lahore, 1985) vol. I, p. 349.
25. Ḥāli, *op. cit.*, pp. 89, 91 and 94.
26. *Ibid.*, p. 93.
27. *Maqālāt* XII, p. 35 (from the article published on 20 September 1867).
28. Ḥāli, *op. cit.*, pp. 95-96.
29. *Maktūbāt* I, pp. 259-261.
30. Ḥāli, *op. cit.*, p. 95.
31. *Ibid.*
32. *Maqālāt* XII, p. 119.
33. Ḥāli, *op. cit.*, pp. 95-96.
34. *The Destiny of Indian Muslims* (Bombay, 1965) p. 29.
35. *Khilāfat to Partition* (New Delhi, 1970) p. 22.
36. Ḥāli, *op. cit.*, pp. 93-94 and 179.
37. *Maktūbāt* I, p. 464.
38. Ḥāli, *op. cit.*, p. 170.
39. *Safarnāmah*, pp. 193-97 and 199-200.
40. *Maqālāt* V, pp. 140-41.
41. Shan Mohammad, *op. cit.*, p. 250.
42. *Khuṭbāt* I, pp. 535 and 537-38.
43. *Maqālāt* XII, p. 118.
44. *Safarnāmah*, p. 195; *Khuṭbāt* I, p. 446.
45. *Maqālāt* XII, pp. 119-120, 135 and 182; *Safarnāmah*, p. 91; *Khuṭbāt* I, pp. 450 and 460.
46. *Safarnāmah*, pp. 194, 199 and 220-21. Ḥāli also cites these addresses presented by Hindu groups, as evidence of Sir Sayyad's impartial efforts for the welfare of all groups during his tenure in the Legislative Council from 1878-83. (*Op. cit.*, pp. 303-04).
47. *Op. cit.*, p. 21.
48. *Khuṭbāt* I, pp. 445 and 448.
49. *Maqālāt* VIII, p. 157.
50. *Maqālāt* X, pp. 52-53.

51. *Khuṭbāt* I, p. 444; *Safarnāmah*, pp. 74-75.
52. *Khuṭbāt* I, pp. 446-48.
53. *Ibid.*, pp. 446 and 536.
54. *Maktūbāt* I, p. 105.
55. *Maqālāt* XII, p. 118.
56. *Khuṭbāt* I, pp. 460 and 537; *Maqālāt* XII, pp. 119 and 134.
57. *Maqālāt* XV, p. 41.
58. *Maqālāt* XII, p. 120; *Khuṭbāt* I, pp. 536-37.
59. *Maqālāt* XV, pp. 41-42.
60. *Khuṭbāt* I, pp. 445-46.
61. *Safarnāmah*, p. 91.
62. *Maqālāt* I, p. 295; vol. V, p. 67.
63. *Maqālāt* XII, p. 118.
64. *Maqālāt* V, pp. 167-171.
65. *Maqālāt* XII, pp. 180-81.
66. *Khuṭbāt* I, p. 443.
67. *Ibid.*, pp. 537-38.
68. *Ibid.*, pp. 445-46 and 450.
69. *Maqālāt* XII, p. 119.
70. *Safarnāmah*, pp. 195 and 200; *Khuṭbāt* I, pp. 537-38.
71. *Maqālāt* XV, p. 41.
72. *Maqālāt* XII, pp. 21 and 24.
73. *Ibid.*, pp. 118-19.
74. *Ibid.*, pp. 180-81; *Khuṭbāt* I, p. 461.
75. *Khuṭbāt* I, p. 461.
76. *Safarnāmah*, p. 200.
77. *Khuṭbāt* II, pp. 74-75; *Maqālāt* V, p. 167; vol. X, p. 190.
78. *Khuṭbāt* I, pp. 435-36.
79. *Safarnāmah*, p. 36.
80. *Khuṭbāt* II, pp. 74-75.
81. *Maqālāt* V, pp. 167-69.
82. *Ibid.*, pp. 170-71.
83. *Maqālāt* VIII, pp. 102 and 104.
84. *Ibid.*, pp. 119, 123-25 and 128.
85. *Ibid.*, p. 119.
86. *Safarnāmah*, p. 91; *Khuṭbāt* I, pp. 445-46 and 450.
87. *Maqālāt* XV, pp. 199-200.
88. *Ibid.*
89. *Ibid.*
90. *Khuṭbāt* II, pp. 249-50.
91. *Maqālāt* VIII, pp. 91 and 94. (The article is dated 1289 A.H. *i.e. circa* 1872-73 A.D.).
92. *Khuṭbāt* I, pp. 599-600.
93. Malik, *op. cit.*, p. 383.

94. *Ibid.*, pp. 383-84.
95. *Ibid.*
96. *Khuṭbāt* II, pp. 290 and 320-21.
97. *Ibid.*, pp. 290-91, 321 and 335.
98. *Ibid.*, pp. 286 and 334.
99. *Ibid.*, pp. 334-35.
100. *Ibid.*, pp. 75-77 and *passim.*
101. Ḥāli, *op. cit.,* pp. 179-180, 182-83 and 304.
102. *Maqālāt* IX, pp. 61-63.
103. Shan Mohammad, *op. cit.*, p. 114.
104. Ḥāli, *op. cit.*, p. 445.
105. *Islamic Modernism in India and Pakistan* (London, 1967) p. 32.
106. *Khuṭbāt* I, pp. 399-400.
107. *Ibid.*, pp. 400-01. It is interesting to compare this with Sir Sayyad's stand on the close relationship between the Indian communities, and his assertion of India's single nationhood during the same period *i.e.* 1883-84 (*supra* p. 10 *ff.*), and not easy to reconcile, nor even to explain the great variation in points of view.
108. Malik, *op. cit.*, p. 354.
109. *Ibid.*, p. 371; *Khuṭbāt* I, pp. 447 and 535.
110. Malik, *op. cit.*, pp. 377 and 394.
111. *Ibid.*, pp. 377-78.
112. *Maqālāt* XII, pp. 181-82.
113. *Maktūbāt* I, pp. 101-05.
114. Malik, *op. cit.*, pp. 348-49 and 378.
115. *Ibid.*, pp. 347-48.
116. *Ibid.*, pp. 357, 372-73, 379 and 394.
117. *Ibid.*
118. *Ibid.*, pp. 357 and 362.
119. *Ibid.*, p. 378.
129. *Ibid.*, p. 357.
121. *Ibid.*, pp. 357-58 and 364.
122. *Ibid.*, pp. 351, 356, 363 and 394; Shan Mohammad, *op. cit.*, pp. 245, 251-52 and 264; *Maqālāt* XV, pp. 43-44.
123. *Maqālāt* XII, p. 182.
124. Malik, *op. cit.*, pp. 363-64.
125. *Ibid.*, pp. 370-72.
126. *Ibid.*, p. 37.
127. *Ibid.*, pp. 350, 353-54 and 370; *Maqālāt* IX, p. 18; Shan Muḥammad, *op. cit.*, p. 263.
128. Malik, *op. cit.*, pp. 351-52, 372-73 and 378-79.
129. *Ibid.*, pp. 356 and 377-78.
130. *Ibid.*, pp. 356, 358 and 360.
131. *Maqālāt* XV, pp. 41-44.

132. Ziya-ul-Hasan Faruqi, *The Deoband School and the Demand for Pakistan* (Bombay, 1963) p. 2.
133. *Maqālāt* I, pp. 158-59 and 175-77; vol. IX, pp. 19-20; vol. XIII, p. 274; *Maktūbāt* II, p. 350; Malik, *op. cit.*, pp. 232-33.
134. *Maqālāt* I, pp. 159 and 176; vol. IX, pp. 56-57; vol. XIII, p. 274; Malik, *op. cit.*, pp. 231-33, 310-11 and 314.
135. *Maktūbāt* II, p. 350; *Maqālāt* XIII, pp. 274 and 276-77; Malik, *op. cit.*, p. 240.
136. *Maqālāt* I, pp. 157, 167-68, 171-72 and 174; vol. XIII, p. 432.
137. *Maqālāt* I, pp. 158-59 and 162-63.
138. *Maqālāt* I, pp. 168-69; vol. XIII, pp. 427-28 and 432; Shan Mohammad, *op. cit.*, p. 254.
139. *Maqālāt* XIII, p. 433; Shan Mohammad, *op. cit.*, p. 254.

Chapter 2

SHIBLI NU'MĀNI
(1857-1914)

Muslim Nationhood

Very much in the manner of Sir Sayyad (*Cf. supra* pp. 13-14), Shibli emphasized in 1907, 1910, and again in 1912, that since Muslim nationhood (*qawmiyyat*) was based not on race or region but solely on religion, he who uttered the *kalimah* became a Muslim, and the brother and equal (in all national and religious rights), of all fellow-Muslims.[1]

From this point however his thought diverges, and he parted ways with Sir Sayyad who notwithstanding his later emphasis on the close link between religion and nationhood, had throughout been preoccupied with his nation (*qawm*) above all else. Shibli on the other hand tried to replace "nation" by "religion" or "Islām" as the central issue since (as he reasoned), Muslim nationhood was in fact equivalent to religion, which alone could revive the "nation." He felt further that the usage of the word "nation" had made national (*qawmi*) progress, education, and life, devoid of the obligation of religious commitment.[2]

Shibli was therefore convinced (like Sir Sayyad in his later years—see *supra* pp. 13 and 19), that for Muslims "national progress" was possible only if religion remained firmly entrenched, for without it, the very definition of their being, they would in fact cease to remain "the Muslim nation." He believed that religion was not only the axis around which revolved the particular nature, needs, life, thought, and action of the Muslim "nation", but it was in fact the only sentiment which could touch their feelings and arouse their zeal for action.[3] Like Sir Sayyad (*supra* pp. 11 and 18), while comparing the Islāmic and other concepts of nationhood in 1912, Shibli twice used the English word "nation", thus implying its current Western political connotations.

Whereas Sir Sayyad's thought and action was totally centered around the "nation", whose welfare was his ultimate goal, Shibli apparently felt that it was being elevated to the detriment even of that which defined it. He therefore attempted to substitute Sir Sayyad's *qawm* by "religion", and give it its rightful place of supremacy.

Religious Dangers and Needs

From 1908 onwards Shibli perceived grave threats to Islām from various quarters : religion was being challenged by modern science, and the atheism of Europe was influencing not only the western-educated but all sections of the population. He was also agitated at the misrepresentation by European scholars, not only of the life of the Prophet (Pbuh) and his Companions, but also of Muslim social and personal law and criminal code. Since their works were sources of information for the English-educated Muslims, the latter were invariably influenced by them. Besides the occasional misrepresentation of Islāmic Law in Indian courts due to the ignorance of alien rulers, he was also disturbed at the fact that thousands of rural Muslims were not familiar with even basic religious commandments.[4]

Besides the influence of western thought and the attacks of the atheists of Europe, Shibli perceived a threat to Islām from other sources too—the vigorous activities of Christian missionaries and the sustained efforts of workers of the Ārya Samāj (which had been founded in 1875), among newly converted Muslims. He found the Muslim community on the other hand, rendered weak by its apathy and lack of religious education.[5]

Shibli was greatly troubled by the reconversion, on a large and well-organized scale, by Hindu missionaries, of newly-converted Muslim Rājpūts. Attributing the former's success to the religious ignorance of their targets, he felt it was the religious duty of all Muslims to combat this grave threat to Islām. He astutely remarked that besides its religious implications, the matter involved grave political dangers too, since reconversion would decrease the numerical strength of Muslims, on which depended the securing of civil and political rights. He therefore felt that even the modern-educated and worldly Muslims had reason to be troubled on this account.[6]

Propagation of Islām

In the light of these developments, Shibli became deeply convinced of the need for the spread (*ishā'at*) and defence (*ḥifāẓat*) of Islām, both among Muslims and non-Muslims, and devoted a large part of his energies to this task. He advocated various measures for "propagation", and visualizing the Nadwah-al'Ulamā'[7] as the institution that would satisfy these needs, even set up a separate department in it for this purpose. This activity was aimed at two groups among the Muslims: new converts, and the English-educated; both of whom he believed were equally ignorant of Islāmic beliefs, practices, and history, and therefore highly susceptible to the attacks of Hindu missionaries.[8]

Some of the measures that Shibli suggested in 1910 and 1912 to stem the tide of apostasy included the setting up of a permanent department for the spread of Islām, with branches in all the districts. He suggested that permanent preachers, specially trained and paid for the purpose, should be appointed to impart basic religious education to rural Muslims by camping for a few months in each village. He also advocated the setting up of elementary religious schools in rural areas, where only the text of the Qur'ān and basic Urdu (sufficient to impart fundamental religious education) should be taught. He suggested that it would be even better to publish small pamphlets on important religious subjects in Hindi, which was easier and quicker to learn. He also believed that religious scholars should be taught Sanskrit, Bhāsha and English, to equip them better to combat the influence of the Ārya Samāj. (The Nadwah had attempted to execute many of these measures.)[9]

Shibli believed that the Muslim community (*qawm*) itself should arrange for the religious education of children studying in English schools, who were deprived of such education. He also suggested the constitution of a central authority, to which Muslims would contribute a part of their income, to be spent for this purpose. Alternatively he proposed the appointment of a scholar in each town, who would impart weekly religious instruction to the students of English schools. He also suggested that in Muslim-populated rural areas, Muslim rather than Hindu teachers should be appointed in primary government schools, as this would incline the students towards Islām.[10] (*Cf.* Sir Sayyad, *supra* p. 15)

Although Shibli was greatly concerned about the activities of the Hindu missionaries and actively involved in countering them, it is significant that he never displayed the slightest rancour or ill-will against them, or against Hindus in general. (In fact he even expressed admiration for the selflessness, devotion, and simplicity of the workers of the Ārya Samāj.[11]) He therefore repeatedly emphasized that the works in refutation of the Hindu missionaries should be written with politeness, refinement, and in a spirit of reconciliation.[12]

At the same time Shibli displayed great missionary zeal. He believed that Muslims should not be on the defensive: since Islām was meant to enlighten the whole world, they should preach and propagate it among other nations (*qawm*) too. He was convinced that if it was rightly presented, thousands in both Asia and Europe would embrace it willingly.[13]

Education

Education and Muslim Nationhood

In his early years, perhaps under the influence of Sir Sayyad (he joined the M.A.O. College in 1883 as Asstt. Professor of Arabic and left it in 1899), Shibli felt the need to nurture a feeling of nationality (*qawmiyyat*) among Muslim students, and realized the importance of education as a potent tool for this purpose. However later he does not seem to have devoted much thought to the subject.

In the second session of the Muḥammadan Educational Conference in December 1887, Shibli agreed with Sir Sayyad that they should aim at nurturing among Muslim youth, the feeling of nationality (*qawmiyyat*), which was the ladder to progress, and more essential than even education itself. He felt that from school-days itself this feeling should be nurtured among the students, and reinforced in youth by studying in a great national (*qawmi*) institution such as the M.A.O. College, whose students viewed themselves as a "national congregation."[14] The similarity with the views of Sir Sayyad is striking, and indeed the words are nearly an echo of his (*Cf. supra* pp. 17-18).

Writing a travelogue of his visit to Turkey and other eastern lands in 1893, Shibli opined that it was very important that the dress, diet, and lodgings of all the students in a boarding school be identical, so as to wipe out different social strata, and allow the spirit of "nationality" to prevail.[15]

Modern Education

For all his emphasis on religion, Shibli was also a great votary of western education, which he regarded in 1886 as an urgent need of the Muslim nation (*qawm*), on which depended its progress. He felt that due to lack of higher education in English, not only were Muslims deprived of a fair share in government employment, but in the absence of a national (*qawmi*) newspaper which could communicate with the government in its own language, they had no suitable means of airing their grievances. Thus unlike Sir Sayyad, he emphasized not only the economic, but also the political handicaps resulting from lack of modern education.[16]

In 1903 Shibli felt that the greatest deterrent in the path of the acquisition of such education was the religious bigotry of Muslims, which led them to mistakenly believe that since the *Sharī'at* prohibited them from following other "nations", it was wrong to acquire European languages, arts, and sciences. He took great pains to demonstrate that it was forbidden to imitate non-Muslims only regarding the Islāmic signs (*sha'ār*) which distinguished believers; that the Prophet (Pbuh) and the Pious Caliphs had approved of cultural exchange with alien "nations", and that throughout its history Islām had been free of religious, political, social, and racial bigotry.[17]

At the same time however, Shibli was also acutely conscious of the need to preserve religious traditions—he wrote in 1893 that for Muslims decline was preferable to a progress unanimated by religion.[18] In 1904 when some Muslim leaders turned down a move for the introduction of Arabic sciences in Aligarh on the plea that it would divert Muslims from western education; he was surprised that a college which called itself "oriental", and claimed to be a centre of "national" and religious education for Muslims, should exhibit such blatant disregard for Arabic education, which he believed would not detract in any way from modern education. He felt that by downgrading their religious language Muslims had reached the pit of degradation *i.e.* self-contempt.[19]

In 1907 Shibli felt that since the scheme of English education could not accommodate proficiency in religious sciences, the only means of reinforcing the religiosity of students receiving such education was that their upbringing should be on religious lines.[20] However by 1910 he was in favour of imparting religious influence both by precept and example. He now believed that the western-educated should also be familiarized with Islāmic beliefs, issues, history, and jurisprudence; and at the college level this instruction should be imparted in the Arabic language. Unlike Sir Sayyad he did not believe that a minimum of religious education imparted alongside modern knowledge was sufficient (*Cf. supra* p. 16). He reasoned that such education was inadequate to preserve the Qur'ān and *Ḥadīth*. Its products could not elucidate complex Islāmic issues, counter the attacks of non-Muslims, execute religious duties, nor incline the people towards religion.[21]

Shibli feared that western education completely devoid of the religious element would produce not only ignorance but also irreligiosity. He therefore felt that while the former should be encouraged, Muslims should also strive to preserve the faith, and it appeared to him in 1908 that the best means of doing so was to set up a magnificent centre for religious instruction.[22] In 1910 he felt that while the hectic efforts to spread modern education were justified, in view of the religious dangers outlined above (p. 36), alongside this Muslims should also work for religious preservation.[23] He felt that the modern education then current in India was insufficient for them, for being totally devoid of religious content, it did not take into account their religious and national (*qawmi*) needs and peculiarities.[24]

Traditional Education

In 1893 Shibli wrote that although he whole-heartedly approved of modern education, he was also a strong supporter of traditional education, which he believed was extremely "essential to keep alive Muslim nationality" (*qawmiyyat*).[25] However he found the prevalent system of religious education not only profitless, but also lacking in religious content. While he believed that all Muslims should work for the progress of religion keeping in mind present needs, he found the religious scholars or *'ulamā'*—products and supporters of this system—sadly lacking in this respect. Unwilling to step out of their narrow confines, they were ignorant of contemporary developments including the current political revolutions in the country; and unconcerned about the daily declining numbers of Muslims not only in government jobs, but in all kinds of organizations.[26] In what appears to be an oblique reference to Sir Sayyad, Shibli wrote in 1909 that after thirty years of western education Muslims had ransomed their sciences, arts, history, civilization, and much more, only to create a service-class. He believed that traditional education had been wiped out due to the decision of their reformers to demolish the old structure before laying the foundation of the new *i.e.* modern education.[27]

Again in 1910 Shibli reasoned that since for Muslims "nationality" was equivalent to religion, it could not survive without religious education. He believed that the group of religious scholars was, and would always remain, an essential part of the Muslim nation (*qawm*), wielding a powerful influence on it. He therefore disagreed with those who felt that Arabic *madrasahs* were now redundant, since as he reasoned, their products could perform the traditional, purely religious functions.[28]

Sir Sayyad on the other hand had lamented in 1872-73 that all the efforts of Muslims were in the field of traditional religious education, which he described as totally useless and unprofitable. In 1881 he had forcefully opposed the proposed scheme for oriental education in the Panjab University, on the grounds that its products could render none but religious services to the country.[29]

Shibli felt that Sir Sayyad's opposition to traditional education on the ground that it would hamper the progress of western learning did not now hold good, since Muslims had realized the importance of the latter, and it was possible to accommodate the former also, whose need would always persist.[30]

Special Scheme of Education

As early as in 1883 and again in 1906, Shibli opined that like the early Muslims who had vigorously combated the challenge of Greek philosophy, modern scholars should learn English, and defend Islām against the attacks of western philosophy which posed an even greater threat. Besides being capable of unravelling the secrets of the Qur'ān, they should also be broad-minded and well-informed.[31]

In 1908 and 1910 he expressed the view that the religious and worldly needs of Muslims were inseparable; to meet these, to counter the religious dangers outlined above (p. 36), and to spread Islām in Europe, both kinds of education were necessary. He therefore felt the need to initiate a special scheme of education incorporating both modern knowledge, and Islāmic science and history.[32] He believed that if the *'ulamā'* became supporters of western education, the whole "nation" would adopt it. He visualized the Nadwah as the institution which aimed at producing scholars who would strive for the preservation of Arabic and religious education, while also directing the people towards worldly education.[33]

Shibli believed in 1909 that whereas in the present both the modern and traditional-educated groups were unhelpful, familiarizing the latter with European languages and research could make it the intellectual group which the "nation" needed.[34] He was convinced in 1910 that Muslims needed a group which was the genuine expositor of religious issues—the *'ulamā'* of the present were not, but should be made competent to fulfil modern religious needs.[35] Besides being specialists in specific religious sciences, they should be able to produce a modern *'ilm-al kalām*.[36] He visualized the Nadwah as the institution that would produce such a group of ideal *'ulamā'*, and strove to mould it on these lines.

Role of the 'Ulamā'

As early as in 1886 Shibli had recalled that among Muslims the sciences had always been subservient to religion. Besides being their religious and ethical guides, religious scholars had also wielded a political influence on the "nation."[37]

In 1911 Shibli felt that Muslims should follow the example of other "nations": despite their pre-occupation with modern education, there was a large group among both Europeans and Hindus, which was engaged in preserving and propagating religion and religious literature and education.[38]

It is interesting that in 1912 Shibli lauded the Hindu caste system, which on the principle of division of labour (which he believed had been taught in the Qur'ān too), had created a group of Brahmans who had been absolved of all but religious duties. He felt that in view of the Qur'ānic injunction to form a group preaching the right and restraining from evil (3:104), it was a *farḍ-i kifāyah* of the Muslim "nation" to create and support a group devoted to religious pursuits (as did other "nations"), without which their axis (*i.e.* nationhood or *qawmiyyat*) would not survive into the future.[39]

Shibli believed that this group should not depend on government service, and thereby on its scheme of education, but should be free to acquire an education replete in religious information, as well as the languages, sciences, and arts of Europe. According to him modern needs demanded that religious leaders master the English language so as to benefit from European research in their study of Islāmic sciences, and to defend and preach Islām in foreign lands and among

English-knowing people at home. He believed that besides fulfilling the religious needs of the Muslim "nation", they must interact freely with the government in religious matters, as equals.[40]

Shibli thus envisaged a lofty and multifaceted role for the '*ulamā*' in society, and developed a special scheme of education to produce such scholars.

Islāmic Unity and the Turkish Caliphate

Shibli's learned biographer Sayyad Sulaymān Nadwi believes that since Shibli was infatuated with Islām—its history, civilization, sciences, and arts, it was only natural that he should hold its rule dear, and wish to see it return. Making much of Shibli's Islāmic sympathies (citing the collection and dispatch of a subscription by him to Turkey during its war with Russia in 1877 as the first display of these feelings), Nadwi describes him as a "confirmed pan-Islāmist." However elsewhere he himself gives a more plausible explanation of this gesture: since at that time Turkey was the only kingdom with a vestige of Islāmic glory, Shibli felt an attachment for it, which also prompted him to visit it in 1892-93.[41]

We can accept that besides scholarly reasons Shibli was also motivated by his love of Turkey to visit this last stronghold of Muslim power; and that by providing authentic information on it for the first time, the *Safarnāmah* may have created a new bond between Turkey and Indian Muslims. But it is perhaps questionable to impute political motives to the visit, and to suggest that behind the "scholarly screen" it was "the first link" in Indo-Turkish relations, Shibli being "the first ambassador of Muslim India to Turkey."[42]

As Shibli clarified in the Preface to the *Safarnāmah*, he was keen to see Muslim countries at first hand, since information regarding them had so far been furnished by Europeans, who tended to be prejudiced.[43] It is questionable whether attachment and sympathy for Muslim lands (which was particularly natural for him, being a student of Islāmic history, whose glorious phase was enacted in these very lands), can be equated with political pan-Islāmism.

By his own admission, Shibli was greatly moved by the splendid view of the Sultān's ceremonial state-drive in Constantinople.[44] According to Nadwi, he was overcome by the display of the remains of Islāmic grandeur, seeing in it "the refulgent face of the national life of Islām"; and painted the scene in a poem which reads like "a martial song of communal life", full of "the zeal of national pride."[45]

Shibli lamented the curbs on freedom of the press and book-publishing in Turkey (which led to tampering and distortion of facts), and the suppression of any debate on the issue of the Islāmic caliphate, but tried to defend the Sultān's position *vis-a-vis* these malpractices.[46] He continued to harbour Turkish sympathies after his return, and wrote in its favour on the Armenian question in February 1896. Nadwi describes his private gatherings as being full of interesting anecdotes about the Turks, and praises for their excellence.[47]

It is interesting that after his return Shibli himself penned an article on the subject of the caliphate, written according to Nadwi in 1897-98 during the Greco-Turkish war, when there was great Islāmic zeal among Indian Muslims.[48] Defining the caliph as the religious and worldly successor of the Prophet (Pbuh), and the universal Islāmic caliphate as implying "a general authority... obedience to which was obligatory on all Muslims"; he however falsified the Turkish claim to it on the ground that they did not fulfil the condition of being from the family of the Quraysh. He further undermined their claim by calling attention to the forceful acquisition of the title by a former Turkish Sultān from the nominal Abbasi caliph of the day.[49] We recall that Sir Sayyad had also denied their caliphal authority, but for altogether different reasons (*supra* p. 29). While his argument had undermined the very office of the caliphate in later Islāmic history, Shibli tries valiantly to keep its authority and sanctity intact.

Notwithstanding the laudatory references in his poetry to the Sultān as the might of Islām, this article belies the "pan-Islāmic" sentiments which Nadwi attributes to Shibli. He however explains away the contradiction by asserting that the article does not represent Shibli's actual views, since he "was made to write it", citing its inconclusiveness (Shibli never completed it), as proof of its having been written under pressure. He also undermines its contemporary religio-political relevance by saying that it has "historical" rather than "religious" significance.[50]

Nadwi would have us believe that the article was written on Sir Sayyad's "advice", but it is difficult to accept that Shibli could be persuaded to express views contrary to his own, on so important a subject, and one so close to his heart. This is more so when in the next few pages Nadwi himself elaborates Shibli's independence of thought, particularly in the light of his differences of opinion with

Sir Sayyad, his fidelity to his own views, and his refusal to do anything against his will. It is also significant that the article was written after Sir Sayyad's demise.[51]

Nadwi believes that although in deference to Sir Sayyad's views Shibli contained his feelings in the Greco-Turkish war of 1897-98, he felt stifled in Aligarh, and his later separation was the result of this political conflict. He was overjoyed when Turkey accepted democracy in 1908, which was for him a vindication of the Islāmic political principle of *shūrá* or consultation. In 1911 he was deeply agitated by Italy's attack on Tripoli, and closely followed the war developments, rejoicing greatly at any good news.[52]

Shibli's Islāmic sentiments were again aroused in October 1912, when due to the incitement and support of the European powers, the Balkan states revolted against Turkey. This created a wave of anti-British feeling among Indian Muslims, which was fanned by Shibli's moving poetry. *'Īd-al-Aḍḥá* fell during the war, and he issued a *fatwá* (or juristic ruling) in consultation with a few other '*ulamā*', that it was better for Indian Muslims to donate to the Turkey Fund, the money which they intended to spend on the sacrificial animal.[53]

To sum up we may say that although Shibli did not regard the Turkish Sultān as the universal caliph, he was for Shibli the embodiment of contemporary Muslim power and glory. Like many Muslims of his day he had deep-rooted sympathies for Turkey, which was then the centre of the Islāmic world and the last bulwark of Islām against the hostile west, pitted valiantly against the European powers. The very fact that Shibli made his poetry rather than prose the vehicle for glorification of the Turkish sultanate, reveals the element of emotion and sentiment in these ideas. In fact in his landmark article "Musalmānoṇ ki Political Karwat" written in 1911-12, which he described as the prose commentary on his political poems,[54] he categorically quashed any pan-Islāmic sentiments that Indian Muslims may have harboured.

Shibli felt it was a disgrace to Islām to reason that Indian Muslims should now unite with their Hindu neighbours because the weakening of Iran and Turkey had lowered their international standing, and they had no other support. He felt on the other hand that even a powerful Iran and Turkey could not help them against their fellow-countrymen and immediate neighbours.[55] Thus in spite of his deep sentimental attachment to Turkey he was acutely conscious of the political and territorial reality at home, and had no illusions about the success for Muslims, of any political alliance outside India.

Loyalism

In an article in 1908, very much in the manner of Sir Sayyad but on different juristic and historical grounds, Shibli attempted to show that Muslims must obey the British government in India. He tried to illustrate with the help of Islāmic history that from the time of the Prophet (Pbuh) to the present, Muslims had always remained loyal to the government of the day since this was a precept of their religion. As a result they had always won the confidence of their non-Muslim rulers, and were appointed to high and responsible posts, even in preference to the co-religionists of the ruler. He further reasoned that since there were no obstacles in the path of the religious observances of Muslims, India under the British (who were also People of the Book), was *dār-al-Islām* rather than *dār-al-ḥarb*.[56]

According to Sayyad Sulaymān Nadwi, Shibli's argument is based on misrepresentation of a juristic text. He further tries to explain away the article by saying that it was written at a time when attempts were underway to effect a compromise between Nadwah and the government, describing it as "the price paid by the Mawlāna for the annual aid of Rs. 6,000 which the government had sanctioned for the Dār-al-'Ulūm."[57]

Although Shibli's argument appears weak, there is nothing unusual in the article to suggest that it does not represent his actual views (which at this stage are the same as Sir Sayyad's), such a display of loyalism being not at all uncharacteristic of the times.

As Nadwi himself admits, even the most liberal person then demanded only reforms from the government, since none could visualize anything beyond that, Shibli being no exception. It was therefore not surprising that in spite of his desire for greater political freedom, he never entertained any thought of turning against the government of the day, and under the slightest pressure, would hasten to prove his loyalty.[58]

Hindu-Muslim Relations

Urdu and Hindi

Shibli was only too conscious of the important position of Urdu in Hindu-Muslim relations. It was a product of the fusion of both cultures, and thus a bond that cemented the two communities; but it could also become a divisive factor—the bone of contention causing a rift between them. He therefore tried his best to make the most of the former, and counter the latter aspect.

As the Secretary of the *Anjuman-i Taraqqi-i Urdu* [a subsidary of the Muḥammadan Educational Conference and constituted during its session of 1902], in his report for Aug.-Sep. 1903, Shibli refuted the allegation of a Lucknow newspaper that the Anjuman had kept the Hindus away from its work for Urdu. He wrote that far from it, in the past few months eminent Hindus had taken a keen interest in the Anjuman. Besides this it had awarded the first prize for a literary work to a Hindu translator, for a book about Hinduism.[59]

An influential Hindu editor had claimed in 1906 that despite their centuries-old rule over, and habitation among Hindus, the religious bigotry of Muslims had prevented them from taking an interest in Hindi literature, and if anyone chanced to do so he was branded a *kāfir*.[60] Shibli perceived that such baseless allegations regarding delicate issues would adversely affect Hindu-Muslim relations, and took great pains to refute what he regarded as not only a grave, but also a grossly misplaced allegation against Muslims. His reply was published in a series of three articles in the *al-Nadwah*. Referring to his own work *Tarājim*, which abounded in evidence of the fact that Muslims had zealously studied the sciences and arts of the Hindus and mastered them thoroughly, Shibli proceeded to document evidence of the generosity of Muslims regarding the preservation, translation, and publication of Sanskrit and Bhāshā works. He took great pains to highlight the fact that far from harbouring any religious prejudice, they held not only the sciences and arts of the Hindus, but also their country, language, and religion in such high esteem as could hardly be expected of an alien nation (*qawm*).[61]

Shibli reminded his readers that Muslim interest in Hindu sciences and arts dates back to the time of Al-Bīruni. Later Sultān Zayn-al 'Ābidīn of Kashmir admitted Hindu *pandits* in his court, and had Sanskrit works translated. He was also the first to stop the collection of *jizyah* and abolish cow-slaughter. Shibli cited historical evidence to prove that in the reign of Fīrozshāh the translation of Hindi works was handsomely rewarded. Ibrāhīm 'Ādil Shāh of the Deccan entrusted his entire administration to Hindus, and even changed the official language from Persian to

Hindi. Countering allegations against Jahāngīr, Shibli cited his own account in the *Tuzūk-i Jahāngīri* to show that he enjoyed the company of Hindu scholars and sages, and would learn from them about Hinduism.[62]

In the second part of the reply Shibli demonstrated that besides translation and publication, Muslims also wrote widely in Bhāshā, especially poetry. The third article in the series is devoted to a book on the art of rhetoric and prosody of the Hindus, written by a Muslim at the instance of Jahāngīr's son A'ẓam Shāh. He also pointed out that although his detractors labelled 'Ālamgīr as a bigot who tried to destroy Hindu literature, yet the progress made by Brij Bhāshā and Hindi in his reign, and the number of translations and original works in both, was unequalled by any other.[63]

In 1912, the Allahabad government initiated a Vernacular Scheme which aimed to introduce an identical course for Urdu and Hindi, with difference only of script. Shibli was a member of the committee formed in this connection. While opposing the scheme he reasoned that the language used by educated Hindus and Muslims was identical: Urdu interspersed where necessary with Arabic and Persian words. He felt that even if a common language such as envisaged by the Scheme was developed, expressing all but the most mundane thoughts in it would require borrowing from some other scholarly language *i.e.* either Arabic or Sanskrit, and this would create a severe conflict. In preparing the syllabus too there would be a severe tussle, with both groups favouring their respective national (*qawmi*) languages.[64]

Shibli felt that whereas the scheme would create a third language, the need of the hour was to develop both Urdu and Hindi independently. Furthermore, the introduction of Sanskrit words in Urdu to make it one with Hindi would rob what was the *lingua franca* of all Muslims if not all Indians, of its universality, confining it to a single province. His views were so influential that the matter was decided accordingly, with the approval of other members.[65]

Yet it is significant that far from perceiving any threat to Urdu from the Hindus, in the same year Shibli wrote that it was unfair to accuse them of trying to wipe out the "national" language of the Muslims. On the contrary, he pointed out, they were publishing and writing in the best Urdu magazines, and by thus enhancing its worth, were instrumental in producing many new writers in the language. Muslims in contrast had failed to show any concern for Urdu: they did not publish any learned periodical in it, Urdu writers were not valued, and their *Anjuman-i Urdu* was totally profitless.[66]

Thus far from betraying the least trace of bigotry or rancour, and in spite of his championing the cause of Urdu, Shibli was not only fair and liberal, but extremely self-critical and honest in his views, which appear very balanced and enlightened. We recall that in the same year he had suggested that Muslims be taught Hindi as a medium for basic religious instruction, since it was easier and quicker to learn than Urdu (*supra* p. 37). It is also significant that he regarded Urdu as the common language of both communities, and Arabic and Sanskrit as their respective "national" languages.

History of Hindu-Muslim Relations

Reviewing the chronology of the Hindu-Muslim relationship in the fourth part of his landmark article "Musalmānoṇ ki Political Karwat" written in 1911-12, Shibli candidly reminded his co-religionists that they had been the aggressors, not only attacking the country of the Hindus, but also destroying many of their places of worship. He felt that these wounds had been kept alive in the family traditions of the Hindus until they reciprocated in full, Akbar's hand of friendship, love, and even marriage. The bonds thus formed were sincere and could not be attributed to Akbar's power, or the sycophancy of the Rājpūts. He recalled the loyalty of the Hindu *rājās*, none of whom had ever committed treachery, although many Muslim courtiers and generals had been guilty of it at one time or another. He attributed to religious misunderstanding, the uprisings by local Hindus in some parts after the reign of Shāhjahān, while the Sikhs and Marāthās were not mutineers but ambitious political contenders.[67]

In fact Shibli was so vigorous in his defence of the Hindus that the article was objected to as being one-sided, and he was obliged to clear the misunderstandings that it might have generated, in the fifth and conclusive part. He now clarified that the iconoclasm of the Muslims was motivated by political considerations rather than religious bigotry: religion and politics were then so inextricable that it was impossible to destroy the political power of an adversary without subduing his religious authority. This was why Muslims had demolished temples only in wartime, and refrained from doing so once their authority was established; and Hindus had also destroyed hundreds of mosques in the period of their dominance.[68]

In an attempt to counter the apparent one-sidedness of the

fourth part of the article, Shibli now credited the initial kindness and generosity of the Muslims with having been able to elicit an equal response from the Hindus. Recalling not only the social, but also the greater political favours of the Muslim rulers, he concluded that no nation (*qawm*) had ever bestowed such dignity, rights, and equality of status on a conquered "nation."[69]

Shibli reminded his readers that even in the present, in towns and villages, members of both communities lived as brothers and friends, sharing each others joys and sorrows. As an instance of the goodwill of the Sikhs (who were generally considered rivals of Muslims), he cited the example of the Mahārāja of Patiala, who used to donate generously from the state treasury towards the construction of mosques.[70]

Politics

Muslims and Politics

Shibli's lone but extremely significant political commentary, the article *Musalmānoṇ kī Political Karwat* was written in 1911-12, on the occasion of the annulment of the partition of Bengal.[71] The first part appeared in print on 12 February 1912, the second on 4 March, the third and fourth were published in the *Muslim Gazette*[72] on 9 October 1912, and the fifth in *Al-Ma'ārif*[73] in July 1916. Having come a long way from the loyalism he had espoused in 1908 (*supra* p. 46), Shibli now displays great political modernism and enlightenment.

The second part of the article contains the core of Shibli's philosophy of Muslim politics. He wrote that Muslims possessed a twin status: as Muslims, and as subjects of the British government; their politics being a sum of these two elements. What is highly significant is his belief that [for the purpose of politics], the second would take precedence over the first.[74]

Shibli attributed to Sir Sayyad's powerful influence, the unnatural indifference of the Muslims of northern and western India to politics. He however felt that in view of the boldness with which Sir Sayyad had demanded rights from, and expressed himself *vis-a-vis* the government, and the fact that his views were peculiar to his own times; those who claimed to follow him in their abstinence from politics were actually cowardly and unambitious people, who clung to only one aspect of his political *Shāhnāmah*.[75]

Shibli made the point that Sir Sayyad had restrained Muslims from the Indian National Congress, not from politics itself. Whereas it may be accepted that a particular school of politics was not beneficial for them, the crucial question for him was whether or not Muslims should participate in politics *per se*, which he incisively restated thus: did they have any right over the government, or the right to participate in governance; and if yes, whether or not they should demand these rights.[76]

Shibli felt that the greatest damage caused by the blind acceptance of Sir Sayyad's political ideas (*e.g.* that the time was not yet ripe for Muslims to indulge in politics; they should first make themselves fit for it; at present all they needed was education; since they were fewer in number representative government was unsuited to them etc.) by the Muslim nation (*qawm*) was that it had lost its "ideal", which alone could enthuse and inspire its members to noble action. Their highest ambition became merely graduation and jobs, and this inferior goal had caused the "nation" to be overcome by low-spiritedness and cowardice.[77]

Shibli felt further that as a result, the political ideals of Muslims had become grossly misplaced, and their "political dictionary" defined legitimate freedom as rebellion; while the Parsis and Hindus participated in the Congress, criticized the government, and yet remained members of Parliament, and of the Viceroy's Council. He felt that as a result of the loss of political consciousness, Muslims had lost the ability to strive selflessly for their national (*qawmi*) endeavours, whereas the Hindus diligently cultivated these qualities (and he admired them greatly for it).[78]

Shibli urged the Muslims to think for themselves, rather than blindly following Sir Sayyad and regarding his views as "a perpetual law of their political life." Using effective religious imagery, he reminded them of their duty to abandon *taqlīd* (rigid conformism) in favour of *ijtihād* (independent opinion). He then proceeded to illustrate how each one of Sir Sayyad's opinions and fears had been proved mistaken and unfounded by time, and concluded that since the circumstances had altered greatly since then, there was no reason to cling to outdated views. He felt that although blind adherence to Sir Sayyad's opinions had led Muslims to nurture a misplaced contempt for politics, the revocation of the partition of Bengal had jolted them out of their delusion and negligence. A new awareness had been created, and the course of their politics had been altered, although the new direction it was to take was yet to be determined.[79]

Shibli felt however that rather than joining the Congress in imitation of the Hindus, Muslims should stand on their own feet and chalk out a course for themselves. Their needs though common with the Hindus, were also different, and therefore they required a separate political stage. He however found the All India Muslim League sadly wanting, and unable to fulfil this function in its present state. Calling it an "illusion", he opined that it could never become true politics due to its misplaced foundation: the mistaken spirit of the Simla Deputation[80] (whose sole aim was that a share be earmarked for Muslims in the civil rights which the Hindus had secured after thirty years of struggle) would always remain an element of its make-up.[81]

Shibli objected to the League ideology on the grounds that it was based on the assumption that the Hindus were dominating the Muslims, who therefore needed to protect themselves. This he felt was the essential element of the League, the rest being merely face-saving devices. Some aspect of broader national aims which it sometimes included in its proceedings was, he felt, only borrowed colour. He incisively pointed out that the mutual disputes, contentions, quarrels, and demands of two subject nations (*qawm*) could not be described as politics, which defined rather the mutual demands of the government and its subjects, and originated in the question as to the extent to which the subjects should participate in governance.[82]

Shibli was astute enough to gauge the importance of politics in the modern age. Describing it as the most potent sentiment in the world, and ranking it as equal in power to religion, he defined it as an intense national (*qawmi*) feeling which could not be forced upon the heart, but which when stirred, animated man's very being, and inspired him to struggle selflessly, and with courage and determination. It quickened all his passions and enkindled his energies—but only if thought and action were true and right. The reason, he felt, why these sentiments had not been generated among Muslims was that their politics was not "true politics", which for him was characterized by universality and wideness of aims.[83]

Shibli therefore believed that besides concentrating on minor issues which concerned only a particular group, the League should set for itself goals on which depended the fate and prosperity of India as a whole. For instance a suitable system of taxation would be a greater blessing for the country than a few more jobs for Muslims. The most important demand was of course that Indians should participate in all administrative matters since they were best acquainted with their own conditions and problems.[84]

Comparing the resolutions passed by the Congress and the League, Shibli found a vast difference in their stature, scope, and significance. The former if executed would change the face of India—he appreciated the fact that already, ever since it had opened the chapter of civil demands, the Congress had marched ahead on the road to self-government through a series of administrative reforms. On the other hand he found the demands of the League characterized by a childish shallowness—he therefore advised it to include in its programme all but a few of the resolutions passed by the Congress, and to undertake constitutional struggle for their acceptance in the manner of the moderates among the Hindus.[85]

Stating emphatically that wealth had no value in politics, Shibli criticized the League for hankering after wealthy and highly placed office-bearers. He demanded that it vacate its Organizing Committee of all landlords and titled nobility, who needed to appease the authorities for their personal gain. Such could never be leaders of the nation (*qawm*), for they could never be independent in their opinions—only those should be made members of the Committee who could express themselves freely and honestly. Expressing great admiration for Gokhale, Shibli believed that the ideal leader should be like him—free of title, property, and wealth, ardent and brave, a keen student of political literature, and a master of politics.[86]

Realizing the importance of political education, and ample and accurate information, Shibli felt that the foremost need was to cultivate a political temper among the people; and for this the vast treasure-house of information regarding the science of politics must be translated into the native language and made available to them. Besides this pamphlets should be published on important political issues, and people must be appointed to furnish information regarding these, as well as to tour the country and deliver learned lectures on these issues, supported by facts, figures, and arguments.[87]

Hindu-Muslim Politics

We have already seen (*supra* pp. 49-50) the breadth of vision with which Shibli recounted the history of Hindu-Muslim relations in the fourth part of this article. We shall now examine his views regarding

"Indian" rather than "Muslim" politics. Shibli explained that in a parliamentary system the people had every right to participate in governance, to express their opinion, and to criticize the government—in fact they were both the ruler and the ruled, abiding by laws enacted by them, for themselves. Whereas this was true in England, he protested against the distortion of this principle in India, and according to him this was the point wherein originated the course of Indian politics *i.e.* in the struggle of Indians for their rights. Significantly employing war imagery to describe this struggle, he felt that despite its stiff resistance, the other side had to daily admit defeat: the English were forced to admit Indians to high posts which they had so far reserved for themselves, and above all the Reform Scheme[88] had laid the foundation of self-government.[89]

Shibli did not agree with Sir Sayyad and the Aligarh School that the Hindus had committed the greatest wrong by forming the Congress, since it had created an insurmountable rift between them and the Muslims. Vigorously countering this argument and defending its formation, he wrote that if Muslims chose to fear politics and lacked the will to demand their rights, there was no reason for the Hindus to do the same. He believed that the argument that since unity between the two communities was impossible they could not share a political stage, was wrong on both counts. (We recall that Sir Sayyad had frequently expressed this view—*supra* pp. 22 and 25). On the other hand he wholly supported Amīr 'Alī's proposal that the two communities should form a joint stage for common issues.[90]

Shibli described as "misplaced logic", Nawāb Viqār-al Mulk's argument[91] that if Muslims participated in the Congress their very identity would be destroyed, as an insignificant river loses itself in the mighty ocean. He believed on the other hand, that if one lakh Parsis could maintain their identity in the midst of nineteen crore Hindus and five crore Muslims, the latter need not feel apprehensive about the loss of their identity.[92]

Another argument that Shibli protested against strongly was that Muslims should unite with the Hindus due to the enfeeblement of their international allies—Iran and Turkey. He felt it was a disgrace to Islām to reason that Muslims should seek refuge with neighbours because they had no other help and support. He stated conclusively and realistically that these allies even if powerful, could not help the Muslims against their Hindu neighbours, unity with whom had *always* been recommended and would always remain so.[93]

Thus although Shibli was a great sympathizer and admirer of Turkey, he displayed astute political realism in dismissing the illusion of Indian Muslims that any foreign Muslim power could help them. He unhesitatingly accepted the political reality at home—that since Muslims and Hindus had been neighbours and compatriots for centuries, and would remain as such, the only way to salvation for them lay in mutual political co-operation. Although he did not say it in so many words, this idea permeates the political thought of Shibli.

Notes and References

All references in this chapter unless otherwise specified, are to the works of Shibli Nu'māni.

1. Sayyad Sulaymān Nadwi, *ed., Khuṭbāt-i Shibli* (A'zamgarh, 1965) pp. 57-58, 93-94 and 127-28.
2. *Ibid.*, pp. 58 and 94-95.
3. *Ibid.*, pp. 58-59 and 126-28.
4. *Ibid.*, pp. 96-97.
5. Sayyad Sulaymān Nadwi and Mas'ūd 'Ali Nadwi, *ed., Maqālāt-i Shibli*, 8 vols. (A'zamgarh, 1932-65) vol. VIII, p. 7.
6. *Ibid.*, pp. 3 and 13-15; *Khuṭbāt*, p. 102.
7. The Nadwah-al 'Ulamā' was founded at Lucknow in 1894 by Shibli and a group of other religious scholars. He actively took charge of its administration in 1904. The next year he was appointed its Secretary and launched it on its new, more vigorous career. In 1908 he took over its principalship and introduced many liberal innovations such as the introduction of English as a compulsory language, for which he had to overcome the stubborn opposition of his conservative colleagues. He however resigned from the post in 1913.
8. *Maqālāt* VIII, pp. 1 and 3-4.
9. *Ibid.*, pp. 2 and 14-15; *Khuṭbāt*, pp. 103-04 and 120-21.
10. *Maqālāt* VIII, pp. 2, 11 and 15; Mushtāq Ḥusayn, *ed., Bāqiyyāt-i Shibli* (Lahore, 1965) p. 108.
11. *Khuṭbāt*, p. 102.
12. *Maqālāt* VIII, p. 2.
13. *Ibid.*, p. 10.
14. *Khuṭbāt*, p. 2.
15. *Safarnāmah-i Rum-o Miṣr-o Shām* (A'zamgarh, 1921-22) p. 58.
16. *Bāqiyyāt*, pp. 25-26.

17. *Maqālāt* I, pp. 172-74; *Khuṭbāt*, pp. 67-68 and 70-85.
18. *Safarnāmah*, pp. 76-77.
19. *Maqālāt* III, pp. 164-65 and 177.
20. *Khuṭbāt*, pp. 59-60.
21. *Maqālāt* III, pp. 140-42.
22. *Maqālāt* VIII, p. 4.
23. *Khuṭbāt*, pp. 95-96.
24. *Maqālāt* III, p. 156.
25. *Safarnāmah*, p. 77.
26. *Bāqiyyāt*, pp. 14 and 17.
27. *Maqālāt* VIII, pp. 143-46.
28. *Maqālāt* III, pp. 140, 143 and 150.
29. Muḥammad Ismā'īl Pānīpati, *ed., Maqālāt-i Sir Sayyad*, 16 vols. (Lahore, 1941-1965) vol. VIII, pp. 49 and 75-76.
30. *Maqālāt* III, pp. 146-48.
31. *Bāqiyyāt*, pp. 14-16 and 107; *Maqālāt* VIII, pp. 141-42.
32. *Maqālāt* III, p. 157.
33. *Khuṭbāt*, pp. 90 and 98.
34. *Maqālāt* VIII, pp. 143-46.
35. *Bāqiyyāt*, p. 108.
36. *Khuṭbāt*, pp. 99 and 101.
37. *Bāqiyyāt*, pp. 25 and 28.
38. *Maqālāt* III, pp. 146-48.
39. *Khuṭbāt*, pp. 135-38.
40. *Maqālāt* III, p. 161; *Khuṭbāt*, pp. 133-34, 139-142 and 147-48.
41. Sayyad Sulaymān Nadwi, *Ḥayāt-i Shibli* (A'zamgarh, n.d.) pp. 94-96 and 585-86.
42. *Ibid.*, pp. 190, 221 and 279.
43. *Safarnāmah*, p. 2.
44. *Ibid.*, pp. 112-18.
45. *Ḥayāt*, pp. 205-06.
46. *Safarnāmah*, pp. 84-87.
47. *Ḥayāt,* p. 587.
48. *Ibid.*, pp. 281 and 631.
49. *Maqālāt* I, pp. 179-184.
50. *Ḥayāt*, pp. 142, 281 and 631.
51. *Ibid.*, p. 281 ff.
52. *Ibid.*, pp. 587-88.
53. *Ibid.*, pp. 591, 593 and 597-98.
54. Mehr Afroz Murad, *Intellectual Modernism of Shibli Nu'māni: An Exposition of His Religious and Socio-Political Ideas* (Lahore, 1976) p. 101.
55. *Maqālāt* VIII, p. 148.

56. *Maqālāt* I, pp. 165-69 and 171.
57. *Ḥayāt*, pp. 631-32.
58. *Ibid.*, p. 630.
59. *Bāqiyyāt*, p. 93; *Ḥayāt*, p. 403.
60. *Maqālāt* II, p. 79.
61. *Ibid*; *Maqālāt* VI, pp. 218-19 and 222.
62. *Ibid.*, pp. 220-21, 225 and 229-233.
63. *Maqālāt* II, pp. 79 ff. and 92-93.
64. *Ibid.*, pp. 72 and 74-75.
65. *Ibid.*, pp. 72 and 75-76.
66. *Maqālāt* VIII, pp. 176-77.
67. *Maqālāt* VIII, pp. 175-77.
68. *Ibid.*, p. 179.
69. *Ibid.*, pp. 179 and 181.
70. *Ibid.*, p. 176.
71. The partition was effected by Lord Curzon in 1906 for administrative convenience; but it greatly benefitted the Muslims of eastern Bengal, and adversely affected Bengali Hindus, who had held a monopoly of all services. It was however annulled after it flared up the flames of communalism.
72. An independent Muslim newspaper which Shibli brought out from Lucknow from 1912 to 1913.
73. The publication of the Dār-al Muṣannifīn, founded by Shibli in A'zamgarh in 1913 to promote the publication and translation of historical, religious, and scientific works.
74. *Ibid.*, p. 151.
75. *Ibid.*, pp. 154-55 and 158-160.
76. *Ibid.*
77. *Ibid.*, pp. 149-151.
78. *Ibid.*
79. *Ibid.*, pp. 148-49, 151 and 155-58.
80. Refers to the address presented by a delegation of Muslim elite led by the Āghā Khān, to the Viceroy Lord Minto, at Simla in 1906, after which the All India Muslim League was formed in the same year.
81. *Ibid.*, pp. 161 and 163-64.
82. *Ibid.*, pp. 164-65.
83. *Ibid.*, pp. 167 and 169.
84. *Ibid.*, pp. 171-72.
85. *Ibid.*, pp. 165-66 and 172.
86. *Ibid.*, pp. 170, 173 and 182-84.
87. *Ibid.*, p. 173.
88. Referring apparently to the constitutional reforms introduced by the British government in 1907 under pressure from the moderate group

in the Congress.

89. *Ibid.*, pp. 152-54.
90. *Ibid.*, pp. 172-74.
91. Expressed in an article "Hindustān Meṇ Musalmānoṇ ki Ā'indah Ḥālat," written in 1911 on the occasion of the annulment of the partition of Bengal, and published in the *Aligarh Institute Gazette*.
92. *Maqālāt* VIII, p. 148.
93. *Ibid.*

Chapter 3

MUḤAMMAD IQBĀL
(1876-1938)

Loyalism

In 1909 Iqbāl expressed loyalist feelings akin to those of Sir Sayyad. He quoted from the Qur'ān and *Hadīth* to show that whereas Islām permitted defensive war, the doctrine of aggressive war against unbelievers was wholly unauthorized by it. He tried to establish that it was essentially a religion of peace, which severely denounced all forms of social and political disorder and violent changes, its ideal being to secure peace at any cost. He also quoted familiar Traditions enjoining obedience to the ruling authority whoever it be.[1] We recall that Sir Sayyad had argued on much the same lines (*supra* pp. 28-29).

At this juncture Iqbāl disapproved of the tendency of those Indian Muslims who were exposed to "an overdose of western ideas", to indiscreetly criticize the government, and wanted "to educate political opinion on strictly Islāmic lines." He felt that their attitude to the government must be guided by the example of the early Muslim emigrees to Christian Abyssinia, and the Qur'ānic verse which describes Christians as being "nearest . . . in love/to the Believers."(5:82)

Iqbāl glorified England for carrying its mission of democracy (which he described as the most important aspect of Islām as a political ideal) to the nations of the east, and thus politically vitalizing them. He reasoned that since an aspect of their political ideal was being worked out in the British empire, it deserved the greatest "sympathy and respect" from Muslims—its democratic spirit even prompted him to call it "the greatest Muḥammadan empire in the world."[3] However later in life we do not find him expressing such strong loyalist sentiments.

SECTION I

In this portion we shall deal with the general principles regarding nationhood which Iqbāl evolved in the early phase of his thought, and later applied to the Indian situation.

Muslim Nationhood

Definition

In Iqbāl's thought we find a fully worked out, complex, and rich philosophy of the concept of Muslim nationhood, which he outlined in various articles, speeches, and notes between 1909 and 1911. In an article published in 1909 he wrote that the basis of nationhood for Muslims was Islām itself, which besides being a religion, was also "a community, a nation", whose membership was not based on birth or naturalization, but on identity of belief. He even went on to say that since Islām was above time and space, phrases such as "Indian Muḥammadan" although convenient, were actually a contradiction in terms. Nationality for Muslims was thus a pure idea, without any geographical basis—its material centre if any, was the holy town of Makkah. The basis of Muslim nationality thus combined the real and the ideal, the concrete and the abstract.[4]

A year later however, Iqbāl appears to have altered his stand slightly in favour of a purer idealism. He wrote in his notebook in 1910 that for Muslims nationality was "a pure idea" without any material basis, their only rallying-point being a mental agreement in their view of the world. Thus whereas Islām constructed nationality out of a purely abstract idea *i.e.* religion, the very lifeblood of the western concept of nationality was a concrete thing *i.e.* country.[5]

Elaborating the point in a lecture that he delivered at the M.A.O. College, Aligarh, in December of the same year,[6] Iqbāl explained that since Islām was in its essence "non-temporal and non-spatial", it could not found its nationality on an external, sensory principle such as country, nor depend on the character and genius of a particular people. Thus true to its abhorrence of all material limitations, Islām based its nationality on "a purely abstract idea objectified in a potentially expansive group of concrete personalities."[7]

Iqbāl thus believed that the essential difference between Muslims and other nations of the world lay in their peculiar conception of nationality, which was not based on identity of language, country, or economic interest; but on unity of belief and, as he now added, participation in the legacy of a common historical tradition which bound them together.[8]

Islām thus held a far deeper significance for Muslims than merely religion. As the very basis of nationality, their communal life depended on a firm grasp of it: if they let go of this handhold—the theological rope of God (*ḥabl-al matīn*)—they would become disorganized. (The similarity with the views of Sir Sayyad and Shibli—*supra* pp. 13-14, 19 and 35—is indeed striking.) Not only this, Islām was the "eternal home or country of Muslims", and thus above everything else for them, as England was for the English, and Germany for the Germans.[9]

Iqbāl developed these ideas further in an article which appeared around the same time, wherein he sketched the first outlines of his theory of Islāmic universalism. He stated that the membership of the ideal Muslim state would not be determined by birth or domicile, but "by a public declaration of like-mindedness", and would terminate with its cessation. He believed that since the general principles of the law of Islām were based on human nature rather than the peculiarities of a particular people, for Islām nationality was not the highest limit of political development. Rather, overlooking natural and historical differences of race and nationality, its political ideal aimed at the creation of a nation born of a "free fusion" of all peoples. The ideal territory for such a nation was the whole earth. Although the Arabs had failed to create such a "world-state" by conquest, he believed it was possible of realization; and nor was it incompatible with the sovereignty of individual states, since it was based not on physical force, but on the spiritual force of a common ideal.[10]

We note the extreme idealism inherent in Iqbāl's conception of Muslim nationhood. Later he developed these ideas more fully, but they never lost their innate idealism. By characterizing Muslim nationality as a pure "idea", he exposes it to the danger of becoming an unattainable ideal; and himself to a paradox which we shall see surfacing later, and which is in a way inevitable when an attempt is made to translate what has been developed as a lofty and abstract ideal, into mundane reality. The abstract nature of his concept of nationhood also creates a certain insecurity, making his Muslim society very fragile, prone to disintegration, and therefore extremely wary of change and external influences—as we shall henceforth see for ourselves.

Iqbāl further believed that uniformity of culture within the Muslim community was as important as unity of belief—this was how he interpreted the theological phrase about dyeing oneself in the colour of God—*ṣibghatullāh*. The "uniform mental outlook" thus created would not only define the community clearly, but also give it "a purpose and ideal of its own", besides linking its past with its present and future, by ensuring a continuity of historical, cultural, and intellectual traditions. Just as the Muslim community aimed at the "subsumption" of all races, so also its culture was universal, and not the product of any particular people.[11] In the latter phase of his thought, we shall see him becoming increasingly preoccupied with the dissemination and continuity of Muslim culture as essential to the solidarity and survival of the community.

Writing his notebook in 1910, Iqbāl vigorously defended Muslim "fanaticism", describing it as "patriotism for religion." He reasoned that if patriotism, which was nothing but "fanaticism for country", was considered a justifiable sentiment, then so also was Muslim fanaticism. He reasoned that since all nations were fanatical concerning the basis of their nationality (*i.e.* country), and Muslim nationality was based on religion, their fanaticism concerning it was equally justified. Defining fanaticism as "the principle of individuation working in the case of a group", he felt that in this sense all groups in all species of life which cared for the survival of their individual and collective life, were fanatical.[12] In the lecture delivered later that year, he clarified that by fanaticism or group loyalty he meant to convey merely regard for one's own community, and not dislike for others.[13]

We shall see Iqbāl using this argument of survival time and again, to defend the Muslim community against similar charges of intolerance, communalism etc., when this question arose later in the Indian context.

Tradition and Change

Iqbāl believed in 1910 that the problem of survival was central to nations, which were as deeply haunted by the fear of extinction as were individuals. Whereas he felt that the assimilation of elements of the civilization of other nations was not only expedient but imperative, he warned against too much haste, or lack of method in emulating others. He therefore believed that in order to maintain the health and stability of a community such as that of Muslims based solely on "the religious idea", it was necessary not only to closely guard against the contradictory forces operative within it; but also to control foreign influences, allowing them to permeate the social fibre very gradually—or else, due to the great strain on its "assimilative power", such a society was liable to disintegrate. The archetypal Muslim character should therefore "hold fast to its own" even while it assimilated the virtues of others, rejecting all that was inimical to its own cherished traditions.[14]

As we shall see, this tension between assimilation and exclusion, universality and exclusiveness, change and tradition, liberalism and conservatism, proved to be a persistent feature of Iqbāl's thought, recurring time and again. He tends towards the former, but the threat to survival which it seems to him to imply when indulged in freely, compels him to temper it with the latter antidote, for as we have seen earlier, the "survival" of the community was to him dearer than all else.

Delivering his Six Lectures in Madras and elsewhere nearly two decades later in 1928-29, Iqbāl welcomed "the liberal movement" in the contemporary Muslim world, but also warned that liberalism had a tendency to act as a disintegrating force: he feared that in their over-zealousness Muslim reformers might "overstep the proper limits of reform." He was also cautious in asserting the necessity of *ijtihād* as the instrument of evolution in Islāmic law; stressing at the same time that "conservatism" was equally important—since the past of a people, which constituted their peculiar identity, could not be summarily rejected.[15]

Iqbāl appears to have found the Afghans true to the ideal type outlined by him. He visited Afghanistan in 1933, and wrote next year in praise of their "conservatism", which even while it kept them "in living contact with their past", was at the same time "fully sensitive to, and assimilative of new cultural forces."[16]

Education

During this period (1909-11) when he outlined his ideas regarding Muslim nationhood, Iqbāl also dwelt on the issue of education as a means of ensuring its continuity. Himself steeped in the best of both worlds, he however appears to have been greatly disturbed by the complete overshadowing of Muslim history and culture, in the sphere of education, by its western counterparts. We notice a shift in his stand later, when not only the political, but also the cultural threat is perceived, not from the west any more, but from the majority community in India.

Iqbāl's views on education were guided by the principle that "a living nation is living because it never forgets its dead." He felt that "a truly national education" should breed intimacy with one's "social and historical tradition", since only this could create that "healthy pride" which was "the very lifeblood of a truly national character." He therefore believed that every Muslim student should be familiar with the glories of Muslim civilization and history, the achievements of its leading figures, and the extent of its influence over modern western civilization. He felt that the present western-oriented system of education in India on the other hand, by breaking away Muslims completely from their past, did not in the least do justice to their needs. He wrote in 1909 that if they did not develop their own educational institutions which would keep alive their social and historical traditions, their very survival would be threatened.[17]

Iqbāl was not satisfied with Muslim educational efforts of the last fifty years, which he felt had been totally oblivious to long-term needs, concentrating only on immediate gains. He felt that the fears of the traditionalist followers of Islāmic culture, who had disputed with Sir Sayyad about western education had been proved true—that a shift in education would change hearts. He was convinced that no nation could abruptly break the link with its past, and for Muslims, whose collective traditions were the lifeblood of their nationhood, it was all the more impossible to do so.[18]

To Iqbāl the modern Muslim appeared to be an intellectual slave of the west, and devoid of that healthy self-respect which is born of a study of one's national history and literature. He felt that the present system of education was creating a new group of quasi-Muslims who, in being intoxicated by western literature and bereft of their national traditions, had moved far away from the Islāmic centre of gravity. He feared that due to the lack of a unifying centre this group would someday lose its identity, and be merged into some other, more vital community.[19] In 1938 he reiterated that imperial powers not only subjugated weaker peoples but also robbed them of their religion, literature, and cultural traditions.[20]

Faced with such a situation, Iqbāl realized and reaffirmed the primacy of religious education in 1910. Significantly enough, he felt that those who had followed the principle that the education of every Muslim child should commence with lessons in the Qur'ān, were wiser than modern Muslims. Having established that the solidarity of Muslims as a community lay in their grasp on the religious principle, he felt that the best way to tighten this hold and thus ensure the continuity of national life was to provide "sound religious education" to the Muslim woman—the "principal depositary of religion", and the virtual "maker of the community."[21] (*Cf.* Sir Sayyad and Shibli, *supra* pp. 16, 18-19 and 39ff.)

Iqbāl denied that he was against western civilization as such, and acknowledged Muslim indebtedness to it in the intellectual sphere, but also insisted that Islāmic culture was an independent entity. While Muslims must keep abreast with the swift pace of modern sciences, their culture should be purely Islāmic, and for this they needed a national university run on thoroughly Islāmic principles. Whereas Shibli had emphasized the need to acquaint religious scholars with modern languages and sciences, since they were already well-versed in religious knowledge (*supra* pp. 41-42), Iqbāl felt on the other hand that Muslim preachers and scholars had a limited knowledge of Islāmic history and sciences, and emphasized that besides economics and sociology they should also have command over Muslim literature and thought. He felt that since present Muslim educational institutions could not satisfy these needs, a new exemplary university should be set up, whose overriding principle should be Islāmic culture, and in which the old and the new should be perfectly blended, even while he realized that this was not an easy task.[22]

We recall that Shibli had also visualized such a model university whose products would embody the best of both worlds. Whereas his views were those of a man of action, accompanied by concrete practical steps to be taken, Iqbāl is essentially a man of thought, and develops his theory of education more as a philosophical ideal. His pre-occupation with education was limited to the early period, politics becoming the field of his thought and action, and the means of safeguarding the Muslim community in his later life.

Islāmic Universalism

We have earlier commented on the tension in Iqbāl's thought between contradictory aspects of the same reality (*supra* p. 63). One such conflict is between the universalism and exclusivity of Islām, which although it obliterated all distinctions among those within its fold, also signified a clearly-defined community, the line of demarcation between those within and without its boundaries being very explicit. In 1910-11 he had emphasized the former aspect, seeing Muslim society as a "potentially expansive group" which did not recognize natural and historical differences, and aimed at a "fusion" of all peoples (*supra* p. 61).

In a letter to Dr. R.A. Nicholson dated 24 January 1921, Iqbāl attempted to reconcile this dualism. He felt that Islām was exclusive only "in the sense of having a creed and well-defined outline", while at the same time it was "ever enlarging its limits by example and persuasion." He clarified that it aimed at "absorption" not through "conquest", but by "the simplicity of its teaching [and] its appeal to the commonsense of mankind."[23] However many years later, in 1938 he described Islām as an "imperceptible . . . biologico-psychological activity" which could influence men "without any missionary effort."[24] If Islām was to take the aid neither of conquest, nor proselytization (which interestingly enough he did not exclude in 1921), it is not clear how it would absorb all of humanity.

In his letter of 1921 Iqbāl had deduced on the basis of the verse: ". . . come, let us unite on what is common to us all . . ." (3:64), that the Qur'ān called for the "universal unification of mankind", overlooking the minor differences between them; and that not only Muslims, but all men were "meant for the kingdom of God on earth"—if they abandoned "their idols of race and nationality."[25]

Iqbāl believed that Islām had proved to be the most successful opponent of the "race-idea", which was "the hardest barrier in the way of the humanitarian ideal", and therefore the biggest enemy not only of Islām, but of all humanity. Since the salvation of man lay in absolute equality and freedom for all, all lovers of mankind should revolt against racialism. He accepted territorial and racial organizations only as "temporary phases . . . of collective life"; and felt that since Muslims were "being lured by the idea of a territorial nationality", forgetting their "ideal of a universal humanity", it was his duty to remind them of it.[26]

Iqbāl expressed similar views in his Lectures eight years later, when he stated that according to the Qur'ān the racial divisions among mankind were only for the purpose of identification—he must have had in mind verse 13 of *Sūrah-al-Ḥujurāt*. He opposed modern Muslim nationalism as a manifestation of the race-idea, which threatened to "wipe off the broad human outlook" of Islām. He felt further that in modern Muslim countries religion was being gradually displaced by patriotism and nationalism; whereas only "a purely religious method of spiritual renewal" could succeed, by expanding man's thought and emotion rather than narrowing it down. He therefore warned Muslims to guard against a movement that might have results similar to the Protestant revolution in Europe, which displaced "the universal ethics of Christianity by systems of national ethics."[27]

Admitting that before Islām, Christianity had brought "the message of equality", Iqbāl however felt that "Christian Rome" had been unable to fully realize the idea, whereas the later "growth of territorial nationalism" destroyed it altogether. For Islām on the other hand, the unity of mankind was not a lofty ideal: as "a social movement" it aimed, and had more or less succeeded, through its institutions, in making the idea "a living factor" in the lives of the "heterogeneous mass" of its adherents, and in creating a "collective will and conscience among them."[28]

Echoing his earlier views on the thoroughly abstract nature of Muslim nationhood (*supra* pp. 60-61), Iqbāl reasserted that Islām was non-territorial, and aimed at a "a final combination of humanity." Since it believed in the spiritual origin of all human life, it rejected the earth-rooted bond of "blood-relationship", positing instead "a purely psychological foundation of human unity" *i.e.*, "the principle of *Tawhīd*."[29]

In the Presidential Address that he delivered at the annual session of the All India Muslim League on 29 December 1930 at Allahabad, Iqbāl again cited verse 64 of *Sūrah 'Āl-i-'Imrān* as the first practical step which Islām had taken towards unifying mankind by calling upon the People of the Book to unite on the principle of the unity of God, which was common to them all. Whereas he felt that this verse could not be realized due to the wars between Islām and Christianity; he now endorsed "Muslim nationalism" in modern countries as helping in its gradual realization. Yet earlier in the same speech he had also expressed the apprehension that nationalism in the modern Muslim world was threatening "the humanizing work of Islām" by racializing the Muslim "outlook", whereas Islām aimed at liberating it from "its geographical limitations." He feared that increased "racial consciousness" signified "the growth of standards different and even opposed to the standard of Islām."[30]

From an interview that he gave in 1931, we learn that Iqbāl interpreted pan-Islāmism too in this way—as "pan-humanism" or "Islāmism" *i.e.* a social experiment (rather than a political project), and a precept of Islām, which did not recognize caste, race, or colour. In a speech the next year he reiterated that overlooking their mutual differences, Islām had accepted all of mankind as brothers.[31]

In a statement in March 1933 Iqbāl said that the rise of nationalism in the west implied an upsurge of racialism, which was for him "the greatest blot on modern civilization." He feared that the birth of a race-problem in Asia would have "disastrous" consequences; and felt that if it did not wish to go the way of Europe, it should "assimilate the ideals of Islām", and think in terms of "mankind" not "race."[32]

Replying to questions raised by Pdt. Jawaharlal Nehru regarding Qadianism, Iqbāl wrote around 1935 that in its message that mankind would perish by internecine war unless it de-racialized itself (which was borne out by modern day events), Islām was in keeping with the spirit of modern times; its institutions aiming to create "an outlook which would counteract the race-building forces of nature." He however held that the adoption by Muslim nations of racial and nationalist ideas did not mean that they had abandoned Islām.[33] We recall that in 1930 he had acknowledged that the ideals of modern Muslim nationalism were opposed to those of Islām, whereas his stand against Muslim nationalism was even more severe in his letter of 1921 and the Lectures of 1928-29 (*supra* pp. 66-67).

In 1938 Iqbāl concluded that not "national unity" but human brotherhood was the only "durable" unifying force, which was above race, nationality, colour and language—it is significant that he does not include religion here. He believed that in order to achieve happiness men needed to obliterate all distinctions, and to "believe that the whole world is the family of God."[34]

In his statement on "Islām and Nationalism" written in response to Mawlānā Ḥusayn Aḥmad Madani's views and published in the *Eḥsān*, Lahore, in March of the same year, Iqbāl reiterated that Islām wanted to replace mankind's "national and racial viewpoint" by a purely human one, and to unite it despite all its natural distinctions. Although it recognized these differences, it wished to purify the world of the abuses perpetrated in their name, and to create a society true to the divine law received by the Prophet Muḥammad (Pbuh). He therefore felt that Islām was the only social order which could ensure lasting peace and security.[35]

Having analysed Iqbāl's views on Islāmic universalism, it is not difficult to see why it drove him to the contradictions which it did. Two factors may be responsible for this: firstly, the dual nature of Muslim society itself—as a thoroughly egalitarian one it did indeed aim at creating a universal brotherhood, yet it was also very clearly-defined, brooking no blurring of its boundaries. Secondly, the ideal and abstract conception that Iqbāl built of Islāmic universalism tended to breakdown when applied to a real life situation. The kind of universal brotherhood he envisaged was possible only if all of mankind followed the ideals, and by implications the religion of Islām (as Iqbāl himself suggests), which is a near impossible situation, especially since he himself ruled out the spread of Islām both by conquest and missionary activity (*supra* p. 66).

Iqbāl appears to have merely replaced other political, ethnic, geographical, and linguistic differences by the religious—he does not seem to regard human brotherhood as being above religion (*supra* p. 68). Since he believed that religion (or Islām) alone could unify mankind, his very universalism drove him to an attitude which could not adjust itself to the kind of religious pluralism that existed in India, producing separatist tendencies instead. It also partly explains the paradox of his situation—in spite of being a firm believer in the need for unifying mankind, since he made religion the basis of this unity, in India he was compelled to present a solution which rather than bringing together the different communities, highlighted their differences. He had spoken of wiping out all distinctions between men, and was a vociferous opponent of geographical divisions—yet in the Indian context he stressed the need for Muslims to maintain their separate identity in a clearly demarcated geographical area. We have seen that he substituted "country" by "religion" in his scheme of things, describing Islām as the motherland of Muslims, and on the same grounds justifying fanaticism as "patriotism for religion" (*supra* pp. 61-62). He thus appears to have succeeded only in replacing the political nationalism which he abhorred, by a kind of religious nationalism.

Nationalism

In the beginning of his poetic career at "the turn of the century",

Iqbāl was attracted to "the surging nationalism of the day."[36] However he visited Europe in 1905 and returned in 1908, "completely disillusioned with nationalism . . . and . . . with a firm belief in Islām as a socio-politico-moral force."[37] In an interview in 1931 he admitted that he had been "a zealous nationalist" in his "college days", but not anymore—his ideas about nationalism having undergone a definite change due to "maturer thinking."[38] His later opposition to "narrow" nationalism goes hand in hand with his championing of universalism.

In 1910 Iqbāl believed that whereas the concept of nationality was a healthy one and necessary for the growth of communities, it was apt to lead to excess, and tended to "kill the broad human element in art and literature." Although it had brought some benefits, it had also vitiated international politics by creating small political groups with abiding antagonism between them.[39]

Iqbāl wrote in an article published in 1938 that he had been repudiating nationalism since very long because the writings of Europeans had led him to believe that the propagation of their concept of nationalism in Muslim countries was a ploy "to shatter the religious unity of Islām", and to further Europe's "imperialistic designs."[40] In his New Year message in the same year he again drew attention to the nexus between nationalism and imperialism, the former providing a cloak and excuse for the latter: "in their hunger for dominion", and to satisfy the "avarice of their own particular groups", nations had subjugated, and shed the blood of weaker peoples.[41]

Nationalism and Islām

One of the earliest arguments which Iqbāl presented in favour of his belief that the two were antithetical to each other, was in his note-book in 1910. He reasoned that since the mission of Islām was to demolish idolatry, it could not approve of patriotism (born of nationalism), which was nothing but "a subtle form of idolatry" amounting to a deification of the motherland, as he deduced from "the patriotic songs of various nations." He even suggested that "the fact that the Prophet (Pbuh) prospered and died in a place not his birthplace", was "a mystic hint" towards undermining the significance of nationalism.[42]

In an interview in 1931 Iqbāl said that he was opposed to nationalism because "as at present understood and practised", it came in the way of the realization of "the higher ideal of Islām" as a social code, which was based on a belief in the spiritual unity of mankind.[43]

In 1935 Iqbāl wrote that whereas "nationalism in the sense of love for one's country, and even readiness to die for it was a part of the Muslim's faith"; it clashed with Islām only when it became a "political concept" and as such, claimed "to be a principle of human solidarity"—for this would necessarily relegate Islām "to the background of a mere private opinion."[44]

Iqbāl elaborated on this aspect three years later, in the article in which he explained his disagreement with Mawlāna Ḥusayn Aḥmad Madani's statement endorsing geographical nationalism. He conceded that "nations" and "countries" had always been associated with each other, and that as such a merely "geographical term", the idea of "country" did not conflict with Islām. He also accepted the sentiments of attachment and sacrifice for one's homeland. However, he reasoned, in modern political theory nationhood had ceased to remain a "merely geographical" term and had become a political concept. This "idea of nation" as "a principle of human society" clashed with Islām—also "a law of human society"—for which any other such law was "inadequate and unacceptable." He believed that by styling Islām as the *"dīn-i qayyim"* or "True Faith", the Qur'ān had also openly declared that any other system must be "rejected" outright.[45]

Iqbāl fully realized that such a stand would generate "political controversies" in India, for it implied that Muslims could not unite with other communities for serving national ends. In spite of this, he did not agree with the nationalists that "in view of present-day needs the Muslim community should take up a different position." He believed on the other hand that "what the divine law has prescribed" was "for all times to come."[46] This pleading the case for strict conformism (*taqlīd*) is in stark contrast to his vigorous advocacy of *ijtīhād* (independent legal opinion) elsewhere (*infra* pp. 87-88), and reflects the recurring tension in his thought between change and stability, referred to earlier (*supra* p. 63). Although a believer in the former, he was also extremely sensitive to the danger of disintegration inherent in it, and therefore advised extreme caution and often, as here, even a strict maintenance of the *status quo.*

We have already referred to the change in Iqbāl's stand regarding Muslim nationalism. In a letter of 1921 and the six Lectures delivered in 1928-29 he had opposed it forcefully as being contrary to Islāmic universalism. By 1930 his views had softened, even reflecting some ambiguity: while he acknowledged that its ideals were opposed to those of Islām, he also credited modern Muslim nationalism with helping to achieve the Qur'ānic ideal by helping to unite the People of the Book. In 1935 he wrote that the adoption by Muslims of nationalist ideas did not signify their abandonment of Islām (*supra* pp. 66-68)—he now appears to have finally reconciled Muslim nationalism with Islām.

Having established that nationalism was opposed to Islām, Iqbāl however exempted Muslim nationalism from the generalization. He now believed that the conflict between Islām and nationalism which threatened to reduce the former's role, did not arise in countries where Muslims were "an overwhelming majority", and the minority comprised People of the Book, with whom Muslim law permitted free social relations including matrimonial alliance. He concluded that whereas in such countries "Islām accommodates nationalism" because there they are "practically identical", nationalism posed a threat for Muslims only when they happened "to be in a minority", for then it demanded their "complete self-effacement." He therefore believed that in such circumstances Islām was "justified in seeking self-determination as a cultural unit."[47]

Thus Iqbāl was faced with the dilemma which confronted many Indian Muslims: the conflict generated by the fact that for them community and country, religion and politics, were not identical, which gave rise to conflicting loyalties; whereas this problem did not exist for Muslims living in majority groups. Sir Sayyad had also perceived this conflict when he differentiated between *watan* and *qawm (supra* pp. 8-9), and feared Hindu domination through the Congress *(supra* pp. 23-24). Shibli does not seem to have been much troubled by the problem—clearly separating religion and politics, he believed that for political purposes the religious status of Muslims was of secondary importance as compared to the political (*supra* p. 50).

In the Lectures of 1928-29 Iqbāl explained that the reason for Islām's conflict with nationalism lay in its being, unlike Christianity, "a civil society" in which church and state were not separate.[48] In his Presidential Address of 1930 he reasoned that in Europe, as a result of the Reformation and the later growth of nationalism, religion became "a private affair of the individual", having nothing to do with his "temporal life." This "mistaken separation of spiritual and temporal" eventually led to "the total exclusion of Christianity from the life of European states."[49]

Iqbāl again underlined that Islām on the other hand did not believe in such "an irreconcilable duality of spirit and matter"; church and state being for it "organic to each other." Religion was therefore not "a private individual experience", but "individual experience creative of a social order." Islām's "religious ideal" was thus inextricably linked to its "social order", the rejection of one eventually involving that of the other too. He therefore concluded that since for Muslims religion was not merely "a private affair", Islām "as a moral and political ideal" could not be permitted to suffer the same fate as Christianity. He was also convinced that it was not possible "to retain Islām as an ethical ideal" while rejecting it "as a polity" in favour of secular "national polities."[50]

In 1935 Iqbāl again wrote that whereas in Christianity the "idea of separation of church and state" was based on the dualism of spirit and matter, in Islām it amounted only to "a division of function." As before he traced this to the difference in their origins: whereas Christianity began as a monastic order divorced from worldly affairs, "Islām was from the very beginning a civil society" based on revealed but civil laws.[51]

Nationalism and Religion

In his lectures Iqbāl condemned both nationalism and socialism for drawing upon "the psychological forces of hate, suspicion, and resentment", and felt that religion alone "which in its higher manifestations is neither dogma, nor priesthood, nor ritual", could help man to triumph over a civilization torn "by its inner conflict of religious and political values."[52]

Whereas Shibli believed that in politics the political status of Muslims held precedence over the religious, and described politics as the most powerful driving force in the world, rating it equal in power to religion (*supra* pp. 50 and 52); Iqbāl constantly upheld the power and relevance of religion, describing it in 1930 as "a power of the utmost importance in the life of individuals as well as states."[53]

In his Presidential Address at the annual session of the All India Muslim Conference at Lahore on 21 March 1932, Iqbāl again asserted the precedence of religion over nationalism. Accepting patriotism as "a perfectly natural virtue" which deserved a place in man's moral life, he however went on to say that what really mattered was "a man's faith, his culture, his historical tradition." For him these, rather than "the piece of earth" with which man happened to be "temporarily associated", were "worth living for and dying for." He further felt that religion and modern European nationalism were incompatible since the latter contained "the germ of atheistic materialism", which was why he opposed it in India.[54]

Europe, for Iqbāl, provided an example of the results of the displacement of religion by nationalism as a means of social unity. In 1938 he wrote that the substitution of Christianity by nationality as the basis of the life of European countries not only led to the breakdown of their "religious unity" and conflict between religion and state, but also to "irreligiousness, religious scepticism, and economic conflicts." He felt that the experiment if repeated in India, would produce equally disastrous consequences. He disagreed with those who believed that religion could coexist with political nationalism; and felt on the other hand that if in a country like India comprising different religions, land was regarded as the basis of nationhood, the communities would die out, leaving behind only a common "irreligiousness." Even if Islām managed to survive, it would be as a purely "ethical ideal", without its accompanying "social order."[55]

Islāmic Unity and the Caliphate

We have seen Iqbāl expressing himself regarding the ideal Muslim nation or "world-state" comprising "the whole earth", yet compatible with individual sovereign states, as early as in 1910 (*supra* p. 61). Later, in 1928-29 he delineated the ideal Islāmic political order as a "League of Nations", in which "artificial boundaries and racial distinctions" would exist only for "facility of reference."[56] (This would be in keeping with the Qur'ānic ideal often upheld by him—*supra* pp. 66-67). In a statement in 1937 he again said that rather than participating in the existing League of Nations which was dominated by European countries, Muslim nations should explore the possibility of forming an "Eastern League of Nations."[57]

In 1935 Iqbāl wrote that the religious solidarity of Islām consisted in "a uniform belief" in its two "structural principles": *Tawhid*, and the finality of the Prophethood of Muḥammad (Pbuh), coupled with an observance of the five obligatory duties; and was threatened when Muslims rebelled against any of these. In the political sphere

Islāmic solidarity encouraged the "political combination of Muslim states", which could take three forms: the first and ideal one was that of a "world-state"; the second "a League of Muslim states"; and the last consisted of independent states whose relations were "determined by purely economic and political considerations." This solidarity would be shaken in case of a war between Muslim states.[58]

Iqbāl is not very clear about how such an abiding unity was to be achieved between Muslim countries. At the same time he categorically rejected the "merely symbolical overlordship" of the Islāmic caliphate (which had now been rendered powerless), as a means of achieving it. In one of his lectures he had merely said that for the time being each Muslim nation should seek to strengthen itself, so that eventually a living family of independent republics may be formed, unified by the "bond of a common spiritual aspiration."[59]

Iqbāl felt that since in recent times the issue of the caliphate had created numerous ruptures and differences among Muslim states, it had succeeded more in keeping them apart from each other than in uniting them. He held that rather than a divine and therefore indispensable institution, "the idea of the universal imamate" was "merely a matter of expediency", which had failed to work ever since the break-up of the Muslim empire, and the rise of independent units.[60]

In 1933 Iqbāl expressed his lack of faith in the feasibility of "political pan-Islāmism" in the sense of the "unification of Muslims into a political state", which he felt had merely been used by Sultān 'Abd-al Ḥamīd as a "diplomatic weapon." He believed rather in pan-Islāmism as a "humanitarian ideal" which did not recognize racial, national, or geographical barriers in its "scheme for the combination not only of races and nations but also of all religions."[61] It is however not clear whether religious differences would persist, or be wiped out in such a unity (*Cf. supra* p. 68).

SECTION II

The Philosopher and the Politician

In 1910 Iqbāl wrote in his notebook: "Nations are born in the hearts of poets, they prosper and die in the hands of politicians."[62] We see him donning both roles, and accordingly his thought reveals an interesting pattern—in the early phase we find him formulating and developing, as a philosopher, his ideas regarding nationhood. In the latter phase, which was also the period of his political activity (he became a member of the Panjab Legislative Council in 1926; presided over the annual session of the Muslim League in 1930 and the All India Muslim Conference in 1932; and attended the second and third Round Table Conferences in London in 1931 and 1932 as a member of the Muslim League delegation), we see him applying these ideas to the Indian situation as it confronted him then. He thus attempted to translate the ideal into the real, and the ensuing tension in his thought may be seen as a natural consequence of the contradictions between the two situations.

A very meaningful observation which he made in 1932 reveals that not only did Iqbāl perform this activity very consciously, but he was also alive to the difficulties inherent in this challenging task, seeing it as the cause of any discrepancy which may be detected in his political philosophy. He remarked that the task of the philosopher—"to reveal an ideal freed from its temporal limitations"—was quite easy as compared to that of the "practical politician"—to show how ideals could be translated into reality; because the former "involves a clean jump over temporal limitations" which continually beset the latter. He therefore believed that the man who had the "courage" to switch from the first to the second role [as he had done] was forced repeatedly to accept, and often even surrender to "those very limitations which he has been in the habit of ignoring." This drove him to "perpetual mental conflict", and even "self-contradiction"[67]—we shall see much of this proving true in his own case.

This was how Iqbāl described his dilemma as a poet-philosopher who had (reluctantly) taken the plunge into politics later in life, the reason for which he disclosed in a letter to Prof. E.J. Thompson, dated 20 June 1933. He wrote that he was "not interested in politics as such", his "interest in Islām as a moral polity" having driven him to it. Since he found Muslims "being swept away" by the forces of "Hindu Nationalism" (due to their "ignorance of Islāmic ideals"), which he felt would ultimately produce atheism, he felt it was his duty to remind his community of their real ideals.[64]

It appears that Iqbāl was conscious of the idealism of his thought: in his Presidential Address of 1932 he referred to himself as "a visionary idealist", while at the same time emphasizing the necessity of vision: "where there is no vision the people perish."[65] In another letter to Prof. E.J. Thompson dated 26 July 1934, he described himself as "a mere poet", referring also to the common perception about poets being "unpractical dreamers."[66]

Armed with these observations, we are perhaps better equipped to analyse Iqbāl's application of his concept of nationhood to the Indian situation, and his attempts at finding a satisfactory solution to its complex problems, which we shall be dealing with in this section.

The Possibility of a Single Indian Nationhood

It appears that the seeds of Iqbāl's political thought regarding India had germinated in his mind soon after his return from Europe (to which time also dates his disillusionment with nationalism), although the mature plant came into view much later. In a letter of 28 March 1909 he wrote that although the vision of a common Indian nationhood held great appeal as a poetic ideal [which he had celebrated in his own poetry at the turn of the century], in the light of present conditions and the trends among its two major communities, it appeared "incapable of fulfilment."[67]

The basic premise on which Iqbāl's political thought about India rested was that it was a country made up of "discordant political units" which, he wrote in 1910, Awrangzeb had tried unsuccessfully to merge into a "universal empire." Unlike Shibli and Mawlāna Ḥusayn Aḥmad who greatly appreciated Akbar's efforts at creating goodwill among the Hindus (*supra* p. 49, and *infra* p. 199), Iqbāl on the other hand appears to agree with Awrangzeb's "political perception": that the "strength" of Islām in India "did not depend as his great ancestor Akbar had thought", on such "goodwill", but "on the strength of the ruling race." Whereas the English had succeeded where the likes of Awrangzeb had failed, Iqbāl emphasized that mere "conquest" could not be equated with "unity."[68]

At this stage although Iqbāl felt the differences among the Indian population, he evidently believed that economic interests were yet capable of uniting them—we recall that Sir Sayyad on the other hand was not willing to admit any field of common participation except the purely social (*supra* pp. 22-23 and 27-28). Iqbāl believed that since economic forces operated alike on all, the leaders of the different communities should strive collectively for the economic upliftment of the country; and for the same reason, a Muslim working for the economic improvement of his community should rid his mind of religious and national prejudices and partisanship. In a manner reminiscent of Shibli (*supra* pp. 52-53), he criticized Muslim leaders for so far having concentrated only on securing a proportionate share for Muslims in government jobs to the neglect of the wider issue of economic freedom.[69] Although he later tended to dwell more on the points of departure, yet more than two decades later, in 1932 we find him repeating that despite separate electorates, unity among Indian communities could still be achieved through "economic questions."[70]

Speaking in the Legislative Council on 19 July 1927, three years prior to presenting his scheme for a Muslim state, Iqbāl described all "talk of a united nationalism" as a fruitless, merely verbal exercise, which Indians had been indulging in "for the last fifty years"; and which was "futile not only in the present", but would remain so for a long time to come. He felt that rather than trying "to become a nation" whose desirability was doubtful, Indian communities should first cultivate mutual trust; for their present distrust caused them to espouse nationalism merely verbally, while the gaze of each was fixed solely on itself.[71]

In his Presidential Address of 1930 Iqbāl emphasized that India was a continent [Sir Sayyad too had described it thus—*supra* pp. 21 and 23], and the differences between its groups, which lacked "a common race consciousness", were not merely territorial as among European countries, but also racial, linguistic, and religious—even the Hindus themselves did not form a "homogeneous group." Denying that India was "a single nation", he called it "Asia in miniature", and "a land of many nations", whose problem was therefore "international" rather than "national."[72] We recall that Sir Sayyad on the other hand had drawn an analogy with Europe for a very different purpose *i.e.* to illustrate India's unity in diversity (*supra* pp. 2 and 12).

Iqbāl felt that the voluntary formation of a common "moral consciousness", which was for Ernest Renan[73] "the essence of a nation", might have been possible in India if the syncretism of the likes of Akbar and Kabīr had appealed to the imagination of its people. On the contrary, its various caste and religious units did not seem inclined to sink their respective individualities in a larger whole, each being "intensely jealous of its collective existence." He therefore concluded that they were not prepared to pay the price for the creation of such a "moral consciousness."[74]

After attending two Round Table Conferences in London, and witnessing the diverse reactions prompted by the Communal Award of the British in 1931 and 1932, Iqbāl was all the more convinced about the essential disparity between India's cultural units; and of the impossibility of such a "land of minorities" ever having "a single national point of view." He felt that those politicians who refused to perceive this were "fact-shy." In his Presidential Address of 1932 he described Indian nationalism as being "theoretically correct" since it rested on "western premises", but "belied by facts" of the Indian situation.[75]

In 1933 Iqbāl responded to Pdt. Nehru's charge against some Muslims of being "anti-national", by saying that to oppose a kind of nationalism which implied merely a "biological fusion" of communities was not anti-nationalism, since it was neither possible, nor desirable to build up a nation in this way. He however continued to believe that there were common interests among the communities, on the basis of which an understanding between them was not only possible, but inevitable. Regarding the political process as an evolutionary one, he believed that the prevailing conditions signified only an intermediate stage in the country's political evolution.[76]

In 1935 Iqbāl felt that the Indian nationalist resented Muslim "self-determination" and "political and religious solidarity" due to his "political idealism", which led him to believe that nationalism in India could be achieved by suppressing its "cultural entities." He felt on the other hand that this would lead only to bitterness, while a rich and enduring culture could be evolved only through interaction. He was convinced that Muslims would not succumb to such idealism, and that they were fully capable of reconciling "the claims of religion and patriotism", though he did not specify how.[77]

Hostility Between Indian Communities

Very much in the manner of Sir Sayyad, Iqbāl was not only conscious of the disparity among Indian communities, but also sensitive to the inequality and antagonism between them.

Like Sir Sayyad (*supra* p. 21*ff.*), Iqbāl felt that due to the mutual hostility between its communities—he perceived each as aiming at the other's "destruction"—the principle of "pure and simple" competition was inapplicable in India. He therefore opposed—in the Panjab Legislative Assembly—a move to implement it in 1927, ascribing it to an "innocent idealism" which evaded "realities." He was in favour of "competition tempered by selection", which he felt would be equally beneficial to all. He also felt that the government had been mistaken in granting to Indians, posts earlier reserved for the British—he welcomed a greater number of British officers (due to their impartiality), and felt that only a "false and shallow nationalism" could pretend otherwise.[78]

We have seen Sir Sayyad opposing the Congress because he felt it heralded the political dominance of the majority, and concomitant subjection for the Muslims (*supra* pp. 23-24). The same fear appears to have haunted Iqbāl, who in 1930-31 apprehended an Anglo-Hindu conspiracy against the minority community: the majority would perpetuate British imperialism in India, which would in return connive in the formation of a "Hindu oligarchy to keep all other Indian communities in perpetual subjection." He warned that the Muslims would be forced to fight such a government tooth and nail.[79]

In spite of his political stand against the Hindus, Iqbāl hastened to clarify that he had no "prejudice" against them—on the other hand he greatly admired their "spirit of self-sacrifice and courage." He even went to the extent of saying that he was prepared to "be ruled by the Hindu alone" (provided he had "the tact and ability to govern"), or by the British alone, but not by both together.[80]

We notice some ambiguity in Iqbāl's stand here, which is a little self-defensive, and not very clearly spelt out. Whereas both Sir Sayyad and Iqbāl perceived political danger to the Muslims from the majority community, which prompted them to adopt a somewhat hostile posture against it, unlike the latter Sir Sayyad was very emphatic regarding social co-operation between the two. Shibli on the other hand perceived only a certain kind of religious danger from a section of the Hindus, while displaying no trace of antagonism. He was wholly in favour of not only social, but unlike Sir Sayyad and Iqbāl, complete political co-operation too.

Democracy

From 1930 onwards Iqbāl expressed the view [earlier held by Sir Sayyad—*supra* pp. 21*ff*], that "undiluted western democracy" based on "uniform franchise" could not succeed in India due to the presence of various communal and economic groups representing varied interests. He therefore felt in 1930 that the imposition of democracy and constitutional uniformity in India's political situation would only create conditions for a "civil war"[81]—we recall Sir Sayyad's repeated usage of identical imagery (*supra* pp. 24-25).

Iqbāl reasoned in 1932 that since the principle of western democracy threatened the "very existence" of minorities as "distinct cultural units", they could not accept it unless it was adapted to suit Indian conditions. They were therefore justified in demanding appropriate "safeguards" to avoid their "complete extinction as a nation." Since the majority refused to concede these, while the British were busy serving their own ends, the two chief Indian communities were locked in a political struggle, driven ultimately to "a kind of civil war." On 6 December 1933 he replied to Pdt. Nehru's charge (that while Muslims believed "in democracy as a religious institution" they shied away from it in practice), thus: they were insisting on safeguards such as communal electorates so that their "poor and backward community" could avail the true benefits of democracy—they wanted to ensure its "substance", "even at the expense of its conventional form."[82]

The Political Solution

In spite of his perception of the "seriousness" of the Hindu-Muslim question, and the "difficulties" in the way of its solution; Iqbāl was hopeful of achieving communal agreement, optimistic about the success of the efforts towards Hindu-Muslim unity, and proposed many solutions for the problem between 1930 and 1933. He felt that the prime need was mutual "readjustment" and "harmony" between the Indian people.[83]

Iqbāl believed that a "united" (not "unitary") India should be built by accepting "the existence of more than one people in the country", rather than by aiming at their "biological fusion." Opposing the imposition of an artificial unity which belied the facts of the situation, he felt that true unity should be based "not on the negation but in the mutual harmony and co-operation of the many." He was convinced that due to the "points of contact" between Indian communities, a "harmonious whole" could be built without compromising their "rich diversity."[84]

Iqbāl was pained to observe that the attempts of the Indian communities to discover "harmony" had so far failed. He attributed this to a mutual suspicion of the other party's intentions, the secret desire of each to dominate the other, and their unwillingness to part with their respective "monopolies" in the interest of mutual co-operation. He felt that the "dishonest nationalism" which they professed led them to simulate "a large-hearted patriotism" in order to conceal their egoism and narrow-mindedness. Each was unwilling to recognize that the other had "a right to free development according to its own cultural traditions."[85]

Iqbāl felt that a federal system was one of the solutions of the communal problem in India.[86] He also opposed territorial electorates as being unable to adequately represent all interests in a country like India, whose "racial and religious variety" justified the need for separate electorates. He felt that the Hindus opposed the latter as being incompatible with "nationalism" because they interpreted "nation" as a "universal amalgamation in which no communal entity ought to retain its private individuality"; whereas for him such a situation was both non-existent and undesirable. He felt that separate electorates would not impede the achievement of "inter-communal unity" since other common issues such as "economic questions" could bind Indian communities together.[87]

Iqbāl felt that since India's constitutional problem could be traced to the present demarcation of its provinces, the best solution for it (which would render obsolete the question of joint and separate electorates), was a proper territorial redistribution, to form autonomous communities possessing linguistic, racial, cultural, religious, and historical homogeneity, besides common "economic interests." [In view of India's infinite and multi-dimensional variety, it is questionable whether such a redistribution was possible or viable.] In 1937 he visualized the formation of "one or more Muslim states with absolute majority", by means of such redistribution.[88]

Whereas earlier Iqbāl had been in favour of obliterating religious differences among Indians, by 1909 his views had undergone a drastic change—he now believed that "the preservation of their separate national entities is desirable for both the Hindus and the Muslims." In 1930 he repeated that the Indian peoples should be allowed to develop "without abruptly breaking with their past." He did not believe that the creation of "communal provinces" was against "nationalism"; and to illustrate his point he quoted the Nehru Report on the separation of Sind, which said that just as internationalism does not preclude the existence of separate nation-states, so also a "harmonious nation" could not be built without allowing for "communalism in its better aspect", which it equated with complete "cultural autonomy."[89]

Iqbāl believed that whereas "communalism" had been used as a taunting "propaganda word", the principle which he espoused—that each group should be allowed to develop "on its own lines"—was not motivated by "narrow communalism." Differentiating between different kinds of "communalisms" he championed its "higher aspect", which was free of "ill will" towards other communities. Rather, as he took pains to clarify, he held their "customs, laws, [and] religious and social institutions" in great esteem; his religion commanding him "even to defend their places of worship, if need be." But, he reasoned, he should not be blamed for loving "the communal group" which was the basis of his very identity, for its religion, literature, thought, and culture—in fact its "whole past" had gone into forming his "present consciousness."[90] These words bring to mind Iqbāl's earlier emphasis (in the period 1909-11), on the "past", and therefore the "history" and "culture" of the community in constituting its peculiar identity, and that of its members (*supra* p. 64).

A year later in 1931 Iqbāl reaffirmed that he did not harbour any "prejudice against any community or nation", desiring only that each should retain its "culture and individuality", and that Islām should "return to its pristine simplicity."[91] It is not very clear what exactly he meant by this. The year before also he had spoken of freeing Islām of the "stamp" of "Arabian imperialism" by bringing its law, education, and culture closer to its "original spirit", as well as to that of modern times, by forming a Muslim state in India.[92]

Having been convinced that the "idea of a single Indian federation is completely hopeless", Iqbāl spoke in 1930 of the formation of both "a consolidated north-west Indian Muslim state", as well as "autonomous Muslim states along the north-west border"; whereas in 1937 he wrote about a "federation of Muslim provinces" comprising Panjab, the Frontier Province, Sind, and Baluchistan. Whatever its form, he believed that this "centralization" of Islām "in a specified territory" would ensure its existence "as a cultural force in India" (which he called "the greatest Muslim country in the world"); while also giving Muslims an opportunity to develop, within the Indian body politic, their law, education, and culture. He felt that only such an arrangement could protect Muslims from non-

Muslim domination, and ensure peace by creating an "internal balance of power." Without it a "civil war" would ensue, which in a way was already taking place in the form of communal riots.[93]

In 1930 and 1933 Iqbāl assured the Hindus and the Indian National Congress that Muslims would join them in the struggle for freedom only if they were granted safeguards for their protection as a minority, and given the right to develop freely, according to their own "culture and tradition", in their "Indian homelands."[94]

The Problem of Muslim Insecurity

It appears that Iqbāl's ideas about Muslim nationhood in India were motivated to a large extent by his perception of the insecurity of the community, and his desire to have its existence, and thus its very identity, protected.

In 1930 Iqbāl assured the nationalist Hindus that the demand of the Muslims for separate states was motivated only by a "desire for free development"; which was not possible under the kind of "unitary government" which they wanted to impose, hoping thereby to achieve their permanent and complete "communal dominance." In 1932 he explained that as a culturally and historically homogeneous people Muslims wanted only to live and develop on their own lines.[95]

Iqbāl also defended Muslims against the charges of communalism, pan-Islāmism, and lack of patriotism, by reasoning that just as the protection of his country was every man's duty; as the member of a cultural community, a Muslim was duty bound to protect his culture, faith, and historical tradition, and this was what Indian Muslims were doing. (We recall that in 1910 he had said that Islām itself was the homeland of Muslims—*supra* p. 61.) He repeated what he had said once earlier that year: that only a man's faith, culture, and tradition were worth living and dying for (*Cf. supra* pp. 72-73). He assured his fellow countrymen that while Muslims were demanding safeguards for the protection of their communal interests, they were equally concerned about the interests of India—in 1936 he was to express his faith in the ability of Muslims to reconcile "the claims of religion and patriotism" (*supra* p. 79)—and believed that for minorities to develop a "national outlook", the principle of their "protection" had to be recognized.[96]

In 1934 Iqbāl explained the reason for Muslim insecurity thus: whereas most Indian religious communities were partly influenced by "the race idea", Islām repudiated it altogether, founding itself solely on "the religious idea." Since its basis was completely "spiritual" and "ethereal", Muslim society tended to be "much more sensitive" to disintegrating forces. For Muslims their "religion" was not only their "faith" but also their "patriotism"; and "toleration" was equivalent to "suicide", intolerance being the other side of insecurity—born of the peculiar circumstances in which they were placed in India[97] (*Cf. supra* p. 61).

Iqbāl believed that it was mistaken to brand a man who was "jealous of the boundaries of his own faith" as intolerant or morally inferior. He felt rather, that this was a defensive mechanism triggered in the members of a group by the perception of any danger to their social organism, and was therefore an essentially "biological" and "life-giving" attitude. [This is comparable with his defence of fanaticism earlier, on the same principles—*supra* p. 62.] He described "true toleration" as the outcome of the "intellectual breadth" of the "spiritually powerful man", who could appreciate other "forms of faith" even while jealously guarding the frontiers of his own. He believed that only the "true Muslim" was capable of such toleration, since the "synthetic" nature of his own faith allowed him to sympathize with other faiths.[98]

Muslims Constitute a Nation

As early as in 1910 Iqbāl regarded Awrangzeb as the founder of Muslim nationality in India, due to his significant political perception that the strength of Islām in India depended not on the "goodwill" of its inhabitants, as his predecessor Akbar had believed, but on the "strength" of the ruling Muslims.[99]

In his Presidential Address of 1930 Iqbāl asserted that due to their homogeneity Indian Muslims were in fact a "nation in the modern sense of the word." He believed that it was Islām which had unified them by providing common "basic emotions and loyalties." Its ethical, political, social, and legal systems had acted as "the chief formative factor" which had shaped, and ultimately transformed them into "a well-defined people." It is interesting that he did not consider the Hindus fit to be called a "nation", due to their lack of homogeneity, which he attributed to their unequal social structure. Having established Islām as the basis of Muslim nationhood in India, in reply to the argument that other modern Muslim countries were proceeding not on religious but "territorial lines", he reasoned that whereas Muslims there were in a majority, and there were no social barriers between them and the minorities who were People of the Book, in India they were "differently situated."[100] We have seen that he would justify Muslim nationalism on the same grounds in 1935 (*supra* p. 72).

Having committed himself to a religious basis for Muslim nationhood in India, Iqbāl could not accept the geographical basis offered by Indian nationalism, since it would displace "the Islāmic principle of solidarity." He objected to Mawlāna Ḥusayn Aḥmad Madani's views for the same reason: he felt that the latter was advising Muslims to regard "land" rather than "faith" as the "basis" of their nationality, and was thus in effect urging them to "lose their identity" in Indian nationality, rather than regarding themselves as a separate nation. This implied that religion was a personal affair, and separate from politics.[101] Iqbāl on the other hand believed that a nation could not follow different religious and political systems. Since Muslims were a nation based on Islām, they could not abandon their "religious unity" by adopting any other social and legal system in deference to the dictates of race or nation (*Cf. supra* pp. 71*ff.*). Indian Muslims were thus not only a religious group, but also a distinct cultural and political entity with a definite "political objective."[102]

The Kind of State Envisaged

It is fruitful to piece together from Iqbāl's utterances and observations, the kind of Muslim state that he envisioned in India. In 1930 he assured his Hindu compatriots that the Muslim state would not have "religious rule", and would protect its non-Muslim minorities.[103] In a letter of 1934 he disowned the "Pakistan" scheme originating in England,[104] which proposed "a separate federation of Muslim provinces directly related to England", whereas he had suggested the creation of a Muslim majority province as part of the Indian federation.[105] Such a state would implement the Islāmic ideal of "social democracy", which would help it to solve modern problems. As for poverty, its solution would be found in the enforcement and further development, according to modern needs, of Islāmic law.[106]

It is interesting to observe that throughout his reflections on the fate of Indian Muslims, Iqbāl is silent about the Muslims of the minority provinces, except for a few stray references—they have been completely sidelined in his schemes for Muslim emancipation.

He appears to have been most concerned about the fate of the Muslims of Panjab (the state from which he himself hailed), and the north-western region, and to a much lesser degree, about those of Bengal. In 1937 he advised both these groups to "ignore Muslim minority provinces" for the present, as this was in their best interest. He was against holding the forthcoming session of the Muslim League in a minority province, suggesting that it be held in the Panjab to bring about "a fresh political awakening" among its Muslims; and advised the League to concentrate all its activities on the Muslims of the north-west.[107]

The Ideal Muslim State

We recall that as early as in 1910-11 Iqbāl had formed some idea about the ideal Muslim nation or "world-state", which could yet incorporate individual sovereign states (*supra* p. 61). Later in 1921 he believed that Muslim society was open to absorption and expansion "by example and persuasion", and the "simplicity of its teaching", rather than by aggression and conquest. However in 1938 he disclaimed "missionary effort" as being superfluous to Islām, which could influence mankind even without its aid (*supra* p. 66). He also believed that the ideal Muslim society should be true to the divine law of Islām, and free of all artificial distinctions between men, the "ultimate purpose" of the Prophet's (Pbuh) mission being the creation of such a community (*supra* p. 68).

From his Lectures we get an idea of Iqbāl's perception of the Islāmic state, which he clarified was not a theocracy in the sense that it was "headed by a representative of God on earth", but in the sense of being an attempt to realize the spiritual principles of *Tawhid*, equality, solidarity, and freedom in a definite human organization. He believed that in this sense every state based not on mere domination, but on the effort to realize ideal principles, was theocratic.[108]

Iqbāl felt that modern Muslims were justified in wanting to reinterpret Islāmic legal principles in the light of their experience. He believed that rather than being static the *Sharī'at* was capable of development, and upheld *ijtihād* as the means whereby it could be rebuilt in the light of changed modern conditions. The "dynamic outlook" of the Qur'ān demanded that "each generation, guided but unhampered by the work of its predecessors, should be permitted to solve its own problems."[109]

However with his characteristic caution Iqbāl hastened to add that life was not unalloyed change—alongwith the need for social change he asserted the "value and function of the forces of conservatism"—for conservation of a people's past helped to keep alive their "personal identity." He felt further that in a "non-territorial" society like Islām's, which was an "atomic aggregate" of the followers of different, often "mutually repellant races", reform and "revision of old institutions" was a greater responsibility, which needed to be executed very carefully.[110] As we have seen earlier (*supra* pp. 62-63 and 71), this caution had become a hallmark of Iqbāl's thought.

Yet, in spite of his concern to keep alive the past of the community as a common cognizable heritage in order to ensure its survival, Iqbāl was totally opposed to any "false reverence for past history and its artificial resurrection", which far from stemming decay, only hastened it. This was how he interpreted the events after the fall of Baghdad in 1258 A.D.—for fear of further disintegration, conservative Muslim thinkers had tried to preserve uniformity by excluding all innovations in the *Sharī'at* as expounded by the four juristic schools. The denial of *ijtihād*, which for him was "the principle of movement" in Islām, made its law static. Throughout the Lectures Iqbāl underlined that the Qur'ān highlighted dynamism, change, creation, and evolution in the universe, and therefore this stasis in law was contrary to its spirit[111] (*Cf. supra* p. 71).

For Iqbāl the Muslim state was essentially a republican one, for this form of government he felt was not only "consistent with the spirit of Islām", but somewhat of a "necessity." He therefore fully agreed with the Turkish *ijtihād* that the authority of the caliph could be vested in an elected group of persons instead of a single individual. He saw *ijmā'* as "the most important legal notion in Islām", which could be developed and adapted to modern conditions to form the basis of the Islāmic republican system, wherein the power of *ijtihād* would be transferred from individual jurists to a Muslim legislative assembly. This would enable even laymen with "a keen insight" to contribute to legal discussions, and thus activate the Muslim legal system. However, since the majority of the members would be ignorant of the details of Islāmic law, he felt that religious scholars would be an essential part of the assembly, to guide it in legal matters. In order to prepare legislators for the future, he suggested the expansion and improvement of legal education in Muslim countries, and the study of modern jurisprudence.[112]

Iqbāl felt that in the light of the idea of the finality of prophethood and revelation, Muslims should be the most "spiritually . . . emancipated" people in the world. Realizing their great responsibility, they should evolve the "spiritual democracy" which was Islām's ultimate goal.[113] In his Presidential Address of 1932 he rejected the unbridled "individualism" of modern western capitalism and asserted that Islām, while recognizing the individual's worth, also "disciplines him to give away his all to the service of God and man." He felt that if emancipated from its "medieval" trappings Islāmic idealism could "create a new world" where a man's status was determined not by birth or wealth, but by his moral stature. The ideal Muslim society was one of perfect social equality, founded not on an economic, but a spiritual basis, "where the poor tax the rich", private ownership was a trust, and capital was not "allowed to accumulate so as to dominate the real producer of wealth."[114]

Notes and References

All references in this chapter unless otherwise stated are to the works of Muḥammad Iqbāl.

1. Syed Abdul Vahid, ed., *Thoughts and Reflections of Iqbāl* (Lahore, 1973) pp. 46 and 48-49.
2. *Ibid.*, p. 50.
3. *Ibid.*, pp. 51-52.
4. *Ibid.*, p. 50.
5. Javid Iqbāl, ed., *Stray Reflections: A Notebook of Allama Iqbāl* (Lahore, 1961) pp. 24 and 30-31.
6. Muḥammad. 'Abd-al Salām Khān, *Afkār-i Iqbāl* (New Delhi, 1991) p. 90.
7. Taṣdīq Ḥusayn Tāj, ed., *Maḍāmīn-i Iqbāl* (Haydarābād Dakkan, 1941) pp. 84 and 86; Vahid, *op. cit.*, p. 377.
8. Taṣdīq Ḥusayn, *op. cit.,* p. 84; Vahid, *op. cit.*, pp. 376-77.
9. *Ibid.*, p. 88; *iIbid.*, p. 378.
10. Vahid, *op. cit.*, pp. 59-60.
11. Taṣdīq Ḥusayn, *op. cit.*, pp. 89-91 and 94; Vahid, *op. cit.*, pp. 378-79 and 381.
12. Javid Iqbāl, *op. cit.*, pp. 23-25.
13. Taṣdīq Ḥusayn, *op. cit.*, pp. 85-86.
14. *Ibid.*, pp. 83, 92-94 and 101; Vahid, *op. cit.*, pp. 380-81.
15. *The Reconstruction of Religious Thought in Islām* (London, 1934) pp. 162 and 167.
16. Vahid, *op. cit.*, pp. 231-32.

17. *Ibid.*, pp. 44-46.
18. Taṣdīq Ḥusayn, *op. cit.*, pp. 95 and 97-99.
19. *Ibid.*, pp. 96-99.
20. Vahid, *op. cit.*, pp. 373-74.
21. Taṣdīq Ḥusayn, *op. cit.*, pp. 97-98 and 102; Javid Iqbāl, *op. cit.*, pp. 29-30.
22. Taṣdīq Ḥusayn, *op. cit.*, pp. 98-100.
23. Vahid, *op. cit.*, pp. 98 and 100.
24. Shamloo, ed., *Speeches and Statements of Iqbāl* (Lahore, 1944) p. 217.
25. Vahid, *op. cit.*, p. 99.
26. *Ibid.*, pp. 98-99.
27. *Reconstruction*, pp. 94, 162 and 188.
28. *Ibid.*, pp. 140-41 and 167.
29. *Ibid.*, pp. 146-47 and 167.
30. Shamloo, *op. cit.*, pp. 7 and 32.
31. Bashir Aḥmad Dar, ed., *Letters and Writings of Iqbāl* (Karachi, 1967) pp. 55-56 and 75.
32. Vahid, *op. cit.*, pp. 353-54.
33. *Ibid.*, pp. 285 and 287.
34. *Ibid.*, p. 375.
35. Shamloo, *op. cit.*, pp. 206-07 and 217.
36. Wilfred Cantwell Smith, *Modern Islam in India: A Social Survey* (Lahore, 1969) p. 117.
37. Ziya-ul Hasan Faruqi, *The Deoband School and the Demand for Pakistan* (Bombay, 1963) p. 63.
38. Dar, *Letters and Writings*, p. 58.
39. Javid Iqbāl, *op. cit.*, p. 95; Taṣdīq Ḥusayn, *op. cit.*, pp. 84-85.
40. Shamloo, *op. cit.*, p. 204.
41. Vahid, *op. cit.*, pp. 373-74.
42. Javid Iqbāl, *op. cit.*, pp. 26-27; Taṣdīq Ḥusayn, *op. cit.*, p. 85.
43. Dar, *Letters and Writings*, p. 59.
44. Vahid, *op. cit.*, p. 287.
45. Shamloo, *op. cit.*, pp. 205 and 215.
46. *Ibid.*, pp. 206 and 219.
47. Vahid, *op. cit.*, p. 287.
48. *Reconstruction*, p. 155.
49. Shamloo, *op. cit.*, pp. 4-5.
50. *Ibid.*, pp. 8-9.
51. Vahid, *op. cit.*, p. 284.
52. *Reconstruction*, pp. 188-89.
53. Shamloo, *op. cit.*, p. 7.
54. Vahid, *op. cit.*, pp. 196-97.
55. Shamloo, *op. cit.*, pp. 207-08.

56. *Reconstruction*, p. 159.
57. Vahid, *op. cit.*, pp. 371-72.
58. *Ibid.*, p. 288.
59. *Reconstruction*, p. 159.
60. *Ibid.*, pp. 157-58; Vahid, *op. cit.*, pp. 283-84.
61. Shamloo, *op. cit.*, p. 187.
62. Javid Iqbāl, *op. cit.*, p. 125.
63. Vahid, *op. cit.*, p. 196.
64. S. Hasan Aḥmad, *Iqbal: His Political Ideas at Crossroads* (Aligarh, 1979) p. 72.
65. Vahid, *op. cit.*, p. 195.
66. Aḥmad, *op. cit.*, p. 82.
67. Javid Iqbāl, *op. cit.*, p. xxi.
68. *Ibid.*, pp. 44-48.
69. Taṣdīq Ḥusayn, *op. cit.*, pp. 104-05.
70. Latif Ahmad Sherwani, ed., *Speeches, Writings and Statements of Iqbal* (Lahore, 1977) p. 223.
71. Vahid, *op. cit.*, pp. 321 and 323.
72. Shamloo, *op. cit.*, pp. 9, 12, 22 and 30.
73. "What is a Nation?" *Modern Political Thought: The Great Issues,* ed. William Ebenstein (New Delhi, 1970).
74. *Ibid.*, p. 9.
75. *Ibid.*, p. 30; Vahid, *op. cit.*, pp. 211 and 346.
76. Vahid, *op. cit.*, pp. 365-66.
77. *Ibid.*, pp. 258-59.
78. *Ibid.*, pp. 319-322.
79. Shamloo, *op. cit.*, pp. 19-20; Sherwani, *op. cit.*, p. 207.
80. Sherwani, *op. cit.*, p. 207.
81. Shamloo, *op. cit.*, pp. 12, 31 and 155.
82. Vahid, *op. cit.*, pp. 205, 211 and 366-67.
83. Sherwani, *op. cit.*, pp. 206-08.
84. Shamloo, *op. cit.*, p. 9; Vahid, *op. cit.*, pp. 197 and 366.
85. Shamloo, *op. cit.*, pp. 9-10.
86. *Ibid.*, p. 17.
87. *Ibid.*, p. 16; Sherwani, *op. cit.*, p. 223.
88. Shamloo, *op. cit.*, pp. 15-16 and 30; Vahid, *op. cit.*, p. 367; Bashir Aḥmad Dar, ed., *Letters of Iqbal* (Lahore, 1978) p. 259.
89. Javid Iqbāl, *op. cit.*, p. xxi; Shamloo, *op. cit.*, pp. 11-12 and 31.
90. Shamloo, *op. cit.*, pp. 11 and 31.
91. Dar, *Letters and Writings*, p. 55.
92. Shamloo, *op. cit.*, p. 15.
93. *Ibid.*, pp. 12-13 and 15; Aḥmad, *op. cit.*, p. 81; Dar, *Letters of Iqbal*, pp. 254 and 260.
94. Shamloo, *op. cit.*, p. 11; Vahid, *op. cit.*, p. 365.

95. Shamloo, *op. cit.*, p. 14; Dar, *Letters and Writings*, p. 71.
96. Shamloo, *op. cit.*, p. 161; Dar, *Letters and Writings*, pp. 72 and 76; Sherwani, *op. cit.*, p. 225.
97. Vahid, *op. cit.*, pp. 248, 252 and 259-260.
98. *Ibid.*, pp. 261-62.
99. *Ibid.*, p. 380; Javid Iqbāl, *op. cit.*, pp. 45-46.
100. Shamloo, *op. cit.*, pp. 3 and 31-32.
101. *Ibid.*, pp. 8-9, 204 and 209-211.
102. Dar, *Letters of Iqbāl*, pp. 249-250.
103. Shamloo, *op. cit.*, pp. 13-14.
104. The reference is to a campaign begun around 1933 by Indian Muslim students in Cambridge, in favour of the creation of a separate state in north-west India, for which they mnemonically coined the name "Pakistan" from Punjab, Afghania (NWFP), Kashmir, and Baluchistan. Chaudhary Rahmat Ali, a Punjabi Muslim, gave the movement shape and form.
105. Shamloo, *op. cit.*, p. 80.
106. Dar, *Letters of Iqbāl*, pp. 254-55.
107. *Ibid.*, pp. 260 and 262.
108. *Reconstruction*, pp. 154-55.
109. *Ibid.*, pp. 157, 162-64 and 167-68.
110. *Ibid.*, p. 167.
111. *Ibid.*, pp. 148 and 151.
112. *Ibid.*, pp. 157 and 173-76.
113. *Ibid.*, pp. 179-180.
114. Vahid, *op. cit.*, p. 212.

Chapter 4

MUḤAMMAD 'ALI JINNĀH
(1876-1948)

Ambassador of Unity

As is quite well-known, in the initial phase of his political career Jinnāh was a great advocate of Hindu-Muslim unity. On 13 February 1915 he appealed to Muslim students to eliminate dissension and work for co-operation, unity, and goodwill, not only among themselves, but also between Muslims and other communities. Since as citizens of India they would have to work alongside others for its progress, he believed that they should first try and understand each other.[1]

In his Presidential Address at the annual session of the All India Muslim League in 1916 [he had begun his career as a Congressman, but was persuaded by Mawlāna Muḥammad 'Ali and Wazīr Ḥasan to join the League in 1913, "at a time when that organization came very close to the views of the Congress, and on the assurance that it would continue to do so"[2]], Jinnāh recognized "the existence of a powerful unifying process", which he saw as "creating out of the diverseness of race and creed, a new India, fast growing to unity of thought, purpose, and outlook, responsive to new appeals of territorial patriotism and nationality", and eager to govern itself. He astutely credited British rule with having indirectly caused the genesis of this "genuine spirit of patriotism", and therefore described it as having conferred the greatest of boons on India.[3]

At the same time, as a nationalist Jinnāh was also fully alive to the "magnitude" of the task of "nation building" in a "vast continent" such as India, with its huge population abounding in racial, cultural, and religious variety, which tended to produce "a great diversity of outlook, purpose, and endeavour." In spite of this, he was quick to dismiss British justification of the total exclusion of Indians from the Simon Commission in 1926 on the plea that the existence of numerous parties and minorities made it difficult to guard the interests of all concerned. He thought it was "grotesque" to imply "that there is such a museum of communities and interests in India that it would be impossible to find a few representative Indians."[4]

In 1916 Jinnāh believed that by bringing together Hindus and Muslims for a common cause, this "newborn movement in the direction of national unity" had engendered a "living and vigorous spirit of patriotism and national self-consciousness." In this rapprochement between the two communities, which was in evidence since a few years, he saw "the first signs of the birth of united India", for so far the Hindu-Muslim question had been the biggest hurdle in the way of the "unifying forces" which were moving towards "the evolution of a common Indian nationality." He felt that the improvement in their relations was all the more significant when compared with the state of things only a decade earlier—in 1906 at the time of the founding of the Muslim League, when "mutual distrust and suspicion were rampant, and communal bigots on either side ruled the roost."[5]

Jinnāh reminded the two communities that for a new India to arise they would have to give up their petty interests, and strive unitedly for "the transfer of power from the bureaucracy to democracy", for no power could resist the force of their united voice. At this stage he went so far as to say that only "goodwill, concord, harmony, and co-operation" were not sufficient—India's progress hinged on the "union" of the "two great sister communities." In this context he hailed the coming closer of the programme of the League to that of the Indian National Congress, by the former's adoption of the ideal of self-government in 1913, which had led to their simultaneous sessions in 1915 and 1916 at Bombay and Lucknow respectively.[6] [He had been instrumental in forging an alliance between the two in 1916, which came to be known as the Lucknow Pact].

Addressing a public meeting in November 1917, Jinnāh appealed to Muslims to join hands with their Hindu brethren, and to the latter to uplift their "backward brothers." Speaking in the Legislative Council the previous month [he was elected to it in 1910 from Bombay, and resigned in 1919 in protest against the passing of the repressive laws of the Rowlatt Act], he had expressed disagreement with those who opposed the holding of the Civil Service Examination in India on the plea of the variety of its population, and the danger of Muslims not getting their fair share. While admitting their backwardness and the numerical strength of Hindus, he announced their preparedness to compete with the latter. Stressing the need for the selection of the best candidates so as to provide an efficient service, he felt that a greater number of Hindus was no more objectionable than more Europeans.[7] This is in marked contrast to the views of Sir Sayyad, and specially Iqbāl who in 1927 would demand a greater number of British officers in the bureaucracy (*supra* pp. 23-24 and 79-80).

In the same spirit, Jinnāh asserted that India would be governed by its people as a whole rather than by any particular class or community, thus allaying Muslim fears of being subjected to a virtually Hindu government. He felt this was a "bogey" which their enemies were using to make them shy away from co-operation with the Hindus, which was essential for the introduction of self-government. He was convinced on the other hand that government could not be conducted by ballot-boxes alone, and if seventy million Muslims did not approve of a measure, the Hindus could not carry it through and enforce it merely on the strength of their majority—he trusted the intellect and past history of their statesmen not to do so. He therefore felt that the demand for Home Rule should be made by "the Hindus and Muslims as one nation",[8] which is significant. Here again his views are diametrically opposed to those of Sir Sayyad and Iqbāl (*supra* pp. 21, 23-24 and 79-80).

It is interesting to see Jinnāh himself drawing a parallel with Sir Sayyad at this point. Commenting on the latter's observation that Hindus and Muslims were like the two eyes of a bride, and injury to one would hurt the other too; he remarked that this indicated a passive stage of national life, with the two groups content with not harming each other, whereas they had now reached the active stage of co-operation for national work.[9]

In his Presidential Address of May 1924 [unless otherwise stated this refers to sessions of the Muslim League] Jinnāh attributed the establishment and continuance of foreign rule in India to lack of unity and trust among its people, particularly the Hindus and Muslims. Characterizing their differences as "the greatest enemy of India", he urged them to find a solution to these as they had at

Lucknow in 1916,[10] emphasizing at the same time that their political unity was essential for achieving *swarāj*. In 1926 he wanted them to realize that the only way to rise to the nationhood to which they were aspiring was through friendship and harmony—if they settled their differences they would be more than half-way to responsible government. He therefore appealed to the Congress and the Hindu Mahāsabha to accept the hand of friendship extended by the Muslims.[11]

In 1928 Jinnāh reiterated that as "sons of the land" Hindus and Muslims had to live and work together, for without their unity India could not progress. Declaring that nothing would please him more than their "union", he urged them to reach a compromise, to be reconciled and united, and to feel that their interests were common. Speaking not "as a Muslim but an Indian", he expressed his desire to see not only the League, but all Muslims marching with others in the struggle for freedom. In 1929 he urged the Hindus and Muslims to settle their differences if they wanted to terminate their present slavery, for the British could not resist their united demand.[12]

As for himself, speaking in the Central Legislative Council in 1924 (he had been re-elected to it the previous year), Jinnāh affirmed that as its member, the only consideration that guided him was his commitment to larger national interests rather than the smaller interests of his city or town, no matter how dear. In 1925, he refuted as "absolutely false", the charge that he had "become a leader of communal strife", stating with "a clear conscience" that he was "a nationalist first, a nationalist second, and a nationalist last." He also appealed to the members of the House to strive to make it a "real national Parliament", rather than degrading it by introducing "the discussion of communal matters in it."[13]

Jinnāh however became increasingly disillusioned with the Indian political scene, and resigning his seat in the Legislative Council in July 1931, decided to retire from politics, and to reside in England. He however returned to India and to politics in 1934 at the entreaty of the Muslim League leader Liyāqat 'Alī Khān, and proceeded to revive the League in the next few years. While still in England he had been elected to the Legislative Council from Bombay, and continued to be a member till independence.

In 1936 Jinnāh reasserted that his sole object was the welfare of his country, whose interest would always remain most sacred to him. Clarifying that his solicitude for Hindu-Muslim unity was "not merely a lip-expression nor a diplomatic statement", he reaffirmed his commitment to it in the past and the future, for without it there was no hope for them to rule India. He reminded Kashmiri Muslims that as a majority it was their duty to make the minority feel secure, or else they would "have a sore festering" in their "body politic."[14] We shall notice this concern for minorities as a consistent streak in his thought.

We have thus seen Jinnāh the devout patriot and nationalist, and the untiring ambassador of Hindu-Muslim unity, which however appears to be only a political unity, forged for achieving political ends. In this he seems curiously enough to be more akin to Mawlāna Ḥusayn Aḥmad Madani rather than Sir Sayyad or Shibli, who constantly emphasized cultural, social and ethnic affinities between Hindus and Muslims. We shall later see him making a complete *volte-face* by turning back with a vengeance on all the sentiments expressed so far.

Change of Heart

Even in the early phase of his political life Jinnāh believed firmly in preserving and protecting the individuality and political existence of Muslims as a community, although he disowned sectarianism of any kind. In fact his efforts appear in this initial stage to be directed towards balancing his nationalistic and patriotic convictions with this other aspect of his political thought. Although he believed in safeguarding Muslim interests, he felt this should be coupled with patriotism and unity with other communities.

In 1916 Jinnāh justified "the value and need of a separate Muslim political organization"—the Muslim League—which had been formed for the "retention" of a "strong" Muslim "communal individuality", "unimpaired" by the future "constitutional readjustments" being vociferously demanded by "Hindu politicians" at the beginning of the century. [The use of the word "Hindu" for the Congress which had many Muslim members too, is significant.] He felt that in the circumstances Muslims were justified in feeling the need to organize themselves politically, "lest the impending changes . . . should swamp them altogether as a community."[15]

However, felt Jinnāh, over the years with the political evolution of the community the creed of the League had also "grown and broadened"; and its present outlook and future goals approximated closely to those of the Congress, so that it was "ready to participate in any patriotic efforts for the advancement of the country as a whole." He believed that the fact that in barely a decade it had prepared dedicated Muslims "to work shoulder to shoulder with other Indian communities for the common good of all", was justification enough for its existence. Refuting the charge of "separatism" against the League, which though a "communal organization", was fast becoming "a powerful factor for the birth of united India"; he affirmed that he himself throughout his public life had been "a staunch Congressman" [which is apparently here used as a synonym of "nationalist"], and opponent of sectarianism.[16]

Jinnāh clarified that Muslims desired neither "favours" nor "partial treatment" from the government, but only that "a healthy and fair impetus be given to [their] aspirations and ideals as a community." Advising them to maintain self-respect even while they were loyal to the government, he at the same time urged them to maintain "goodwill" towards the Hindus, for India could progress only through "harmonious relations between the two great sister communities." He encouraged them to co-operate "in the cause of [their] Motherland", and to work for "a healthy national unity" rather than mere "self-interest and self-gain."[17]

Yet Jinnāh believed that before the "broader political sense" of a minority could be "evoked for co-operation and united endeavour in the national task", it should "have a complete sense of security" (Iqbāl would say much the same thing from 1930 onwards—*supra* pp. 83-84); which for Muslims could come only through "adequate and effective safeguards as regards their political existence as a community." He therefore pleaded for safeguards from this early date, urging his "Hindu brethren" to "win the confidence and trust" of the Muslim minority by granting their demand for separate electorates, on which they were insisting—"rightly or wrongly."[18]

Jinnāh was consistent in his stand a decade later—even while he appealed for unity in 1926 (*supra* p. 96) and again in 1927, he felt that Muslims were insisting on separate electorates only because they were anxious to ensure that their future position in the country was thoroughly defined and secured. He felt that whereas neither would separate electorates impede the growth of representative government, nor could nationalism be created overnight merely by a mixed electorate; the question was really one of means to an end—that of giving "a real sense of confidence and security to the minorities." Clarifying that he personally did not favour separate electorates, he felt however that if Muslims believed that it was the only method by which they could be safeguarded against the oppression of the majority, they should be made secure by granting it to them. He now believed that there was no escaping the fact that communalism did exist in the country, and could not be removed by mere talk and sentiment.[19]

In 1928, 1931, and 1935, while dwelling on the need for friendship, harmony, and a Hindu-Muslim settlement, Jinnāh also emphasized that the problem of minorities had to be faced squarely. Majorities, he felt, and "particularly religious majorities", tended to be "tyrannical and oppressive", making the minorities fear that "their interests and rights" would suffer unless clearly and definitely safeguarded." He felt that since the minorities would not support any proposed system unless they felt that under it they were secured "as an entity" [he apparently means a political entity], in order to ensure stability it was necessary to instil complete security and confidence in them by providing due safeguards for their rights and interests; since without their willing allegiance any constitution would breakdown, leading to "a revolution and civil war." He therefore requested the majority for an "adjustment" that was fair to Muslims, who as a minority, could give them nothing—the majority alone was in a position to be generous.[20]

In 1935 Jinnāh admitted that considerations of religion and race should not be allowed to enter into politics (language was not so objectionable), since religion was an individual and private affair. However, he felt, the question of minorities was a political issue rather than purely a question of religion or language, and as such it should be faced and solved, rather than evaded. He defined a minority as a "separate entity in the state" which may differ in religion, language, race, or culture; and "desired safeguards as an entity."[21]

In 1936 Jinnāh wrote that it was perfectly natural for Muslims to wish to ensure that as a minority their future position should be protected. Although at face value such a demand might appear to "an amateur politician" to smack of "communalism", he felt it did not in any way question their patriotism, of which they had given ample proof by their equal participation in the struggle for responsible government. He declared that the League was working for friendship between Muslims and others and for a responsible government, but coupled with "adequate and effective safeguards for Muslims." Whereas so far he appears to have been concerned about protecting only the political individuality of Muslims (*supra* p. 97*ff.*)—although he realized even a year back that this was linked to their religious, linguistic, racial, and cultural identity—there is a marked change in his stand now, when he defines the object of the League as the protection of "the political, religious, and other rights and interests of Muslims."[22]

Dismissing the view which regarded Muslims as intruders, Jinnāh exhorted them to stand firmly by national interests, to prove "that their patriotism is unsullied, and that their love for India and her progeny is no less than of any other community"; even as they organized themselves and put "their own affairs in order." He expressed the conviction that the only way to face and resolve political issues was by political leaders collectively facing the dangers that confronted them "as politicians and statesman, and not as Hindus, Muslims, or Christians." Speaking at the Dayal Singh College which did not "believe in any creed", he felt himself "among kindered spirits" due to his consistent commitment to the belief that India's "salvation" lay in "non-sectarian feelings." Yet only a few lines later he remarked cryptically that although like the students present there he had started "life as a dreamer and an idealist", he had now "begun to realize the realities"[23]—one wonders if this hints at his later disillusionment with idealist notions such as non-sectarianism.

After its overwhelming success in the provincial elections of 1937 the Congress formed governments in almost all the Hindu majority provinces. During their period of office which lasted till 1939, these governments, specially that of the Central Provinces, initiated and adopted religious, cultural, and economic measures which the Muslims considered detrimental to their survival as a religious and cultural entity. As a result hostility between the Congress and the League deepened, and in response to this challenge, within two years, the League emerged as the chief party in opposition to the Congress, and the representative organ of the Muslims, with Jinnāh as their principal leader. We hold that it was this experience of Congress rule which, "led to his final breach with Indian nationalism", rather than Gandhi's failure to solve the communal problem in the Round Table Conferences of 1931 and 1932, as suggested by Aziz Ahmad.[24] This is borne out by the fact that as late as in 1936 he had espoused the nationalist cause, and that of Hindu-Muslim unity (*supra* pp. 96-97 and 99-100).

Accordingly, Jinnāh's post-electoral Presidential Address of October 1937 is marked by a definite change in his attitude to the Hindu-Muslim problem. He now stated categorically that any settlement with the majority was impossible since no Hindu leader showed any concern or genuine desire for it. He even went to the extent of declaring that an honourable settlement could be reached only between two equals who respected and feared each other; and believed that without such equality there could be no agreement, for offers of peace by the weaker party amounted to confessions of weakness and an invitation to aggression. Politics now meant for him "power—and not relying on cries of justice or fair play, or goodwill", for all agreements and safeguards were meaningless and ineffective unless backed by the power to enforce them.[25]

Jinnāh expressed much the same sentiments in his Presidential Address at the special session in April the next year. Yet it is interesting to note that in the very same speech, while referring to the communal tangle created by the demolition in 1936, of the Shahidganj mosque at Lahore, he reminded both parties of their "moral obligation" and "moral responsibility" to strive for an "honourable settlement", a "just solution", and "permanent peace and goodwill between the two great sister communities."[26]

Thus we now find Jinnāh appealing to those very sentiments which he had twice denounced. Perhaps he felt that while a rapprochement was possible on minor issues at the local and micro-level, on the macro or national plane it was much more elusive—it certainly reflects a conflict between two opposing modes of thought.

In 1939 Jinnāh wanted to know why Muslim leaders were branded as "communal" merely because they were mindful of the interests of their community, although this did not imply that they were hostile or even indifferent "to the larger interests of India." While reaffirming his belief in a Hindu-Muslim pact, he clarified that it should be an "honourable" one, rather than aiming at "the destruction of one and the survival of the other community."[27]

We thus find Jinnāh moving further away from the goal of Hindu-Muslim unity which he had so fervently espoused in his early days (*supra* p. 93*ff.*), a gradual change having come over his thought in a period of about two decades. It would do well to study his own analysis of the shift in his stand, and the reasons for it.

In his Presidential Address of 1943 Jinnāh described himself as the "arch-culprit" in the mission to dispel misunderstanding between Hindus and Muslims; who by his laborious efforts had succeeded in getting the Congress and the League to meet simultaneously in Bombay in 1915. He however accused Gandhi who arrived on the scene in 1920, of introducing religion into politics, and sabotaging all efforts made from 1925 onwards by the Muslims for resolving mutual differences. He felt that whereas the latter repeatedly approached Gandhi and the Congress with their proposals as "petitioners and supplicants", they always replied in the negative, never making any counter-proposals either. He therefore accused Hindu leaders of deliberately, systematically, and with ulterior motives, destroying—in the name of nationalism and democracy, any chance of adjustment between the two communities.[28]

Thus although Jinnāh began his political career as a champion of unity, he became gradually disillusioned with such ideas, and more and more embittered, which culminated finally in his giving up all hope, and presenting his proposal for a division of India in his Presidential Address to the Muslim League on 23 March 1940.

The Congress and Hindu *Rāj*

As remarked earlier, the year 1937 marks a turning-point in Jinnāh's political career (*supra* pp. 100-01). In his Presidential Address in October that year he launched his "bitter anti-Congress campaign", and "ridiculed rather than criticized", without suggesting any alternative, its demand for a constituent assembly. He also "ridiculed" it "for the failure of the two previous nationalist struggles, and for the acceptance of office under the new 'reactionary' constitution."[29]

Jinnāh also accused the Congress leadership of increasingly alienating Muslims particularly during the last decade, by following an "exclusively Hindu policy." He felt that its policies in the six provinces where it had formed governments after the recent elections had conclusively proved that Muslims could not "expect any justice or fair play from it." As soon as they secured the least power, its Hindu leaders had demonstrated by their actions that they considered India to be the sole domain of the Hindus, even while they continued to "masquerade under the name of nationalism." He felt that such tactics would only tighten Britain's imperialistic hold by producing bitterness and communal war, and thus make unity unattainable.[30]

In the same speech and again in his Presidential Addresses at the Muslim League sessions in April and December the next year, Jinnāh accused the Congress of displaying an "aggressive attitude" after coming to power; and of attempting to foist Hindi as the national language, and *Bande Mātaram* as the national song, upon Muslims. He described the latter as an "idolatrous", "hymn of hatred of Muslims", and violative of their religious beliefs. As for the scheme of Hindi-Hindustani, he felt that in contravention of its nationalistic claims the Congress had initiated it in order to "stifle and suppress Urdu" and Muslim culture; and to nurture Hindu literature and culture, and impose it on Muslims by making Hindi a compulsory language. Muslims, he felt, were compelled to accept this state of affairs—if they protested they were "branded as communalists and disturbers of the peace", and subjected to repressive measures. In fact, in the face of complaints of interference in the observance of their religious rights, and of "hardship, ill-treatment and injustice" by the Congress governments, the League had appointed an inquiry committee headed by Rājā Muḥammad Mahdi of Pīrpūr.[31]

Jinnāh described as mere "paper resolutions", the "high-sounding declarations" of the Congress regarding the guarantee of fundamental rights to freedom of religion, culture, language etc. [passed at Calcutta and Haripura in 1937 and 1938], which were never enforced. He therefore accused it of a contradiction between its preaching and practice, and of masquerading under the guise of nationalism, whereas it was mainly a Hindu body. He felt that by opposing the communal award [announced by the British Premier in August 1932], separate electorates, and reservation of seats, it wanted to deny adequate representation in government to Muslims. In July 1942 he accused the provincial "Hindu Congress" governments of having violated the fundamental rights of Muslims by suppressing and ridiculing their culture, language and customs, and exalting those of the Hindus.[32]

In 1937 Jinnāh felt that the Muslims in the Congress were betraying a "defeatist mentality" by urging their co-religionists to throw themselves at the "mercy and goodwill of others." For him such a policy amounted to "unconditional surrender", and would "seal" the community's "doom" by depriving it of "its rightful part in the national life." He again called the Congress a Hindu organization which did not represent Muslims and other minorities; among whom he interestingly included in 1938, "scheduled castes and non-Brahmans" too. Demanding a "fair deal" for them all, he felt that despite its claims the Congress had done nothing towards making them secure. He even accused it of wanting "to crush all other communities and cultures in the country"; equating its declared aims of *swarāj* and "national government" with Hindu *rāj* and Hindu government. He believed that Gandhi, who aimed at a revival of Hinduism, was single-handedly responsible for making the Congress an instrument for furthering these ends, and for destroying the ideal for which it had been founded[33] (*Cf. supra* p. 102).

Jinnāh asserted that the League was struggling not only for Muslims but for all minorities; and demanded for them a sense of security, and freedom from the danger of being "ground down by caste tyranny and rule." As for the Muslims, he spelt out their determination not to surrender to the dictates of the Congress, or be dominated by those dreaming of "Hindu *rāj*." He felt that "besides the question of religion, culture, language, and personal laws", that of securing their political rights and their fair share in government was equally a matter of "life and death" for Muslims—since "their future destiny" depended on it, they were determined to "fight for it to the last."[34]

We have remarked before that whereas earlier he seemed primarily concerned with safeguarding the political existence of Muslims; by 1935 the realization had dawned on Jinnāh that this was inextricably linked to their religious, linguistic, racial, and cultural identity; leading him to declare in 1936 that the League aimed at protecting "the political, religious, and other rights" of Muslims (*supra* pp. 97-100). He appears now (in 1938) to have come full circle in that political rights seem to have been subordinated to religious, cultural, linguistic and legal issues, the defence of which appears to have acquired precedence.

In March 1939 Jinnāh accused the Congress of being not only hostile but inimical to the League, which precluded the possibility of co-operation between the two. He however warned the Hindus that in spite of their economic strength and greater numbers they would be unable to overpower and oppress Muslims, who were determined to go down fighting (*Cf.* Sir Sayyad, *supra* p. 24). In January 1940 he again described the Congress as "mainly a Hindu body" which was "led by an astute Hindu politician of the first rank." He felt that the Congress was insisting on the adoption of complete democracy because through it, it could maintain "a permanent all-India dominance."[35]

Democracy and Partition

In his Presidential Address of March 1940 Jinnāh explained that whereas the rule of the "Congress caucus" would imply the "slavery of Muslims and other minorities"; the League, through its scheme of partition first proposed in that very session, desired the freedom of all Indians rather than of one section. [It is however not clear how partition, which held no promise even for the Muslims in minority provinces, would ensure freedom for other minorities.] He urged Muslims not to bear ill will or malice toward others, but to depend only on themselves for the protection of their rights and interests. He wanted Gandhi to abandon all deception, and honestly admit that he was a Hindu representing a Hindu body; just as Jinnāh proudly acknowledged himself to be a Muslim leader representing his people.[36]

This is in marked contrast to his stand only four years back, when in 1936 Jinnāh had opined that the only way to resolve political issues was by political leaders confronting common dangers as "statesmen" rather than as followers of different faiths (*supra* p. 100).

Jinnāh again deplored the behaviour of the Congress governments in the provinces, which had made the League all the more distrustful of it, and had proved that "any repetition of such a government must lead to civil war." (*Cf.* Sir Sayyad and Iqbāl—*supra* pp. 25, 81 and 83-84). He believed that the experience had been an instructive lesson in the working of democracy—by yoking together the majority and minorities under it, the Congress desired a Hindu *rāj*, which was unacceptable to Muslims since it "would mean the complete destruction of what is most precious in Islām." [It is not clear exactly what he is alluding to here.] In reply to the observation that Islām too advocated democracy, he retorted that a democracy wherein merely by virtue of their majority non-Muslims would dominate over Muslims, was unacceptable to them and to Islām. In his Presidential Address of April 1943 he asserted that whereas Hindu society was caste-ridden and undemocratic; democracy, "equality and brotherhood" had been a part of the Muslim ethos for the past thirteen centuries, but they could not accept a democracy in which the majority would destroy the minority and all it held dear.[37] We recall that Iqbāl had also replied to similar charges by defending safeguards as a means whereby Muslims wanted to ensure real rather than merely formal democracy (*supra* pp. 80-81).

In 1940 and 1942, while ruling out any agreement with the Congress which although a Hindu body, claimed to alone represent all of India, Jinnāh repeated that it desired not independence but Hindu *rāj i.e.* the power to dominate, with the help of the British, the Muslims and other minorities. The Muslims on the other hand, who regarded themselves as a separate entity rather than a minority, and desired freedom for themselves *and* the Hindus, would not tolerate being shifted from the subjection of one to the other—as he would emphatically and bitterly say to Gandhi: "I do not want to be ruled by you."[38]

This is again a far cry from Jinnāh's earlier attitude of "let the best man win", when he had supported the holding of the Civil Service Examination in India, and had denied that co-operation with the Hindus would subject Muslims to their rule (*supra* pp. 94-95). His words and sentiments here are very close to those of Iqbāl who way back in 1930-31 had expressed similar fears about a British-Hindu conspiracy against the minorities, and had ambiguously declared his preparedness to be ruled by either of the two, but not by both together (*supra* p. 80).

In reply to a clarification sought by Mawlāna Āzād in 1941 Jinnāh bitterly charged him with betraying the confidence of the Muslims, and of representing neither them nor the Hindus. He called Āzād a "show-boy", installed as President of the Congress to give the "Hindu body" national colour, and mislead world opinion. In his Presidential Address of December 1943 he remarked that it was since 1923 that the Congress had turned hostile (*Cf. supra* pp.102-04), with ambitions to dominate over Muslims in a Hindu *rāj*, which he now for the first time interestingly enough defined as Hindu government based on ancient Hindu religion and culture, which was totally unacceptable to the Muslims. During his talks with Gandhi in 1944 he again vehemently asserted that Gandhi represented not all Indians but only the Hindus.[39]

On 23 March 1940 Jinnāh proposed, in his Presidential Address to the session of the Muslim League at Lahore, that the two communities be provided their separate homelands to enable them to coexist "as two honourable nations." Although the Congress branded this as "the quintessence of communalism", he felt that it was much more practical than Gandhi's ideal, which would artificially bind the two nations with the majority dominating the minority. In 1943 he repeated that the Hindus desired only their own independence, and the enslavement of the Muslims—a united India was therefore unacceptable to the latter, since they were convinced that the Congress was pressing for it only with the selfish motive of setting up a Hindu *rāj*.[40]

In December 1946 Jinnāh asserted that a united India implied the perpetual rule of the majority over the minority by means of the ballot-box. Such a government, if at all possible, could "only function by force", for the Muslims would never accept it willingly. [We recall that three decades earlier he had assured the Muslims that it was impossible to run a Hindu government on the strength of the ballot-box alone-*supra* p. 95]. He repeated that Muslims demanded freedom from both British and Hindu domination, and would not accept merely a change of masters.[41]

In his Presidential Address of April 1941 Jinnāh had emphasized that in order to find a solution to India's problems, any ambition of domination must be abandoned. It is however a little surprising that he also stressed the need to "promote goodwill and harmony" by respecting each other's rights, and through "equality, fair play, and reciprocity", which he described as the aim of the League;[42] although he had denied the efficacy of such sentiments in 1937 and again in 1938 (*supra* p. 101).

In 1916 Jinnāh had expressed the desire of young, educated Indians "intoxicated with the ideas of freedom, nationality and self-government", to establish a representative government based on democracy.[43] However his views appear to have undergone a radical change later, in that he fiercely opposed democracy in India for reasons that we shall soon examine.

By January 1940 Jinnāh had come to believe like Sir Sayyad before him (*supra* pp. 22-23), that since western democracy was based on the concept of a single homogeneous people, it was unfit for India—a subcontinent of totally different nations and societies. Not only were its people divided on religious lines, but their political decisions too were ruled by their religious sentiments—he was convinced that they would always vote for their "caste-fellow" or co-religionist irrespective of the ideology and programme of his party (*cf.* Sir Sayyad—*supra* p. 21). Whereas only five years back he had described religion as a personal matter between man and God (*supra* p. 99), he now did not hesitate to contrast the western view of religion as a private affair with the religions of India—mainly Hinduism and Islām, which he now claimed were "social codes" that governed not only man's individual, but all aspects of his social and cultural life—not so much his relation with God as with his neighbour. He further reasoned that since these mutually "exclusive" faiths would not permit that union of "identity" and "thought" which was the soul of democracy, it would divide further rather than unify.[44]

In the same article and again in 1941 Jinnāh expressed the view that the implementation of a parliamentary system in India would mean the permanent hegemony of the Hindu majority; whereas the Muslims and other minorities would be rendered impotent by being deprived of their right to share in "the governance of their common motherland." The last words are significant, as also the fact that he used them in January, barely two months before propounding his scheme of separate states in March. It is also significant that whereas in this article he wrote that if at all democracy was to be implemented in India it should be subject to certain qualifications; in his Presidential Address in March he would assert that the different Indian "nationalities" would never accept the writ of a central government unless backed by armed power.[45]

In his Presidential Address of April next year Jinnāh reasoned that India really belonged to the Dravidians; and if three per cent high-caste Brahmans managed to secure a majority by underhand means, it would be a farce rather than a democracy. Expressing "sympathy and support" for "non-Brahmans", he urged them to live their own life in keeping with their "culture and history", and even to establish "Dravidistan" where Muslims would live peacefully with them.[46]

It is however interesting that later Jinnāh did not hesitate to advocate democracy for Pakistan although the objections to democracy in India were equally applicable to it : a parallel situation existed there with a Muslim majority amidst Hindu and other minorities.

India is Not a Single Nation

In February 1939 Jinnāh expressed the view that rather than chasing the noble but impossible ideal of becoming one nation, its inhabitants should accept the fact that India was "a state of nationalities, communities, castes, and creeds", for to ignore it was folly (*Cf.* Iqbāl, *supra* p. 78). In January 1940, in support of this view he cited the report of the Joint Select Committee on Constitutional Reforms according to which India was composed of different "races, often as distinct from one another in origin, tradition, and manner of life as are the nations of Europe." It further described Hindus and Muslims as "two distinct, separate civilizations" with not only religious, but also legal and cultural differences.[47]

In October 1940 Jinnāh asserted that India never was, and never could become a "national state." Advocating its division as the only solution, he felt it was futile to attempt to govern a vast sub-continent of many nationalities on the basis of the visionary ideal of a single united nation. He alleged that such notions did not exist, but were encouraged by those who desired to serve their selfish interests; whereas true statesmanship demanded that facts be faced squarely, and a course of action be charted accordingly.[48] Here we sense an echo of Iqbāl's Presidential Address a decade ago: "True statesmanship cannot ignore facts . . . . The only practical course is not to assume the existence of a state of things which does not exist . . . .."[49]

Three years later Jinnāh was to indirectly acknowledge his debt to Iqbāl by writing (in the Foreword to a collection of Iqbāl's letters to him), that his study of India's constitutional problem led him to conclusions which concurred with Iqbāl's views on the political future of Indian Muslims, and were expressed in the Pakistan Resolution of 1940. Again echoing Iqbāl, who had described India's problem as "international" rather than "national" (*supra* p. 78), Jinnāh defined it as "international" rather than "inter-communal." He felt that if this reality was ignored while determining India's political future, it would result in disaster not only for Muslims but the British and Hindus as well.[50]

In his Presidential Address of 1942 Jinnāh reiterated that the problem of India which never was "a country or nation" (whereas he is here using the terms as synonyms he would later in the same year differentiate between them), was international—"social, political, and economic differences" being too real and "fundamental" to be brushed aside. In a speech in November 1942 he repeated that never in history had India been governed as a united nation by a single power, and even in the present one-third of this "subcontinent" had eluded British rule. In December he wrote that it was futile to hope to unify India under a central government because it was neither a "country" nor a "nation" (the first apparently referring to political, and the second to cultural unity), but a subcontinent of nationalities and races. He felt that "the diversity of its races, religions, cultures, and languages" was unparalleled; the differences between its two major nations being a thousand times greater than those within the European continent.[51]

From 1940 onwards Jinnāh often repeated that the false impression of Indian unity had been created in modern times by "British power" and bureaucracy which held it together as a single "administrative unit." Since "the present artificial unity" dated back to the British conquest and was "maintained by the British bayonet", he predicted like Sir Sayyad before him (*supra* p. 25) that the end of British rule would herald "break-up" and "disaster." In reply to C. Rajagopalachari's reminder that great men like Tipu, Ḥaydar 'Ali, Awrangzeb, and Akbar had looked upon India as one and indivisible, he retorted that they had done so "as conquerors." Contending that the Hindus had not willingly accepted their rule, he wanted to know if this was the kind of government which Rajaji envisioned for the future. He reminded the Congress, which opposed partition, that India, whose real natives were the Dravidians, was not its sole property, the Aryan claim preceding that of the Muslims only by a few centuries.[52]

As we have seen, Jinnāh believed that the conception of a unified India was an unreal "self-deception", for it was composed of nationalities, castes, and sub-castes. He could not comprehend why the Lahore resolution produced such a hue and cry, and accusations of "vivisection" and "cutting the baby into two halves"; for according to him India was "divided and partitioned by nature", its Hindu and Muslim parts already existing on its "physical map." In May 1940, and again in September 1944 he reminded Gandhi and the Congress that the Muslim demand did not amount to "severance or secession from an existing union"; for the country being divided, the nation being de-nationalized, and the constitution or central government being violated were non-existent.[53]

It is interesting that while he advocated India's partition, in March 1947 Jinnāh strongly opposed any division of the provinces of Bengal and Punjab on the flimsy grounds that it was "not based on any sound principle." Whereas he had denied that its partition amounted to a "vivisection" of India, he now accused their Hindu minorities of wanting "to cut up" the provinces and their inhabitants. Although he refused to recognize the existence of a unified India, in the matter of the provinces he insisted that "for nearly a century" they had been "developed and built" as "autonomous units", and any division would strike at the root of their administrative, economic, and political life. Yet he refused to see any parallels between the two divisions, insisting that it was "a mistake to compare the demand for Pakistan and the demand for cutting up the provinces." In April he again attempted to convince the Sikhs that they would suffer rather than profit by the proposed partition of Panjab which would split their population, with more than half of it moving to Pakistan; whereas as a large, undivided majority in a united Panjab they could play a major role in Pakistan.[54]

It is interesting that exactly the same argument could be, and in fact was, addressed by many to the Muslim minority of united India to persuade them against demanding its partition, which Jinnāh held to be essential in their interest. Similarly he raised those very points against the division of the provinces which he had earlier summarily rejected when his detractors had used them to plead against India's partition. While he dismissed Indian unity as an illusion generated by the superficial administrative oneness imposed by British rule, in the case of the provinces he used this very administrative unity as a plea against division. At the same time, while citing India's religious, racial, regional, and caste variety as an impediment to its nationhood, he appears to have overlooked the fact that his proposed state of Pakistan would incorporate nearly as much diversity. As Wilfred Cantwell Smith[55] has incisively commented:

> "The logic of the situation becomes ridiculous. If Muslims in the present India, constituting a minority of 23.5 per cent, deserve the right to secede, how can one visualize a Pakistan with non-Muslim minorities of 40 per cent and more? Surely the Pakistani ought to be the first to let those minorities secede, back to 'Hindu' India."

Hindus and Muslims are Separate Nations

In the context of the lack of Indian homogeneity Jinnāh laid special stress on the differences between the two communities, describing them in January 1940 as "two different nations" representing "separate civilizations." In March he emphasized that Islām and Hinduism were not merely religions, but completely divergent social orders and civilizations based on conflicting ideas, with different sources of history and epics, the hero and victory of one often being the foe and defeat of the other. He therefore ruled out the possibility of such basic differences ever being smoothened out to pave the way for the evolution of "a common nationality." [This is in marked contrast to his early views—*supra* pp. 93-94.] He felt this was borne out by the history of the past twelve centuries which had failed to produce unity, India having always been divided into Hindu and Muslim parts. He was convinced that nationalities so divergent even after a "thousand years of close contact" could not be expected to transform themselves into one nation "merely by yoking them together" under a single state, which would lead rather to the "final destruction" of the social and political fabric.[56]

In March 1941 Jinnāh reasoned that upon their change of faith more than a thousand years back, Hindu converts to Islām had been branded as outcastes and boycotted by the parent community. Ever since then they had developed as a separate, even antagonistic order—not only religiously, but socially and culturally too. He therefore dismissed the argument that mere difference of religion was no ground for demanding Pakistan. In December 1942 he wrote that it had not been born, but had always been there—only they had not been conscious of it—although the two groups had been living in close proximity they had never "blended into one nation", each maintaining its separate identity. He outlined their differences in a long and oft-repeated, but not very meaningful formula : that the

> ". . . culture and civilization, language and literature, art and architecture, name and nomenclature, sense of value and proportion, laws and jurisprudence, social and moral codes, customs and calendar, history and traditions, aptitudes and ambitions, outlook on life and of life . . ."

of Hindus and Muslims were "fundamentally different" if not "antagonistic."[57]

We find Jinnāh enumerating the same points of departure again and again, as in July 1942, September 1944 (*infra* p. 114) and December 1946—he felt that due to their disparate and even conflicting ideology and goals, there was "no common ground for co-operation" between Hindu and Muslim India. Since their union was not workable, the only solution was separation through partition.[58]

Muslims Constitute a Nation

Whereas Iqbāl in 1930 had regarded Muslims (but not Hindus) as a nation, in December 1938 Jinnāh expressed the contrary view. He felt that whereas the Hindus had acquired moral, cultural, and political—in short national consciousness—the Muslims as a community had lost it; although he credited the League with having to a large extent reawakened it by stirring their "political conscience." He wanted Muslims to develop a "national self" and "individuality" (which would make them a force to reckon with despite their small numbers)—Iqbāl, we recall, had credited Muslims with already possessing these qualities (*supra* p. 85).[59]

From 1940 onwards Jinnāh repeatedly asserted that Muslims were not a "minority" but a "separate entity." When reminded that he had not thought thus before 1920, he replied that the idea "had been at the back of the Muslim mind" since the Lucknow Pact of 1916, which presumed the existence "of two separate entities." In his Presidential Address in March that year and again in December 1946, he repeatedly asserted that Muslims were not a "minority" but a "nation", even dominating as an overwhelming majority in many provinces. As such they were entitled to their "homeland", so that as a free people they could fully develop their "cultural" and "political life" according to their own "genius" and "ideals".[60] Again we notice echoes of Iqbāl's Presidential Address of 1930:

> ". . . the Indian Muslim is entitled to full and free development on the lines of his own culture and tradition in his own Indian homelands . . ."[61]

In his Presidential Address of 1941 Jinnāh asserted that since Muslims in India were an "independent nationality", the League would resist any attempt at merging their "political identity." Since he felt that an all-India government at the centre would mean that Muslims would be "absolutely wiped off", he insisted on "the establishment of completely independent states" in the north-west and the east. He felt that this was "a matter of life and death" since they were struggling not only for "material gain", but also for the very existence of "the soul of the Muslim nation." In October 1942 he emphasized that the early Muslims had brought their own civilization to India and further developed it here, which had been inherited by their present successors, becoming their distinct national cultural traits; and they now represented the largest compact Muslim population anywhere in the world.[62]

In July 1942 and September 1944 Jinnāh repeated that "by all canons of international law" Muslims were "a nation" with their own "culture and civilization . . ."; repeating on both occasions exactly the same definition of distinctness which he had elsewhere used to highlight differences between Hindus and Muslims (*supra* p. 112)—he seems to have been greatly enamoured by the formula as is evident from his frequent employment of it. In November 1942 he denied that like the Muslims every other community too had a right to "self-determination." In this context, he differentiated between "national" and "sub-national" groups. While the former (to which belonged the Muslims of the north-west and north-east) were in a majority in the territory of their homeland, and as such could claim self-determination and their own state as a birthright; the latter, like the fourteen per cent Muslims of the United Provinces, were a "scattered" minority who could only demand safeguards. In his Presidential Address in April 1943 he expressed the determination of Muslims to "seize the territory" that was theirs as a nation, and to "rule over" it.[63]

Jinnāh's inclusion of Sikhs among sub-national rather than national groups apparently offended them, whereupon in an apparent bid to appease them he later clarified that this was "only a constitutional phrase" signifying the scattered people of a nation, such as the Muslims of the minority provinces. He appealed to them to forget the past and place their demands before the League which was ready to meet them in every way, and wanted the minorities to be happy. Indeed he went so far in his efforts to placate the Sikhs as to undermine the very definition he had formulated, by hastening to add that by calling the Sikhs a sub-national group he did not mean that they were not a nation : "I do not dispute that the Sikhs are a nation."[64] Having classified them thus it follows that they had an equal right to "self-determination", and to demand a "state" of their own in their majority areas; whereas as we have seen earlier, he was opposed even to a partition of the Panjab into Muslim and Sikh majority areas (*supra* pp. 110-11).

Even before its formation Pakistan was threatened by casteism, as is evident from Jinnāh's vehement criticism, in March 1944, of the "sinister move" initiated by the Jāts in Panjab : that "the Muslim Jāts and Hindu Jāts were one." In order to counter it he emphasized that Islām did not recognize caste differences, the Prophet (Pbuh) having levelled down all distinctions to create national unity among the Arabs.[65]

We may see this as an ominous hint of the regional, caste, racial, and linguistic nationalism that was to raise its head in Pakistan later. As Wilfred Cantwell Smith[66] remarks, the League would "have as much difficulty in coming to terms with the vigorously independent" Pathān and Sindhi movements "as the Congress has been having with the League." Jinnāh was right in perceiving in it a threat to the religious basis of his state, and quick to nip it in the bud.

However he preferred to remain silent regarding the question of a world-wide Muslim unity or nationalism, raised by this issue. In fact when he was questioned by Gandhi in 1944 about whether or not an Indian Muslim was different from a Turk or an Arab, he replied that it was irrelevant to the issue at stake.[67]

Partition, Independence and Minorities

In his Presidential Address on 23 March 1940, Jinnāh for the first time demanded a division of India into "autonomous national states" in order to provide "separate homelands" for its "major nations", as the only way to ensure "peace", a solution of India's communal problems, and independence for all Indians. In March 1945 he reiterated that whereas the "deliverance, defence, and honour" of Muslims lay in Pakistan, the acceptance of a united India would mean complete extinction for them and for Islām in the subcontinent. However, although they stood for "free Islām", they also wanted a "free India"—while they were struggling to defend themselves, they did not wish to harm any other community, nor block its progress. While Pakistan was the means of Muslim salvation, he repeatedly tried to convince the Hindus that far from being prejudicial to their interests, it would be beneficial to all Indians—once he even said that Hindus would "be the greatest gainers"[68]—although he did not specify how.

Jinnāh believed that by giving the two major communities a "national home" and "state" in their majority areas, partition would ensure equality of status and rights to both; while also allowing them to develop according to their own "culture" and "genius", and thus contribute to the advancement of the world as a whole. He did not agree with those who predicted a civil war as the aftermath of partition, saying that there would be no "conflict" unless Gandhi and the Congress tried to "obstruct the achievement of the Muslim ideal." Rather, he felt, division would ensure a stable government for both Hindustan and Pakistan, who, he was confident would settle down as friends, seeing no reason why they should be antagonistic to each other. On the other hand it would end once and for all, the rivalry between the two communities, and the desire and efforts of each for supremacy over the other—the goodwill and harmony thus produced would find expression in pacts and treaties.[69] We can see for ourselves how mistaken he was proved on both counts.

However, in spite of these pronouncements about the desirability and advantages of partition Jinnāh perhaps had some nagging doubts, for in his speech to the Constituent Assembly of Pakistan on 11 August 1947 we find him questioning whether "it was possible or practicable to act otherwise than what has been done." Conceding that many on both sides did not agree with it, he however felt that a division had been inevitable as it provided the only solution to India's constitutional problem; for the idea of a united India could never have worked, leading only to "terrific disaster." Even while he expressed the confidence that this would "be proved by actual experience", and that history would "record its verdict in favour of it"; yet at the same time we also sense a gnawing uncertainty in his last words: "May be that view is correct—may be it is not, that remains to be seen."[70]

This subdued and wary tone seems all the more out of place in what should have been a moment of rejoicing. At a time when one would expect exultation and triumph, we find Jinnāh in a pensive, self-questioning mood. However this may also be partly attributed to the fact that he did not really get what he had demanded, *i.e.*, the whole of Kashmir, Panjab, and Bengal, but only a 'moth-eaten' version of his original ideal.

The question of whether partition should precede independence or *vice versa*, became a hotly debated one. In 1940 and 1944 Jinnāh opposed the Congress proposal that the British should first withdraw, effecting the transfer of power to an Indian Constituent Assembly or democratic government which would then decide all further matters such as partition. He felt that this would in effect vest all power in the overwhelming Hindu majority, whereas Muslims would have no say in government due to their smaller numbers. He conversely proposed that the Hindus should secure Muslim co-operation for their efforts towards independence by first accepting the latter's proposed scheme of partition. Whereas Gandhi and the Congress insisted on the achievement of independence by the joint action of all Indian parties as a pre-condition to the exercise of the right to self-determination by Muslims, for Jinnāh this amounted to putting the cart before the horse.[71]

The issue led to a great deal of contentious dispute and verbal quibbling, each group accusing the other of obstructing freedom. The British, taking full advantage of the situation, pretended to be only too anxious to part with power, but rendered helpless by the two groups refusing to unite. Jinnāh therefore urged the Hindus to foil British designs by securing power as a "divided" if not "united India." He reasoned that partition was the quickest way to freedom for both groups, whereas wrangling over an "imaginary one and united India" would only prolong their "submission to foreign rule"—forcing the Muslims to remain in an unnatural union would thus have the most disastrous consequences. He felt that although the Congress was opposing Pakistan because it desired the freedom of one group and slavery of the other; in effect, by insisting that a solution to the communal tangle should not be made a pre-condition for independence, it was obstructing the freedom of both groups.[72]

Muslim leaders ranged themselves on either side of the debate. Whereas Iqbāl had insisted, like Jinnāh, that Muslims would co-operate with the Hindus in their struggle for independence only if their demands were first met (*supra* p. 84), Mawlāna Āzād and Ḥusayn Aḥmad Madani more or less supported the stand of the Congress (*infra* pp. 165 and 197). Jinnāh's insistence on 'partition first' may be understandable in the light of his conviction that all agreements were meaningless unless backed by the power to enforce them (*supra* p. 101). Distrustful as he was of the Congress, he was perhaps apprehensive that in the absence of an arbitrating third party it could not be relied upon to live upto its commitments once it had secured power after independence.

It is interesting to observe how Jinnāh justified partition for the Muslims of the minority provinces, for whom it promised nothing. It requires little political ingenuity to see that far from benefitting them in any way, it appeared detrimental to their interests—by further reducing their numbers, and leaving them scattered all over a divided India completely at the mercy of the majority, it threatened to render them more weak and helpless. Moin Shakir[73] has aptly quoted S.A. Latif as writing that partition meant "eternal orphanage" for Muslims in Hindu India. Conversely they could be much more effective as part of a large, powerful, and consolidated minority in united India. It is therefore not surprising that Jinnāh's arguments in this context appear a trifle fallacious.

Jinnāh wanted the minority Muslims to believe that it was pointless for them to favour a united India, which would not improve their status—that of a perpetual minority—in any way. He tried to convince them that they were wrongly being made to believe that partition would leave them worse off; and that by opposing it they would be subjecting all Indian Muslims to perpetual Hindu majority rule. By supporting it on the other hand they would help at least the majority Muslims to acquire their own homeland. However he appears to contradict himself by admitting that the minority Muslims had "suffered" for their brethren, but also dismisses their sacrifice in the very next breath with these words: "But never mind, it is all in the role of a minority to suffer." Speaking for all the minority Muslims [it is not clear what sanction he had to do so], he affirmed their readiness to suffer and "face any consequences" if only they could "liberate" their Muslim "brethren."[74]

Jinnāh dismissed as totally unjustified, the apprehension of the Muslim minorities regarding their "en bloc" migration, attributing it to "false propaganda" aimed at rousing their fears. He however did not rule out some "exchange of population" wherever "necessary and feasible." As Moin Shakir[75] has remarked, without complete exchange of population, which was impracticable, partition was no solution. While for the present he appealed to the majority in every Indian province to deal fairly with the minority, Jinnāh felt that partition would ease the present tension created by the ambition of each community to dominate over the others.[76] It is not easy to fathom why such ambitions were expected to vanish at a time when they would become easier to fulfil, with each minority having become smaller and weaker.

Jinnāh naively supposed that the interests of minorities would be safeguarded through friendly settlements between the two states, involving "reciprocal arrangements." He repeatedly assured the minorities in Pakistan that in keeping with Islāmic traditions and teachings, they would be "treated not only justly" but "generously." While reminding them of their duty to remain loyal to the state, he assured them that they would be full citizens enjoying all rights without discrimination, and would play their part in the affairs of the state.[77]

While Jinnāh's concern for the minorities is touching, one cannot fathom why they should accept his assurances, when as the leader of a minority in India he refused to believe the assurances of the majority; whereas the situation in Pakistan would be exactly parallel—except that the balance of population would be reversed.

Repeatedly asserting that the Muslim League was "the only authoritative and representative organization" of Muslims, Jinnāh dismissed as untrue, Gandhi's contention that many Muslim groups did not support its proposal of division. Mawlāna Ḥifẓ-al Raḥmān, General Secretary of the Jamī'at-al 'Ulamā'-i Hind suggested that a conference of all Muslim parties be held to evolve a consensus without which, according to the Qur'ān, no decision of any organization could be deemed lawful. In his reply dated 11 April 1947 Jinnāh affirmed the need for unity among Muslims, but according to him it was to be arrived at by every Muslim joining and loyally supporting the League which was, he repeated, "the only authoritative" organization of Indian Muslims. He therefore appealed to the Mawlāna to do so without delay, and thus contribute to the struggle for Pakistan.[78]

Jinnāh's attitude to dissent and difference of opinion is quite transparent here—not giving it a chance to express itself, he summarily dismissed all opposition rather than attempting to arrive at a consensus through dialogue.

Pakistan

The question of the form of government to be followed in Pakistan was much discussed in the years preceding its formation. Jinnāh's stand on this crucial question is quite obscure.

In a speech in November 1941 Jinnāh denied that Pakistan "would be a religious state" excluding its religious minorities "from all power." In his Presidential Address of April 1943 he dismissed as mischievous and premature, the question whether Pakistan would be an Islāmic government, since it did not arise until the state actually came into being. [This argument appears flawed, for those who were struggling for its formation had every right to know what exactly they were striving for.] At the same time he also affirmed that it was the people who would decide the nature of the government, since they would elect the members to the constitution-making body. While assuring that the proposed state would have a "people's government", he also promised that its constitution could "only be framed by the *millat* and the people."[79]

Jinnāh used the words as synonyms, apparently oblivious to their difference of meaning, specially in a country with a mixed population—whereas "*millat*" denotes only the Muslim population, "people" encompasses all communities and religions. His statement is thus not free of ambiguity, and even contradiction.

In an interview in October 1944, while Jinnāh asserted that Muslims wanted "to establish their own real democratic popular government" in Pakistan; he also went on to say that it would "function with the will and sanction of the entire body of people in Pakistan, irrespective of caste, creed or colour."[80] Here again the subtle difference between a Muslim government or a government of Muslims; and a democratic, popular, people's government, seems to have been glossed over. Perhaps he felt that because Muslims would be in a majority, democracy in Pakistan would amount to Muslim rule, just as he had reasoned that in India it would mean a virtual Hindu *rāj* (*supra* p. 104).

In an interview in November 1945, while Jinnāh repeated that Pakistan would be a democracy, he also assured the minorities of adequate representation in the government. Even while he ruled out the possibility of "social barriers" against any minority as being contrary to the Muslim belief in "equality of manhood"; he visualized Pakistan as "a Muslim state as far as the Muslims are concerned."[81] He however does not make it clear as to exactly how, and to what extent Pakistan would be a "Muslim state" and if it was so for Muslims, how it could be otherwise for non-Muslims. Perhaps he was trying to pander to popular sentiment, and the desire among the masses for an Islāmic state, even while he tried to reassure the minorities of equal treatment, and to remain true to the ideals of democracy and equality.

While only eight years back in his Presidential Address in October 1937 Jinnāh had accused the Congress of leading "the people towards socialistic and communalistic ideas" for which they were "far from prepared"; he now hoped that in Pakistan "major industries and public utility services would be socialized."[82] One wonders what changes had come about in this period to make socialism not only acceptable, but also desirable. Moin Shakir[83] has an interesting explanation to offer : he feels that the Muslim League was obliged to "pay lip-service" to socialism in order to counter the

Congress programme on the one hand; and to win over the Muslim masses on the other"—since Pakistan could not be established without their support, Jinnāh assured them that it aimed at their welfare. Shakir cites his biographer Hector Bolitho who quotes Jinnāh as having once said: "A political organization which gives no promise of improving the lot of the average Muslim cannot attract the masses."

In an interview on 21 May 1947 Jinnāh repeated that the government of Pakistan would be "popular, representative, and democratic"; responsible to all the people (irrespective of caste, creed, or sect); and they would be the ones to determine its policy and programme. When he was asked on 13 July whether Pakistan would be a secular or a theocratic state he dismissed the question as "absurd" for, as he said, he did not know "what a theocratic state means."[84]

In June 1945 Jinnāh had described Pakistan as signifying not only "independence but the Muslim ideology which has to be preserved, which has come to us as a precious gift and treasure and which we hope others will share with us"—but he did not explicate exactly how this was to be achieved. In September 1945 he remarked that Islām was not limited to religious, moral, and spiritual doctrines, duties, and rituals, but was a complete ("religious, social, civil, commercial, military, judicial, [and] penal") code, regulating all aspects of Muslim individual and collective life.[85] Iqbāl had also insisted on the all-pervasive nature of Islām, but while he also asserted its right to mould the law and polity of the Muslim state (*supra* pp. 73 and 86), it is not clear how far Jinnāh intended to apply the universal Islāmic code to the government and politics of Pakistan.

It is interesting that in his speeches to the Constituent Assembly of Pakistan on 10 and 11 August 1947 Jinnāh reminded its inhabitants that they were first and last equal citizens of the state, with equal rights and obligations; for their religion, caste, or creed had "nothing to do with the business of the state." He now lamented the divisions among the people of India (drawing attention to regional and caste-differences within each group—Pathāns, Panjabis, Shī'as, Sunnīs etc., among Muslims; and Brahmans, Vaishnavas, Khatri, Bengali, Madrasi etc. among Hindus), which he felt had been responsible not only for its conquest and continued subjugation, but had also proved the greatest stumbling-block in the way of its freedom. He exhorted the people of Pakistan to learn a lesson from this, and to set before themselves the ideal of England where religious categories had gradually been obliterated; so that in course of time "all these angularities" of "majority and minority", "Hindu" and "Muslim" would "vanish", and

> ". . . Hindus would cease to be Hindus and Muslims would cease to be Muslims, not in the religious sense, because that is the personal faith of each individual, but in the political sense, as citizens of the state."[86]

These sentiments, couched in such language, appear strange and incongruous (to say the least), coming from Jinnāh—the chief architect of the two-nation theory, leading many to surmise that he "took the earliest opportunity to bid goodbye" to what was merely "a convenient tool."[87] Nationhood is suddenly liberated from religion, whereas all along he had pressed for the formation of Pakistan on the very basis of religion. As for his declaration that it had "nothing to do with the business of the state", we recall that more than a decade earlier in February 1935, even while conceding that religion which was a personal matter should not be admitted into politics, he had clarified that the problem of minorities was a political issue rather than a merely religious one (*supra* p. 99). Later of course he came a long way from this view, stating in January 1940 that since in India religion was not merely a private affair but governed all aspects of life, the religious differences between Hindus and Muslims precluded their blending into a single nation (*supra* pp. 107-08). Now we find him calling for that very merging of religious identity into the political which he had earlier deemed impossible. By underscoring religion he appears to be actually undermining the very basis of the new state—how can the very ground of the state dissolve once it is formed?

Since Pakistan was founded on the basis of religion, one would expect religious ideology to continue to guide its politics and society. However it is surprising to see that once the state has come into existence, religion is suddenly abandoned in favour of what appears to be a wholly secular polity. In fact all that was anathema in India—democracy, secularism, socialism—is now being eagerly embraced. Jinnāh appears to have come full circle in that whereas earlier he had emphasized differences (*supra* p. 109 *ff.*), we now find him again preaching that very unity which he had so fervently espoused in the initial stages of his career (*supra* p. 93*ff*). When it could not be forged in India despite his former efforts and those of the nationalists, one wonders how he expected to achieve such unity in Pakistan, which would abound in nearly as much variety. It may well be said that the fact of Pakistan being a Muslim state altered everything, but that is the very question: in what sense was it a Muslim state—could merely the presence of a Muslim majority suffice to make it so, and to radically alter all former perceptions of religion and politics?

In this sudden reversal of his stand Jinnāh has chosen to go only half way with his precursor Iqbāl, who had first floated the idea that religion is the basis of nationhood. However Iqbāl had fiercely opposed the subsumption of religious identity in the political and national consciousness, which Jinnāh is here calling for. He had written in 1935 that as "a principle of human solidarity" nationalism conflicted with Islām by pushing it "to the background of a mere private opinion." Although in the last year of his life he had reconciled nationalism in Muslim majority lands with Islām, he believed that it was not possible to retain Islām as an "ethical ideal" while substituting it as a polity by secular "national polities" (*supra* pp. 71-73 and 85-86).

Pan-Islāmism

Jinnāh did not believe in pan-Islāmism as a "theory", which he felt had "long ago exploded." He therefore did not envisage the establishment of a pan-Islāmic state after the formation of Pakistan. He however affirmed that it would certainly strive for friendship and co-operation with eastern nations. Throughout his political career he had always displayed sympathy for other Muslim countries—in 1936 he had declared that one of the aims of the Muslim League was to "strengthen brotherly relations" between Muslims of India and other countries. In his Presidential Addresses of 1937, 1938, and 1940 he affirmed the support and sympathy of the former for the cause of the Arabs of Palestine. Criticizing the imperialistic policy of the British government for betraying the Arabs, he demanded an assurance from it to the effect that Indian troops would not be deployed against any Muslim country. In his 'Īd message of October 1942 he expressed sympathy and support for other Muslim countries fighting for their freedom who, he observed with satisfaction, were displaying equal concern for the Pakistan movement.[88]

The Muslim League

We have already seen (*supra* p. 97) Jinnāh justifying in 1916, its formation by Muslims, who had so far refrained from political action, but had felt the need for safeguarding their interests in the face of the threat posed to them by the imminent political reforms. He however felt that its creed had "broadened" with the political evolution of the community. In 1936 he recalled that in December 1912 it had adopted the aim of securing "responsible government"; safeguards for Muslims; the protection of their religious, political, and other rights and interests; and the promotion of friendship between them, and other Indian communities as well as Muslims of other countries. In the forthcoming elections its programme included the protection and promotion of "the religious rights of Muslims" and the Urdu language; to work for their general amelioration; and to resist all repressive measures encroaching on their fundamental rights and leading to their economic exploitation.[89]

In 1936 and in his Presidential Address next year, Jinnāh asserted that the League had always stood for full, national, democratic, responsible, self-government. In the Presidential Address of 1938 he vehemently denied the Congress charge that the League supported imperialism—he felt that even those few who had believed in the past that Muslims could profit by an alliance with it had been disillusioned. However his intentions become suspect when he asserts in the same breath that if the interests of Muslims demanded it, the League would ally itself even with the devil, not for love of imperialism, but because one had to play one's game in politics as on the chess-board.[90] We are left to make what we may of this, and the light it throws on his political tactics.

While Jinnāh repeatedly denied that the League was supporting foreign domination, in March 1942 he justified its non-participation in the civil disobedience movement [launched by Gandhi in 1940 for the attainment of free speech], on the rather flimsy grounds that no Provincial League had made out a sufficient case for it. In his Presidential Address of 1943 he dismissed as "vicious propaganda" the Congress charge that the League was indifferent to independence and reconciled to British *rāj*, clarifying that it was only opposed to Hindu *rāj*. On the other hand he turned the tables on the Congress by alleging that it preferred British *rāj* to conceding to the demands of the League, and was holding up freedom by refusing to come to a settlement (*Cf. supra* pp. 116-17). In October 1944 while he denied the charge of being pro-British, he refused to accept the Congress demands on the grounds that it would subject the Muslims to "a Hindu majority triumphant with British co-operation."[91] We recall that Iqbāl had expressed similar fears way back in 1930-31 (*supra* p. 80).

Divide et Impera[92]

It is interesting to observe that while both the nationalist and separatist groups perceived the British to be playing this game, they drew completely divergent conclusions from it by means of contrary arguments.

While repeatedly referring to this policy in his Presidential Address of 1943, Jinnāh recalled that in keeping with it the British government had contrived to break up the session of the League at Bombay in 1915, since he had arranged for the Congress to meet at the same time and place as part of his efforts towards rapprochement. He felt that the government continued to play its old game by saying different things at different times, while it was concerned only with prolonging its own rule. He did not believe its claim that by resisting the demand of the Congress to "Quit India" [made in August 1942], it was actually protecting Muslim interests—it was not for love of Muslims that the British were delaying a Hindu-Muslim settlement, but because they knew that when it came they would have to part with power.[93]

While Jinnāh conceded that the British took advantage of the folly of Indians, he felt it was pointless to keep blaming them for keeping apart the two communities, who were themselves equally responsible for their disunity. He felt that they should come to a settlement despite the obstacles being placed in their way—the only means of countering the British policy of divide and rule was to unite and get them out. He felt further that it was a part of their divisive policy to encourage Indians to pursue the idea of a united India, and explained the paradox thus: they were convinced that since Hindus and Muslims could never agree, such an arrangement would be virtually "a cock-pit of feud . . . with the Englishman on top." He believed that they were "still dangling the carrot before the donkey by saying that geographically India is one", because they knew that they could thus prolong their lease of supremacy: without their arbitration Indians could never agree among themselves to frame a constitution for a united India.[94]

As Wilfred Cantwell Smith[95] has remarked, from 1942 the India Office authorities prohibited negotiations between the Congress and the Muslim League as long as they could, and began to announce, after years of dividing and ruling, that they were unfavourable to separatism. In the end of 1942 the Viceroy Lord Linlithgow emphasized India's geographical unity, and the need to conserve it.

Religious Terminology

Although Jinnāh was primarily concerned with safeguarding the political existence of Muslims; since this was defined by their religious identity, religion was bound to creep in, and we should not be surprised to find him couching his discourse in religious terminology. However this is rare, and even where it occurs, seems superficial, and unlike Iqbāl whose politics is steeped in religion, there is very little religious content in his political thought.

Not surprisingly, Jinnāh's 'Īd messages always carried religious overtones of a very general kind. In November 1939 he said that for Muslims "all social regeneration and political freedom must finally depend on Islām and Islāmic spirit", and appealed to them to be guided by their "rational interpretation of the Qur'ān." In his 'Īd message of October 1942 he would have Muslims establish their place in the world order "according to the light of Islāmic heritage." However later we find him using vaguely religious terminology on other occasions too. Speaking in the Legislative Council in March 1939 he warned the Congress that it could never destroy the souls of Muslims, nor their Islāmic culture and spirit. In his Presidential Address next year he urged the workers of the League to "come forward as servants of Islām [and] organize the people economically, socially, educationally and politically." In December 1942 he vowed to continue his "service of the Muslims and Islām."[96]

In April 1943 Jinnāh told Muslim students that the greatest message for the guidance of Muslims was in the Qur'ān. In his Presidential Address that month he asserted that even "the tallest poppy in the Muslim world" would have to bow to "the voice of the League", the "people", and "the authority of the *millat*." He also appealed to the delegates from Panjab "to substitute love for Islām and your Nation in place of sectional interests." In his speech at the session in December that year he characterized Islām and the Qur'ān as "the bed-rock and sheet-anchor of the community", which kept it "united as one man." He hoped for greater unity in the future :

"one God one Book, one Prophet and one Nation." In an attack on the Communists in March 1944 he proclaimed that Muslims wanted neither any flag except that of the League; nor any "ism", for Islām was for them a complete code of life.[97] He however did not hesitate later to advocate nationalism and socialism in Pakistan (see *supra* pp.119-20).

In another speech in the same month, in the light of the "many impurities and un-Islāmic things" which had permeated Muslim society, Jinnāh urged Muslim institutions to educate their children with a view to enabling them to live the Islāmic life. In November 1944 he proclaimed that the ideal of Muslim commerce was Islāmic rather than capitalistic *i.e.* to equalize the standard of living rather than encourage the concentration of wealth. He declared that if the Muslim League controlled the resources of the government, it "would be the Muslim government." In June 1945 he declared that Pakistan meant, besides freedom, the preservation and sharing with others of their legacy *i.e.* "the Muslim ideology." In November the same year he proclaimed that Muslims could never be crushed, for their religion, culture, and Islāmic ideals were their "driving force to achieve independence."[99]

Notes and References

All references unless otherwise stated are to the works of Muḥammad 'Ali Jinnāh.

1. *Muhammad Ali Jinnah: An Ambassador of Unity: His Speeches and Writings (1912-17)* (Madras, n.d.) p. 135.
2. Aziz Ahmad, *Islāmic Modernism in India and Pakistan (1857-1964)* (London, 1967) p. 164.
3. M. Rafique Afzal, ed., *Selected Speeches and Statements of the Quaid-i Azam, Muḥammad Ali Jinnah (1911-34 and 1947-48)* (Lahore, 1973) pp. 32 and 49.
4. *Ibid.*, p. 52; Ahmad Saeed, ed., *Writings of the Quaid-i Azam* (Lahore, 1976) pp. 16-17.
5. Afzal, *Selected Speeches,* pp. 54-55.
6. *Ibid.*, pp. 42-44 and 55.
7. *Ambassador of Unity,* pp. 155 and 275-76.
8. *Ibid.*, pp. 159-161 and 165.
9. *Ibid.*, p. 194.
10. Referring to the alliance between the League and the Congress through a pact, on the basis of a draft prepared by him. It was a joint declaration for self-government, including a communal constitutional

agreement between the two bodies.

11. Afzal, *Selected Speeches*, pp. 132-33 and 249-250.
12. *Ibid.*, pp. 294-95 and 298.
13. M. Rafique Afzal, ed., *Quaid-i Azam Muhammad Ali Jinnah: Speeches in the Legislative Council of India (1924-30)* (Lahore, 1976) pp. 46 and 96.
14. Waheed Ahmad, ed., *Quaid-i Azam Muhammad Ali Jinnah; The Nation's Voice Towards Consolidation: Speeches and Statements (March 1935-March 1940)* (Karachi, 1992) pp. 27 and 56.
15. Afzal, *Selected Speeches*, p. 56.
16. *Ibid.*
17. *Ibid.*, pp. 62-63.
18. *Ibid.*, pp. 43 and 56.
19. *Ibid.*, pp. 249 and 252.
20. *Ibid.*, pp. 289, 294-95, 315 and 354-55; Saeed, *op.cit*, pp. 75-76.
21. Waheed Ahmad, ed., *Quaid-i Azam Muhammad Ali Jinnah's Speeches in the Legislative Council (1935-47)* (Karachi, 1991) p. 31.
22. Saeed, *op. cit.*, pp. 74-76.
23. W. Ahmad, *Nation's Voice*, pp. 29, 32 and 43.
24. *Op. cit.*, pp. 165 and 170.
25. *Quaid-i Azam's Presidential Addresses, All India Muslim League (1937-43)* (Delhi, 1945) Address I, p. 9.
26. *Ibid.*, Address II, pp. 4-5 and 11.
27. W. Ahmad, *Speeches*, p. 449; Rizwan Ahmad, ed., *Sayings of the Quaid-i Azam, Muhammad Ali Jinnah* (Karachi, 1976) p. 45.
28. *Presidential Addresses,* Address VII, pp. 8-9 and 17.
29. Wilfred Cantwell Smith, *Modern Islam in India* (Lahore, 1969) p. 302.
30. *Presidential Addresses,* Address I, pp. 6-7.
31. *Ibid.*, Address I, p. 7; Address II, pp. 7-9 and Address III, pp. 5-7.
32. *Ibid.*, Address II, pp. 8-9; *Quaid-i Azam Speaks: His Vision of Pakistan* (Karachi, 1991) p. 52.
33. *Presidential Addresses*, Address I, pp. 10-11; Address III, pp. 4-7.
34. *Ibid.*, Address II, pp. 9-10.
35. W. Ahmad, Speeches, p. 431; Mohammad Hanif Shahid, *ed., Quaid-i Azam Muhammad Ali Jinnah: Speeches, Statements, Writings, Letters* etc. (Lahore, 1976) p. 122.
36. *Quaid-i Azam Speaks*, pp. 4-5 and 10-11.
37. *Ibid.*, pp. 20-21; *Presidential Addresses,* Address VII, p. 18.
38. W. Ahmad, *Speeches,* pp. 490 and 492-93; Shahid, *op. cit.*, p. 151; *Presidential Addresses*, Address VII, p. 19.
39. Shahid, *op. cit.*, p. 191; *Presidential Addresses*, Address VIII, pp. 23-24; *Gandhi-Jinnah Talks: Text of Correspondence and Other*

Relevant Matters (July-Oct. 1944) (New Delhi, 1944) p. 18.
40. Shahid, *op. cit.*, pp. 24-25 and 27; *Presidential Addresses*, Address VIII, pp. 14-15.
41. *Quaid-i Azam Speaks*, p. 30.
42. R. Ahmad, *op. cit.*, p. 51.
43. Afzal, *Selected Speeches*, p. 32; W. Ahmad, *Speeches,* p. 72.
44. Shahid, *op. cit.*, pp. 120-21.
45. *Ibid.*, p. 128; *Quaid-i Azam Speaks*, p. 17; R. Ahmad, *op. cit.*, pp. 50-51.
46. *Presidential Addresses*, Address V, pp. 4-5.
47. W. Ahmad, *Speeches,* p. 419; Shahid, *op. cit.*, pp. 120-21.
48. Shahid, *op. cit.*, pp. 146-47.
49. S.A. Vahid, ed., *Thoughts and Reflections of Iqbal* (Lahore, 1973), p. 168.
50. *Quaid-i Azam Speaks*, pp. 17-18.
51. R. Ahmad, *op. cit.*, p. 31; Shahid, *op. cit.*, p. 150.
52. R. Ahmad, *op. cit.*, p. 31; Shahid, *op. cit.*, pp. 22-23, 25 and 150. *Quaid-i Azam Speaks*, pp. 19-20.
53. Shahid, *op. cit.*, p. 25; *Gandhi-Jinnah Talks,* p. 21.
54. Shahid, *op. cit.*, pp. 63-64.
55. *Op. cit.*, p. 324.
56. Shahid, *op. cit.*, p. 121; *Quaid-i Azam Speaks*, pp. 17-19.
57. R. Ahmad, *op. cit.*, pp. 21 and 55-56; Shahid, *op. cit.*, p. 152.
58. Shahid, *op. cit.*, p. 50; *Quaid-i Azam Speaks*, p. 29.
59. *Presidential Addresses*, Address III, p. 8.
60. *Quaid-i Azam Speaks*, pp. 14, 20 and 29
61. S.A Vahid, *op. cit.*, p. 169.
62. *Presidential Addresses*, Address V, p. 4; R. Ahmad, *op. cit.*, pp. 30 and 50-51.
63. *Presidential Addresses*, Address VII, p. 1; R. Ahmad, *op. cit.*, pp. 28 and 31-32.
64. R. Ahmad, *op. cit.*, pp. 57-58.
65. *Ibid.*, p. 56;
66. *Op. cit.*, p. 329.
67. *Gandhi-Jinnah Talks,* pp. 13 and 17.
68. Shahid, *op. cit.*, pp. 25, 27-28 and 151-52; *Gandhi-Jinnah Talks,* pp. 6 and 17-18; R. Ahmad, *op. cit*, pp. 46 and 75.
69. *Quaid-i Azam Speaks*, pp. 18 and 29-30; Shahid, *op. cit.*, pp. 27-28 and 62.
70. *Quaid-i Azam Speaks*, pp. 34-35.
71. *Gandhi-Jinnah Talks*, pp. 7, 20, 23, 26, 29, 49-50 and 87; *Quaid-i-Azam Speaks*, pp. 6-10.
72. Shahid, *op. cit.*, pp. 28 and 147; *Presidential Addresses*, Address VII, pp. 13, 23 and 25, Address VIII, p. 15; R. Ahmad, *op. cit.*, p. 29.

73. *Khilafat to Partition* (New Delhi, 1970), p. 206.
74. Shahid, *op. cit.*, pp. 19-20; *Presidential Addresses*, Address VII, p. 4.
75. *Op. cit.*, p. 206.
76. Shahid, *op. cit.*, pp. 19-20, 27, 52, 61, 64, 70 and 147; R. Ahmad, *op. cit.*, p. 46; *Presidential Addresses*, Address V, pp. 5-6; Address VII, pp. 35-36 and 39; Address VIII, p. 21.
77. *Quaid-i Azam Speaks*, p. 18; Shahid, *op. cit.*, pp. 75 and 84.
78. *Gandhi-Jinnah Talks,* pp. 14, 17 and 52; Shahid, *op. cit.*, pp. 54-55.
79. Ziya-ul Hasan Faruqi, *The Deoband School and the Demand for Pakistan* (Bombay, 1963) p. 126; *Presidential Addresses*, Address VII, p. 34.
80. R. Ahmad, *op. cit.*, p. 60.
81. *Ibid.*, pp. 64-66.
82. *Ibid.*, p. 64; *Presidential Addresses*, Address I, p. 11.
83. *Op. cit.*, p. 204.
84. Shahid, *op. cit.*, pp. 73 and 86.
85. R. Ahmad, *op. cit.*, pp. 22-23 and 61.
86. Shahid, *op. cit.*, pp. 90 and 94; *Quaid-i Azam Speaks*, pp. 35-37.
87. Shakir, *op. cit.*, p. 207, quoting Chowdhry Khaliquzzaman in *Pathway to Pakistan.*
88. Saeed, *op. cit.*, p. 74; *Presidential Addresses*, Address I, pp. 14-15; Address III, p. 9; *Quaid-i Azam Speaks*, pp. 12-13; R. Ahmad, *op. cit.*, p. 89.
89. Saeed, *op. cit.*, pp. 74-75 and 80; Afzal, *Selected Speeches*, p. 56.
90. Saeed, *op. cit.*, p. 76; *Presidential Addresses,* Address I, p. 5; Address III, p. 12.
91. Saeed, *op. cit.*, p. 95; R. Ahmad, *op. cit.*, pp. 26 and 60; *Presidential Addresses*, Address VII, pp. 25-26.
92. Smith, *op. cit.*, pp. 193-94 "On 14 May 1859 the Governor of Bombay said: *'Divide et impera'* was the old Roman motto and it should be ours."
93. *Presidential Addresses*, Address VII, pp. 8 and 14.
94. *Ibid.*, pp. 19-20 and 24.
95. *Op. cit.*, pp. 330-31.
96. R. Ahmad, *op. cit.*, pp. 19-20, 88 and 110; W. Ahmad, *Speeches*, p. 431; *Quaid-i Azam Speaks*, p. 22.
97. R. Ahmad, *op. cit.*, pp. 22 and 100-02; *Presidential Addresses*, Address VII, pp. 4 and 52.
98. R. Ahmad, *op. cit.*, pp. 61 and 114; *Quaid-i Azam Speaks*, pp. 27-28.

Chapter 5

ABU'L KALĀM ĀZĀD
(1888-1958)

Muslim Nationhood

Writing in the *al-Hilāl*[1] in October 1912, Āzād appears to be affirming the value of religious nationalism for Muslims, while rejecting the validity of secular nationalism—he emphasized the power that their religion and God wielded over Muslims—whereas the rest of the world was swayed by patriotism and nationalism, Muslims could be moved only by appeals to their faith. In October the next year he denied the validity for them (unlike the Hindus), of secular nationalism as a means to self-awareness. For them only Islām could perform this function since their nationality, rather than being racially or geographically exclusive, transcended all man-made barriers.[2]

In a speech a year later in October 1914 we find Āzād propounding familiar views regarding the universal brotherhood of Islām, which negated man-made divisions and earthly relationships, and was based on the commonness of divine servitude (49:13), the only real bond being that which connected man with his Lord. Since He is one, His devotees should also remain one (23:52) despite apparent geographical and racial differences which were only one of the "signs of God" (30:22), and should not be regarded as the basis of any real distinctions. Whosoever accepts the *kalimah* instantly becomes, as a Muslim, a member of this community created by God, whose home is the whole world. He believed that before the dawn of Islām, mankind, though a single family, was divided by dissensions created by Satan. But as the call of Islām spread, it reunited different nations (*qawm*), and people of far-flung lands as brothers and co-sharers in each other's joy and grief (3:103). All other relationships could be severed, but not that between Muslims of the world.[3]

In this speech and in his Presidential Address to the Provincial Khilāfat Committee of Bengal in February 1920 (which was later published with some changes as the work *Mas'alah-i Khilāfat*), Āzād quoted numerous *Hadīth* in which the united nationhood (*muttaḥidah qawmiyyat*) of Muslims has been likened to a single organism which participates in the suffering of each of its constituent parts. The *millat* is also described as a wall wherein each Muslim serves as a supportive brick unto every other fellow-Muslim. As is to be expected, the whole argument was developed in order to arouse sympathy among Indian Muslims for their co-religionists in the Balkans and Turkey, who were facing the bullets of Christians.[4]

We recall that it was in 1914 that the First World War began, in which Turkey participated as an ally of the Central Powers. The Italo-Turkish war had been sparked off in 1911 by Italy's attacking and seizing Tripoli; and the Balkan wars in 1912 by the Balkan states revolting against Turkey under European (including British) instigation and support. This gave rise to a country-wide pan-Islāmic agitation. According to Smith, Indian Muslims perceived that through these wars, western and particularly British imperialism was conquering and destroying their Islāmic culture, and oppressing Muslims. "Literary figures" such as Akbar, Shibli and Iqbāl "poured forth their discontent" in verse.[5] This anti-British feeling is also noticeable in Āzād's speeches of this period, which appear to aim primarily at rousing his co-religionists in India, and garnering their support for those Muslims who were fighting the British.

In his Presidential Address to the Jamī'at-al 'Ulamā'-i Hind at Lahore in November 1921, Āzād described the basis of the true nationhood (*qawmiyyat*) of Muslims as "only the knowledge and practice of the *Sharī'at*", according to which they were "the best of peoples" (3:110), and "witnesses over the nations" (2:143).[6]

Islāmic Unity

During his speech of 1914 and in the *Mas'alah* Āzād tried to demonstrate that whereas this feeling, in the form of the universal Muslim brotherhood, dates back to Islām itself, due to its evil intentions Europe had tried to interpret it as a novel phenomenon of Muslim political unity, which it called "pan-Islāmism." Criticizing their attempts to attribute the spread of this movement to the efforts of Sultān 'Abd-al Ḥamīd to extend the power of the Turkish caliphate outside his own domains, Āzād attempted to show that the Turkish Sultāns had always been accepted as universal Islāmic caliphs by world Muslims. He felt that Europe's nightmares of a violent attempt by the Muslims of the world to unite against it was only a reflection of its own bloody intentions; whereas it accused Muslims of sinister designs in the form of pan-Islāmism. Since half a century the Christian powers of Europe had formulated a common strategy to wipe out the remaining political power of Islām, and divide the spoils, *i.e.* the Muslim world, among themselves.[7]

In 1914 Āzād had strongly criticized Europe's double standards in projecting the natural unity of Islām as a great offence, even while it regarded wiping off Muslims as a service to civilization. While it falsely accused them of barbarism, he contrasted their kindness to prisoners of war with European excesses in the Muslim world, and its violation of all natural laws of international justice. He felt that it realized that whereas a severed Turkey alone could not combat Christian unity, the Muslims of the world together were a formidable power. Although their international unity was weakened by western atheism and local preoccupations, it wanted to uproot this potential resistance even before it had fully taken root. He lamented that despite the fact that their only defence against European strategy lay in genuine Islāmic unity or pan-Islāmism, Muslims were lost to the religious brotherhood to which they had been invited from the beginning (3:103), and this was the cause of their weakness and decline. Had such unity existed among them, it was impossible that Indian Muslims be unmoved by the oppression being inflicted on their co-religionists elsewhere.[8]

Attacking the Aligarh movement on this count Āzād asserted that no national (*qawmi*) movement, which would produce only local changes, could benefit Muslims as a nation (*qawm*), who were scattered all over the world. He even described as ill-founded all local Muslim efforts including those being made in India, and was therefore severely critical of the preoccupation of Indian Muslims with the Aligarh University, which he felt had rendered them indifferent to the fate of their co-religionists in the rest of the world. He felt it had acquired precedence for them over the fate of Islām itself, which was for him more important than the survival of "nations"—if the political strength of Islām was destroyed, Aligarh, and even the fulfilment of all their other plans of progress would be profitless for Indian Muslims.[9] This concern for Islām and world

Muslims is not seen later in his thought, when he is ready to sacrifice the *khilāfat* for *swarāj* (*infra* pp. 151-53).

Āzād was also severely critical of the Aligarh school (although he does not mention it by name), for rejecting international Islāmic unity; the validity of the Islāmic caliphate beyond the Pious Caliphs; and the sovereignty of the Turkish caliph over Indian Muslims (*cf.* Sir Sayyad, *supra* pp. 29-30). He accused them of abandoning the Qur'ān and the cause of the "oppressed *millat*" in order to pander to the English, and to serve as tools in the hands of European politicians who desired to wipe out the international influence of the Islāmic caliphate. Using very strong language, he described such persons as being inflicted by a divine curse in that they were severing the bond established by God between the Muslims of the world. In a way they were willing that lakhs of Muslims defending the faith should suffer at the hands of Christians, and were thus causing torment to God and His Prophet (Pbuh) (33:57).[10]

In the *Mas'alah* Āzād dwelt at some length on the concept of the "centre" of the nation (*qawm*), in order to arouse Indian Muslims against any kind of Jewish or Christian influence over the Arabian peninsula and Jerusalem. He expressed the view that no "nation" could survive without an earthly centre, particularly Islām, the diverse constituents of whose nationhood (*qawmiyyat*) were scattered over the whole earth. In order to keep them together it was essential to define a centre-point of unity which was the Ka'bah, and by implication the Arabian peninsula—the native land of Islām. He felt that the institution of the Hajj, and the Ka'bah as the *qiblah* for prayer, was meant (among other benefits) to repeatedly reinforce the links of the whole *ummat* with this central point. He believed that in order to maintain the permanence of this centre it was necessary to perpetually confine it only to Islām, and therefore Muslims had been commanded (in 9 A.H.) to keep the unbelievers out of the sanctuary (*haram*). In the light of this command and a *Hadīth* in which the Prophet (Pbuh) had willed his followers to purge the Arabian peninsula of polytheists, he asserted that Muslims would not tolerate the attempt to bring any part of their sacred territory (in which he included, on the basis of *Hadīth*, the *Bayt-al Muqaddas* and its territory, which as their first holy *qiblah* was equally sacred for Muslims), under Christian or Jewish influence in the present; and regarding it as a challenge to their faith, would be forced to relive the Crusades.[11] This was a response to European, and particularly

British efforts to gain control over parts of the Arab world during and after the First World War (*Cf. infra* pp. 142-43).

Collectivism

In the *Mas'alah* we find Āzād laying great emphasis on this concept, rendered in Urdu by the word *ijtimā'iyyat*. He wrote that on this very factor depended the progress and decline, not only of the Islāmic *ummat*, but of all the nations of the world. The Qur'ān had therefore everywhere described "collectivism" as the foundation of national life, which he interpreted as "holding on fast to the rope of God" (3:103). Whereas revelation produced collectivism, division was the consequence of transgression against it (45:16-17). The Prophet (Pbuh) had therefore given Islāmic life the name of *jamā'at* or community (*i.e.* a group of persons which has unity, order, and discipline); and had exhorted Muslims to remain a part of it, for he who separates himself is destined to go astray. The forceful commands in numerous *Ḥadīth* for Muslims to obey the leader or *amīr* of the community (even if he was a transgressor and tyrant, so long as he was a Muslim and established prayers), was according to him, also meant to strengthen it. He believed that this very communal reality was the foundation of every command of the *Sharī'at*—the emphasis on congregational prayers; the concourse (*ijtīmā'*) of *ḥajj*; and the sustenance of communal life by determining a share for the community in the wealth of the individual through *zakāt*.[12]

In an early but dateless article also Āzād wrote that the Qur'ān has everywhere characterized Islām as "collectivism" and unbelief as disunity, discouraging Muslims from dissension and schism as vehemently as it warns them against unbelief and polytheism (30: 31-32). Yet they had not lived up to the principle of *tawḥīd* which demanded that a people worshipping a single Creator should also remain undivided (*Cf. supra* p. 131). He attributed their decline and afflictions to the fact that they became divided into numerous groups after Islām had bound them together as a single *ummat*. He quoted Ḥaḍrat 'Ali as having instructed Muslims to abstain from dissension, and always remain with the majority *i.e.* the national (*qawmi*) group (*jamā'at*) of Islām, for God's hand is over it; whereas he who separates himself becomes earmarked for Satan. He had even exhorted them to kill anyone who sowed discord in the "group", no matter what his stature. Repeating much the same points in his Presidential Address to the Jamī'at-al 'Ulamā'-i Hind in November 1921, Āzād added that the office of the caliph had been instituted, and obedience to it strictly enjoined, in order to strengthen this very "collectivism."[13]

In the *Mas'alah,* while emphasizing the need for the whole *ummat* to agree upon a *khalīfah* or *imām* who was the national (*qawmi*) centre of their collective existence, Āzād quoted a *Ḥadīth* according to which he who abandoned the *jamā'at*, disobeyed the caliph, and died unrepenting in this state; would die as an unbeliever rather than a Muslim. Attributing the decline of the *ummat* to the conversion of the *khilāfat* into kingship, he interpreted it as the displacement of unity by disunity—whereas the Prophet (Pbuh) and the Pious Caliphs had simultaneously executed the functions of caliph, king, *imām*, jurist etc., these were later divided among different individuals. He welcomed the attempt in the period of Sultān 'Abd-al Ḥamīd to transform the Uthmāni caliphate from dictatorship to *shūrá*, as a step towards the Pious Caliphate.[14] [This refers to the adoption of a democratic constitution by Turkey in 1908.]

Āzād has devoted a whole chapter in the *Mas'alah* to the enormity of the sin of killing a Muslim, as a crime against this very "collectivism." He inferred from the Qur'ān (4:93) and various *Ḥadīth* that since the murder of a fellow-Muslim is unpardonable in the sight of God, raising arms against any group of Muslims disqualified one from remaining within the fold of Islām, even if it was done due to constraints of duty (as in the case of soldiers) and not followed by repentance. Joining hands with unbelievers in a war against Muslims was a worse stage of the sin.[15] Such arguments were frequently employed to dissuade Indian Muslims from contributing in any way to British war efforts, which were often directed against their co-religionists in other parts of the world.

The Jamā'at in India

Āzād urged Indian Muslims that in the light of the Islāmic command to unite in obedience to a single *imām* or *amīr*, in order to remove the root cause of all their ills, they must adopt the truly Islāmic *i.e.* the collective life. In his Presidential Address of November 1921 he repeated that they could not follow the *Sharī'at* unless they did this—in fact he regarded all future action and reform as dependent on this very issue. He believed that the community (*jamā'at*) had existed in India so long as an "Islāmic" government was in power [it is questionable how far this word applies to the Mughal and other Muslim governments]. Thereafter Indian Muslims became totally disorganized, and in the present, in the absence of an *amīr* or leader, any bond of unity, and an operative religious law; ten crore of them (comprising the world's single largest Muslim population), were leading an un-Islāmic life as a scattered multitude. He tried to illustrate to them that since Islāmic law obliged even Muslims living under non-Muslim rule to either appoint an *amīr* (to organize the community and establish the *Sharī'at*) or else emigrate, it was unlawful to remain without an *imām*, and they too must choose between these two limited options.[16]

At this point Āzād launched into a highly stylized discourse on the need for a "superman" (*mard-i ghayb*) to establish the truth—faithful to the Qur'ān and *Sunnat* and enlightened by divine law, a man of initiative, effortlessly combating all hardships, he would command the world, with the angels as his helpers (*Cf. infra* p. 155). After this highly poetic digression he returned to practical realities, recounting his efforts from 1914 onwards to have an Indian *amīr* appointed. He had met Mawlāna Mahmud-al Ḥasan in this regard, who expressed complete agreement and even his readiness to accept the post, so that a beginning could be made towards organizing the community in India. But these plans were thwarted when he suddenly decided to journey to Hijaz [in 1915]. Āzād however continued his efforts during his preventive detention that followed [in 1916], and after his release in 1920; but circumstances proved unfavourable for the execution of his plans. Ultimately when he despaired of establishing an organization at the national level he decided to go about it province-wise, and accordingly first turned his attention to Bihar where, in the session of the Jamī'at in 1920 three hundred '*ulamā*' appointed their *amīr-i sharī'at*. However the matter does not appear to have progressed further, for he opined that in the absence of an *imām*, only the group of religious scholars or '*ulamā*' (represented by the Khilāfat Committee and the Jamī'at-ul 'Ulamā'-i Hind), was authorized to carry out his duties [of guidance and leadership].[17]

True to his belief in "collectivism", in his Friday sermon as Imām of a Calcutta mosque sometime after 1934, Āzād appealed to Muslims not to give *zakāt* individually—he believed that in the absence of an Islāmic government they should themselves form an organization for its collection and expenditure. To him the prevalent way of giving *zakāt* smacked of that very individualism which had caused their present decay, and threatened to rob them of their Islāmic peculiarities unless replaced by "collectivism."[18]

This emphasis on "collectivism" is not in evidence in Āzād's later thought and politics, and appears to have been replaced by more secular Indian concerns. Apparently he developed these ideas in the context of the *khilāfat* movement, and abandoned them after the Turkish *khilāfat* was abolished.

The Islāmic Caliphate

Āzād's emphasis on "collectivism" is in keeping with his preoccupation with the *khilāfat*, the caliph or *imām* being the centre of collective life. He believed that in keeping with the principle of *tawḥīd* which was the foundation of Islām, its *Sharī'at* had ordained that at all times the government of Muslims on the whole earth be one, with a single *khalīfah* or *imām* as its head—an independent ruler who had the power to protect them and enforce the *Sharī'at* (*Cf. supra* pp. 135-36). He felt that although division had set in in this as in other matters, a special central power (held by the ruler of Syria, Iraq, and Arabia) had always been in evidence. Interestingly enough he also posited a single "language" and "nationality" for Muslims.[19]

Āzād inferred from authentic *Ḥadīth* and the consensus of the Companions that Muslims had the right to democratically choose the caliph—the Prophet (Pbuh) had urged them to select the most deserving candidate rather than being covetous of the post for themselves. [In a simplistic view which is belied by history, Āzād believed that this would eliminate conflict and facilitate making the correct choice.] Muslims were duty-bound to obey him to whom they had first pledged their loyalty, and reject any subsequent claimant. If due to some constraints they were unable to choose the caliph and a Muslim secured the position for himself and established his authority, it was obligatory on them to accept him as the rightful caliph even if he was undeserving; and to support him against any rival claimant—who no matter how superior and eligible, was a rebel who deserved death. Āzād reasoned that this was meant to ensure peace and stability by ruling out counterclaims and revolts, or else even the most deserving caliph would perpetually be threatened by violence. While the caliphate of an undeserving person might entail many evils, permission for revolt would lead to anarchy, suspension of the *Sharī'at*, and disorganization of the *jamā'at,* besides rendering it vulnerable to external attacks.[20]

Āzād quoted *Hadīth* to show that Islām had enjoined complete obedience to the caliph so long as he abided by the Qur'ān and *Sunnat*, whereas disobedience was equivalent to flouting God and His Prophet (Pbuh), and death in such a state was the death of an unbeliever. One must thus forbear and not disobey the *amīr* even if he did something that one did not approve of. He felt that there were strong reasons to believe that *ul'il 'amr* (4:59) referred to the *khalīfah* or *imām* of Muslims, who sustained the organization of the *ummat*, enforced the commands of the *Sharī'at*, and held the power of *ijtihād*. Accordingly, in one *Ḥadīth* the caliphs had been compared to the prophets of the Jews, who were responsible for the guidance and governance of their people.[21]

Āzād believed that whereas the Pious Caliphs were true to Islāmic ideals, the caliphate later degenerated into kingship. He concluded from an analysis of *Ḥadīth* that for this very reason, although Muslims were enjoined obedience and emulation of the Pious Caliphs, the later caliphs were only to be obeyed (irrespective of their actions and beliefs)—unless they were guilty of open disbelief (*kufr*), or commanded something that was a sin, or against Islāmic tenets. In that case the pledge of loyalty and obedience stood dissolved. He believed that in keeping with their duty at all times to do good and prevent evil, Muslims had been directed in *Ḥadīth* to prevent, as far as possible, the evil of an unrighteous caliph—without challenging his authority—*i.e.* without violence and revolt. He believed that in such a situation Muslims should either oppose the caliph or emigrate. From this command, by implication he drew the significant conclusion that the Muslims in a country over which non-Muslim rule had been established, should either rise in revolt against such rule, or emigrate, rather than reconciling themselves to the empowerment of unbelief (*kufr*).[22] This would apparently apply to the situation of Muslims in India too, although he did not elaborate the point (*Cf. supra* pp. 136-37).

The Turkish Caliphate

Āzād believed that since for centuries upto the present times, the Uthmāni Sultāns had been the *khalīfah* and *imām* of the Muslims of the world, all that had so far been said regarding the rights of the caliph would apply to them. Their support and obedience was obligatory on all Muslims, and equivalent to the support and obedience of God and His Prophet (Pbuh)—he who raised arms against them and died in a state of disobedience would be reckoned as an unbeliever. He thus concluded that Muslims were bound to obey the Turkish Sultān as the caliph of Islām under all circumstances, even if he was evil. He reasoned that the caliph owed his Muslim subjects the duties of military defence and offence (for the spread of Islām); and by single-handedly performing this function against European Christians for the last five centuries, the Turks had proved themselves the only rightful heirs to the caliphate. In his speech in October 1914 too he had tried to convince Muslims that the Uthmāni caliphate alone could defend Islām in the present. He had also said that no nation could survive without a political centre, which in the case of the world-organism of Islām was Turkey. He therefore urged every Muslim who desired the survival of Islām to nurture his link with the Islāmic caliphate, regarding the friends and enemies of the Turks as his own.[23]

As for the condition of the caliph's being a Qurayshite, which many (such as Shibli, *supra* p. 44) believed to have been stipulated by *Ḥadīth*, Āzād reasoned that far from laying down any such qualification, the relevant traditions amounted only to predictions—that the *khilāfat* would remain with the Quraysh as long as they proved themselves worthy of it. He believed that there was no categorical statement in the Qur'ān either, to prove that it had confined the caliphate to this tribe—in fact it was unacceptable that a religion which aimed at complete equality and brotherhood should place such narrow conditions for its universal caliphate. Even if the qualification was accepted, he reasoned, it would not be applicable to the Turkish caliphate, since it was operative only while selecting the caliph, who once he is established, must be obeyed irrespective of his qualities[24] (*Cf. supra* p. 138).

Āzād held that the belief in the Uthmāni caliphate was not a recent development among Indian Muslims. Although so long as there was an Islāmic government in India they did not feel the need to maintain direct links with any external Islāmic government; after the fall of the Mughal empire they were compelled to establish a relationship of devotion and obedience with the Uthmāni Sultāns, who had always been acknowledged by Indian scholars as repositories of the central Islāmic caliphate. He believed that although the Muslim rulers of India had always accepted the sovereignty of the Abbasid, and later the Turkish caliphs, regarding themselves as their vicegerent and the *imām* in India; in countries such as India which were ruled by Islāmic governments, the relation with the central caliphate did not take root instantly and prominently due to inter-government rivalry, and because the subjects of such governments owed allegiance to their local rulers, and were not dependent on any external Muslim government. However, he hastened to add, where Muslims did not have their own government they accepted the Uthmāni Sultāns as the caliph of Islām.[25] (There seems some ambiguity and even contradiction in his stand here.)

Jihād

In his speech of October 1914 Āzād had reminded Muslims of their duty of *jihād*—to "strive" in the way of God with their wealth, and if need be with their lives. In the *Mas'alah* too he elaborated at great length on the importance of *jihād* as the basis of the existence and stability of the *millat*, quoting the Qur'ān (9:20-22; 61:4 and 11-12) to illustrate its excellence. As the ultimate test of faith and hypocrisy *jihād* was superior to all other forms of obligatory worship—aiding in it was as meritorious as actual participation, and the *mujāhid* was exalted above all believers. He clarified that *jihād*, which meant "utmost striving in the way of God", could also be undertaken through means other than war. During a war too, those unable to fight could contribute in other ways—what was important was that each one should strive the utmost—in the manner that he is best able to. He used the adverse circumstances in which the Tabūk expedition was undertaken by the Prophet (Pbuh) against the mightiest power of the day, and the fact that even those pious Muslims who did not join it merely due to indolence rather than any evil intentions, were strictly boycotted by the whole community, to illustrate the importance of *jihād*, and impress upon Indian Muslims that in neglecting this prime duty they would be guilty of a grave sin.[26]

Āzād elaborated that *jihād* through war (*qitāl*) was of two kinds: offensive (*hujūm*) and defensive (*difā'*). He reasoned that the former was at all times obligatory, and therefore the Qur'ān had commanded Muslims to fight till universal peace and security were established *i.e.* till the whole world submitted to the call of Islām, as it was sure to. Until such time it would be necessary to constantly combat rival evil forces obstructing the spread of the Islāmic mission. He believed that such constant pre-occupation in offensive combat was a *farḍ-i kifāyah i.e.* a collective obligation on the Muslims of every country and region at a given time. He criticized world Muslims for neglecting this duty and leaving it solely to the Turks for the last five centuries; and warned Indian Muslims that they could not be absolved of their obligation by the Turks' performing this duty. Defensive warfare, he believed on the other hand, was a *farḍ-i'ayn i.e.* obligatory on every individual Muslim. This duty of defence was extremely important because, as emphasized in the Qur'ān and *Ḥadīth*, national (*qawmi*) life depended on it—Muslims could not be subjugated so long as they remained alive to the obligation—he cited the example of the Jews in this connection (2:246).[27]

Āzād tried to establish on the basis of the Qur'ān (2:190; 22:39) and *Ḥadīth* that whenever a non-Muslim power jeopardized the independence of Muslims, the duty of defending them (particularly when they were insufficient to combat the enemy), became by degrees obligatory on all the Muslims of the world. In two cases this gradual widening of the circle was abandoned, and defence became simultaneously obligatory on all Muslims : when the caliph was threatened by enemies he was unable to combat; and when the Arabian peninsula—the centre of Islām—was attacked by non-Muslims. He reasoned that since defence of the *millat* and *jihād* in the way of God was individually obligatory in such circumstances, Muslims should strive their utmost with their lives and property, suspending all other pre-occupations. If any population of Muslims lacked an *imām* or *amīr* to lead them, they should first appoint one; whereas neglect of this duty would make them all guilty of a sin which was next only to unbelief (*kufr*).[28]

The Caliphate and the British Government

Āzād recalled that at the onset of the First World War, besides trying to convince its Muslim subjects that Turkey was the aggressor, Britain had taken great pains to assure them that their religious sentiments would not be hurt, and nor would the sanctity of their holy places be violated, for the war was not against Islām or the *khalīfah*. He believed that they were deliberately misled about the actual conditions and British intentions, in order to check the slightest tendency towards unrest among Indian Muslims, which would have completely upset the history and outcome of the war; and therefore they had committed the greatest error by believing British promises. As a result they had ungrudgingly spent their lives and resources—only to ensure Britain's victory, and to wipe out the besieged caliphate, whereas the *Sharī'at* demanded that they rise to its aid.

He brought to their notice the manner in which Britain had flouted its assurances—it had defiled the sanctuaries of Hijaz by causing bloodshed there, and occupied the *Bayt-al Muqaddas* (which he regarded as a part of Muslim sacred territory) and Baghdad (he regarded parts of Iraq upto the River Tigris also as a part of the Arabian peninsula, and therefore sacred). He reasoned that in the light of the command of the *Sharī'at* to keep the sacred territory free of non-Muslim influence (*supra* p. 134), it was the simultaneous (not gradual) duty of all the Muslims of the world to strive their utmost to prevent the passing of these areas from caliphal to Christian control and occupancy.[29]

Āzād recalled that the treaty [of Sevres signed in August 1920] deprived Turkey not only of its Christian, but also Muslim provinces (which were divided by the Allies among themselves), and independent economic and military rights over the greater part of its territory. Not only had Britain dishonoured the Islāmic caliphate by occupying its seat Constantinople, but the Sultān had been robbed of all religious rights over the Muslims of the rest of the world, thus rendering his *khilāfat* impotent. We have seen Āzād reasoning that it was forbidden for a Muslim to raise arms against fellow-Muslims (*supra* p. 136). He repeated the point in the context of the Turko-British conflict, reminding Muslims that being a part of a non-Muslim army fighting Muslims, or even helping or supporting it, would exclude them from the *jamā'at*. Not only this, it was forbidden for them to even remain loyal citizens of the British government which had proved itself to be an aggressive enemy (*farīq-i muḥārib*) of Islām, to which they owed their first and greater loyalty. In an article of 1921 and his Presidential Address to the Khilāfat Conference in August that year, he repeated that so long as it remained pitted against the Islāmic caliphate; persisted in its policy of attempting to occupy or destroy Muslim countries; and did not fulfil the joint demands of *khilāfat* and *swarāj*; they were obliged to give up all support and co-operation with it, and try their utmost to fulfil their Islāmic duty of defence (*difā'*)[30] (see *supra* pp. 141-42).

Āzād elaborated that in keeping with its principle of universal love (60:8-9) Islām recommended good behaviour towards unagressive non-Muslims, but complete non-co-operation with those enemies and aggressors who were in a state of war with it (3:118). In such a situation Muslims were advised only to befriend each other (3:28). Reminding them that the Qur'ān did not permit any relations with those fighting Islām even if they were the closest of family members (9:23; 60:1), and those who did not obey this command ceased to be Muslims (58:22); he was severely critical of those who refused to give up the titles conferred upon them by the government, and continued to support and co-operate with it. He described them as hypocrites who had sold their faith to bow in servility before their evil masters. He inferred from the Prophet's (Pbuh) instructions to boycott those who did not join the Tabūk expedition, that non-co-operation should be practised against those present-day Muslims who were violating the interest of the *ummat* by not joining in the fight against its enemies.[31]

Sir Sayyad and the Muslim University

Āzād began his career as an admirer of Sir Sayyad, and appreciated his services. In an early article—of April 1904 to be precise—he had described the latter as a benefactor of the country and nation (*qawm*), whose name would live on so long as the Muslims of India survived as a "nation."[32] In 1905 he came into contact with Shibli who had "already emerged in revolt against the loyalism and radical modernism of the Aligarh movement."[33] As we have already observed, in 1914 he severely (albeit indirectly) attacked Sir Sayyad's stand on the caliphate (*supra* p. 134). In his Presidential Address to the session of the Jamī'at-ul 'Ulamā'-i Hind in November 1921 he was once more critical of Sir Sayyad and his followers—for being awed and bewitched by European civilization—he felt that instead of combating it with resistance and opposition, their own weakness led them to fall into obedience and conformity.[34]

Āzād often appeared critical of the Aligarh University and those connected with it. Recalling the unprecedented zeal which it had generated, he however lamented in an article of Aug.-Sep. 1912 that such national (*qawmi*) ardour and sentiment had been spent on an unworthy cause, and an excellent opportunity for national mobilization lost. Attacking the university's tradition of loyalism, he blamed its patrons for employing zeal that could be channelled towards freedom and patriotism, only to further strengthen the bonds of slavery. In a dateless article he accused its authorities of hypocrisy—while they pretended to be great votaries of Islām in order to appease Muslims and elicit subscriptions from them, they were actually least concerned about it. Instead of setting an example of religiosity for the students, these "self-proclaimed reformers" who neglected even the daily canonical prayers, tried to pass off atheism as devotion to Islām. While he agreed in principle with Sir Sayyad's desire to develop the college into a "national" educational centre for Muslims, and even conceded that it had acquired this status; he did not agree with its founder on the point that the "national" life of Muslims depended on it. He felt further that Sir Sayyad had been mistaken in insisting that all other scattered educational efforts be abandoned in favour of complete devotion to this single cause;[35] and believed instead that a greater number of good colleges were desirable for solving the ever-increasing needs of Muslims.[36]

Muslim Politics

The Former Scene

In the article of Aug.-Sep. 1912 (which is strongly reminiscent of Shibli's "Musalmānoṇ ki Political Karwat" written only a few months earlier), Āzād analysed the manner in which the British government had sought the support of one section of the population in the aftermath of 1857, and Muslims had willingly offered to sacrifice their own national (*mulki*) interests for those of the government, thus becoming a severe obstacle in the way of all true progress in India. By estranging them from the Hindus (who were fighting for their "national" demands), the government had ensured its victory in the struggle; whereas Muslims had become its puppets by leaning on its support. In what appears to be another veiled attack on Sir Sayyad, he saw their preoccupation with higher education as a ploy on the part of the government to turn their attention from the real issues at hand. Their energies, which would otherwise have been channelled towards "national" movements, were thus wasted for a worthless cause at a time when their fellow-countrymen—the Hindus—were struggling for "national" freedom and rights. He appealed to them to acknowledge their mistake in concentrating only on higher education and closing their eyes to the country and its manifold problems, regarding it as a sin against God and rebellion against the government to get involved in these. [The veiled reference to Sir Sayyad is obvious]. In spite of living in India, they had left these issues solely to their Hindu neighbours, who were alone striving for "national" welfare.[37]

In a language and style closely resembling Shibli's, Āzād recalled that later the government had distracted Muslims with a new toy—

the Muslim League—which deceptively appeared as politics, although it was neither born of a political awakening, and nor did it have any national (*mulki*) or *milli* strength. They were made to believe that the factors for their abstinence from politics thirty years ago (lack of education, fewer numbers, pressure of the majority in the race for advantages etc.) still held good, and therefore politics for them signified first securing their rights against those who had usurped them *i.e.* the Hindus. Consequently, whereas the demand for rights should have been targetted at the government, it was turned towards Hindu neighbours, and thus the political awakening of Muslims posed no danger to the government (*Cf.* Shibli, *supra* p. 51*ff.*). However he did not blame the government for this situation, for it had never prevented anyone from demanding their rights. Rather he felt that the fault lay with the leaders of the community, who did not give it an opportunity to tackle the real issues by engaging it first in higher education, then in the spell of the League, and finally in the movement of the Muslim university, at a time when the country was undergoing great upheavals.[38]

In what appears to be an indirect reference to the reverence in which Sir Sayyad's political views were held and their close adherence by the community, in an article of December 1912 Āzād criticized Muslim leaders not only for advocating complete trust and loyalty for the British government, but also for never giving the Muslim nation (*qawm*) a chance to exercise its judgement. They believed that since it lacked education it should content itself with conformism, and must obey without protest. He lamented that in politics, as in religion, Muslims were so overawed by their leaders that they did not dare to think for themselves. The "nation" thus had no political opinion of its own, but blindly followed a few men of authority who formulated all its policies. He was however glad to note a change—the awe of Muslim leaders, and the myth regarding the soundness of their policy had been shattered. In the ensuing political change the "nation" had felt its power, and tried to reflect on its own rather than merely following its leaders, which for him signalled signs of national (*qawmi*) life and spirit in the *millat*.[39]

Āzād also observed with satisfaction that as a result the "nation" was freely criticizing the political *sharī'at* of those leaders who had so far been regarded as unassailable. [Shibli we recall had referred to Sir Sayyad's political *Shāhnāmah*—*supra* p. 50]. Anyone advocating the demand of rights through political struggle was no longer branded a *"Congressi"*, which formerly denoted utter moral, cultural, and religious decline. In this and another article which appeared in Feb.-Mar. 1913, like Shibli (*supra* pp. 51-52) he attributed this change to the agitation and zeal aroused by the annulment of the partition of Bengal [in the previous year]. However he would also give some of the credit to a section of the Urdu Press—lauding its role, he felt it was instrumental in bringing about the new movement among Muslims by adopting an independent and bold posture. In this connection he made special mention of Shibli's *Muslim Gazette*, his article "Political Karwat" (which he felt had aided the change the most by striking a blow at the "accepted national policy" of Muslims), and Viqār-al Mulk's article ["Hindustān Meṇ Musalmānoṇ ki Ā'indah Ḥālat"] in the *Aligarh Gazette*.[40]

The points of similarity between these two articles of Āzād and Shibli's "Political Karwat" are many and striking: ridicule for the Muslim League; criticism of the loyalism and political apathy of Muslims, and their attitude of confrontation towards the Hindus rather than the government; an attack on Sir Sayyad's political philosophy, and on Muslims for their continued blind adherence to what had become outdated reasoning; attributing to the annulment of the partition of Bengal, a revolution in Muslim politics; and admiration for the political awareness of the Hindus.

Al-Hilāl and Muslim Awakening

Later Āzād would credit his own newspaper *al-Hilāl*—begun in 1912 as an organ of the freedom movement—with the creation of a new religious and political awakening among Indian Muslims. In a statement of January 1922 he recalled that as a part of its divisive policy the British government had deluded Muslims into believing that due to the greater number of Hindus, their government would be set up in a free India. This had not only estranged the Muslims from the political activity of the Hindus, but had made them serve as a tool against it. He credited *al-Hilāl* with persuading Muslims to rely on faith rather than numbers, and to unite fearlessly with the Hindus, which led to the united movement of *khilāfat* and *swarāj*. In his Presidential Address to the special session of the Congress in December 1923, he recalled that not very long back Muslims had believed in communal organizations, and preferred not to associate with the Congress due to their insecurity (bred by their backwardness in education and wealth), and fear (that due to their lesser numbers they would lose their identity and be destroyed). He claimed that he was the first to remind them in 1912 that they should make India's freedom their aim, and that their policy of separation was contrary to its interests. He urged them to trust the Hindus and participate in the Congress; and claimed that they eventually accepted the truth of his words, and began to enter it in droves by 1916.[41]

In his Presidential Address at the session of the Congress in March 1940 [incidentally he remained President until 1946], Āzād recollected that through *al-Hilāl* he had persuaded Indian Muslims that by viewing a future free India with suspicion and distrust they would be forced to tolerate the continuance of a third power; whereas looking at it with courage and confidence would enable them to march towards freedom. While reaffirming his faith in this course of action he felt his efforts were not in vain, for the period between 1912 and 1918 marked a new phase in the political awakening of Muslims—towards the end of 1920 their political ideology had broken through its former mould to take new shape.[42]

These lofty claims are however not borne out by an article of December 1912 in *al-Hilāl*, in which Āzād had outlined his and the paper's political philosophy. While advocating complete adherence to solely Islāmic principles and ruling out both loyalism and emulation of the Hindus; he however appears to favour an issue based support to whoever appeared to Muslims to be in the right on any particular issue.

Āzād had then emphasized that the aim of *al-Hilāl* was only to invite Muslims to act solely on the Qur'ān and *Sunnat* in all educational, cultural, political, and other issues; for the Muslim who accepted any other guide was guilty of polytheism (7:43). He reasoned that those who bowed only before God could not emulate the policy of the Hindus or any other group (4:48 and 116)—rather they should invite and enroll others in their ranks as they had been doing for centuries. *Al-Hilāl* thus neither encouraged Muslims to place unwarranted confidence in the government, nor to follow the Hindus, but only to adhere to Islāmic principles. However in keeping with their religious obligation of promoting good and preventing evil [3:110], they should aid those who were in the right—be it the government or any other nation (*qawm*).[43]

Āzād believed, like Sir Sayyad before him, that the British government had conferred security on Muslims, and the freedom to fulfil their religious obligations. However, whereas Sir Sayyad had made this the plank of his argument in favour of loyalty and obedience to the government (*supra* p. 28), Āzād used it to plead in favour of adopting non-violent means against it. He reasoned that Muslims should not spread mischief on the earth after it had been set in order, since this was a sin in the sight of God (7:56,85). However Islām had taught them freedom and they would strive for it—but strictly according to their religious principles *i.e.* within the bounds of law and peace. He was thus able to assert that this path was not the innovation of a human mind, nor demanded obedience to a human group, but was the way shown by God. He would reiterate in the *Mas'alah* that his views, which had remained unchanged for the last decade, were derived from the permanent guidance of revelation.[44]

Religion and Politics

In the article of December 1912 Āzād asserted that since the two were inseparable, political issues could not be treated apart from religious teachings. The Qur'ān for him was the sole guide for Muslims, and every branch of knowledge (including politics) which did not originate in it amounted to blatant unbelief (*kufr*). He felt that Muslims had gone politically astray due to their refusal to be guided by it, and in fact all their afflictions could be attributed to their folly in abandoning this divine source of knowledge in their political, educational, and cultural endeavours, mistakenly believing it to be relevant only to matters of worship and religion. He believed that as the final word of God Islām was uncompromising, and did not approve of its followers taking recourse to anything else (*Cf.* Iqbāl, *supra* p. 71)—if Indian Muslims had realized its true greatness as a perfect law for all aspects of life, they would not be obliged to follow the government or the Hindus in their political policy. As for himself, he claimed to view every branch of human action purely in the light of religion, and to have imbibed his political thought too from it.[45]

In his Presidential Address to the Jamī'at-al 'Ulamā'-i Hind in November 1921, Āzād repeated that the *Sharī'at* was responsible for the guidance of all aspects of man's life, without any distinction of religious and mundane. He reasoned that the Pious Caliphate was the period of the greatest prosperity and progress of Muslims since they were then guided solely by it—their decline set in when they abandoned it for the sciences of former nations. He therefore believed that the only way they could regain their past glory was by reviving knowledge of, and action on, the *Sharī'at*. He felt that as its guardians, Muslim scholars were responsible for its abandonment by the masses, and only they could initiate its revival. [He however gave no indication of the concrete steps to be taken in this regard.] He warned Muslims not to be dazzled by the ways of the world, specially Europe—for them reform demanded merely renewal and revival, not the founding of something anew—as the final and perfect religion, the teachings of Islām would fulfil all their individual and collective needs, and were valid for all times to come. In a sermon as Imām of a Calcutta mosque sometime after 1934, he repeated that unlike other religions Islāmic laws were complete, and therefore beyond reform and amendment—Muslims needed only to hold on faster to their *Sharī'at* for their welfare and prosperity.[46]

Khilāfat and Swarāj

While Wilfred Cantwell Smith[47] writes that after being released from internment in 1920 Āzād devoted himself "to the *khilāfat* and nationalist cause", Aziz Aḥmad[48] sees this as the beginning of his "participation in the Indian nationalist movement as distinct from pan-Islāmic anti-imperialism", after "he met Tilak and Gandhi for the first time." In 1921 Āzād saw the *khilāfat* movement as one with the struggle for *swarāj*, involving the lives of forty crore world Muslims and thirty-two crore Indians. For Muslims the two-pronged activity entailed the dual obligation of struggling for their aims within India; while simultaneously aiding their co-religionists without—the Congress and the Khilāfat Committees had, as it were, divided these functions among themselves. He shrewdly remarked that the former, being a secular political organization, could not enthuse, nor influence Muslims in the manner that the Khilāfat Committees could. Describing these as religious rather than political organizations, he felt that they therefore enjoyed the exclusive "right to appeal to Muslims in the name of Islām and the *Sharī'at*." He further felt that Muslims could succeed in their twin duties of *khilāfat* and freedom only if they faithfully followed the *Sharī'at* and fulfilled their religious obligations; and that the members of the Khilāfat Committees should take the lead in not only preaching such religious devotion, but also setting the best practical examples of it.[49]

Āzād believed that as followers of Islām which was the greatest teacher of human freedom, the Khilāfat Committees should not only call Muslims to the Indian struggle, but also see to it that they did not lag behind the others; or else the efforts of the Hindus would also be wasted, for India's common goal could not be achieved unless each group fulfilled its own duties. Since he believed that the real solution of the *khilāfat* issue depended on India's freedom, he saw the former as leading to the latter—by showing the way of non-co-operation, which was first mooted by the Khilāfat Committee [in May 1920], and later adopted by the Congress [in September that year]. He also credited the Committee with achieving, for the first time, unity of action among the two major Indian nations (*qawm*). He felt that it was due to its efforts that the movement for *swarāj* had become so strong, and ambitiously hoped that it would prove to be the means to the freedom of the whole Muslim world.[50]

In his Presidential Address to the Khilāfat Conference in August that year, Āzād reiterated that working for India's freedom was as obligatory for Muslims as the preservation of the *khilāfat*. In fact he now felt that the first field of action for the *khilāfat* movement lay within India, and not in countries where Muslim blood had been shed; for Muslims could not succeed in the world unless they did not first conquer their own country.[51]

We recall that he had expressed exactly the opposite view a few years back, opposing in a speech of 1914, all local and "national" efforts by Muslims, and instead espousing the cause of the world community of Islām (*supra* pp. 133-34). This is also in marked contrast to the views he had expressed only a year back regarding the inviolability of world-wide Muslim nationhood, and the duties of sympathy with and defence of the world community of Islām (*supra* pp. 131*ff.*, 136 and 141-42). We may thus not be mistaken in seeing him gradually moving from a world-wide Muslim nationhood to composite Indian nationalism, marked here by a subtle shift in emphasis from *khilāfat* to *swarāj*, this perhaps being the general mood of the times. As Wilfred Cantwell Smith[52] writes, in 1920 a deputation led by Muḥammad 'Ali visited London, and placed before the government its demands relating to Turkey and its caliphate. While they were away the "Khilāfat Committee came more and more under the influence of Gandhi and the nationalists." The deputation returned in October without achieving anything and this turned the Indian khilāfatists more to national questions"—

even Muḥammad 'Ali upon his return urged Muslims to join with "the Hindus in freeing India, for without that no *khilāfat* freedom was possible."

Believing that it was essential to show Muslims a religious course of action for achieving freedom, Āzād consciously tried to demonstrate the religious sanctions for his views; and that non-co-operation was a religious duty of Muslims since its adoption by the Khilāfat Committee was in keeping with the commands of the *Sharī'at*. (It is interesting that even while he appealed to Muslims on the authority of specific Qur'ānic teachings, he urged the Hindus not to be dismayed at the peculiar terminology, since the ultimate reality was one, although it may be approached differently.) Later both Hindus and Muslims decided to adopt non-co-operation jointly as a nation (*qawm*) [at a conference of their leaders at Allahabad in June 1920]. This is perhaps the first mention we find in Mawlāna Āzād's thoughts of both communities jointly constituting a single nation. He believed in fact that the first challenge for the *khilāfat* movement was to unite the Muslims and other Indian "nations" (*qawm*); and it had achieved this in a few months—from being confined to a particular group, it had become a national movement. He also credited it with having successfully revived the dormant issue of India's freedom more effectively than ever before.[53]

Displaying an idealism in marked contrast to Mawlāna Ḥusayn Aḥmad's political expediency, Āzād clarified that since Muslims relied not on numbers but on their faith in God, they were not obliged to call on others for help for the success of their movement. The sympathy and support of the Hindus was thus essential for them—not because their success depended on it, but because India's problem could not be solved without a common agitation (*Cf.* Madani, *infra* p. 183 *ff*). He fondly recalled the spectacle of comradeship afforded by the sincere and sympathetic welcome with which the Hindus had greeted the initiation of the *khilāfat* movement in India. At this stage there were only a few who associated it with the question of India's freedom, the Mahātma being foremost among them—later of course it became a national issue.[54]

In a message issued towards the end of 1921, we find Āzād using a mixed language of patriotism and religious fervour, and repeatedly bearing testimony to the khilāfatist's love for Islām and his country; which appears to be symbolic of the merging of *khilāfat* and *swarāj*. From a conversation he had in prison with Dr. Sayyad

Maḥmūd (Honorary Secretary of the Central Khilāfat Committee, Bombay) in early 1922, it is evident that not only had the twin issues of *khilāfat* and *swarāj* merged for him, but the latter appears to have gained precedence over the former. As reported by Dr. Maḥmūd, he expressed confidence that if Muslims continued to work for the *khilāfat* in co-operation with Gandhi, they would very soon succeed in their aims. He ruled out any exclusive agreement of Muslims with the government in this regard—although it was a religious affair, since the demand had been made jointly with the Hindus, only the Congress led by Gandhi was authorized to settle the issue, for no component of united India could now take any action independently. Repeating that the struggle for *swarāj* was as important a religious and national (*qawmi*) duty for Muslims as *khilāfat*, he clarified that if the latter demand was granted, the struggle for the other would continue. But if India attained *swarāj*, it was ready to immediately forsake the demands of the *khilāfat*, for its real solution lay only in the former.[55]

Although thus summarily abandoning the cause of *khilāfat* appears to be in stark contravention of Āzād's earlier stand, the logic behind it is apparently this: since the *khilāfat* demands were being made by Muslims as subjects of Britain, once it relinquished its right to govern them (by granting *swarāj*), such demands would become meaningless. However the shift in emphasis from religious to secular nationalism appears quite marked.

In a statement of January 1922 Āzād reiterated that since fighting for one's freedom was a part of Islāmic teachings, Muslims should co-operate with their compatriots for the liberation of their country—the only solution lay in establishing a "national government of Indians, in India, for Indians." Whereas earlier he had advocated non-violence as an Islāmic principle (*supra* pp. 148-49), he now acknowledged that Islām had prescribed civil struggle only against tyrannical national (*qawmi*) rulers, and recommended armed conflict to combat alien occupancy. He justified Indian Muslims taking up the first rather than second course of action against foreign rule on the grounds of their weakness and helplessness, and "the peculiar situation in India." He however also made it clear that he approved of the circumstances in which Islām had permitted the taking up of arms, and therefore differed with Gandhi's creed of total non-violence, although he believed in the validity of all Gandhi's other arguments regarding the freedom struggle.[56]

In his Presidential Address to the Congress in December 1923 Āzād repeated that the *khilāfat* movement under Gandhi's stewardship had helped to surmount the long-standing obstacles in the way of Hindu-Muslim unity, without which India's freedom was but a distant dream. He appreciated Gandhi's efforts for the *khilāfat* as one of his "greatest services to India"—Āzād's own endeavours in this direction were motivated by the conviction that striving for the *khilāfat* demands was his "national" duty, both as a "Muslim" and an "Indian." After the abolition of the caliphate in 1924, his shift from *khilāfat* to *swarāj* and from pan-Islāmism to patriotism appears final. In his Presidential Address to the All India Khilāfat Conference in December 1925, he told its workers that their five-year-long struggle for Islāmic and eastern issues outside India had produced whatever results it could—now they should devote themselves to the service of their country, for their present enslavement was a deterrent not only to their own deliverance, but also that of all of Asia and the east.[57]

Islāmic Government

In an article of March 1912, Āzād wrote that an organization or group could never be accepted as Islāmic unless it incorporated the principle of *shūrá* or counsel, which allowed for the participation of the people—in the *Mas'alah* he would compare it to the working of the modern imperfect republic. In another article of Aug.-Sep. 1912 he emphasized that according to Islām no one besides God and the Prophet (Pbuh) held sovereign authority over Muslims, each of whom was himself a leader *i.e.* accountable to God and his fellow creatures. In another article in December that year, while emphasizing the importance of mutual consultation in all matters (3:159; 42:38), he reiterated that the Qur'ān opposed individual power and hegemony of any kind—since authority was vested in the *millat* or *jamā'at*, government should be in its, rather than in individual hands. He inferred on this basis that Muslims should strive for legitimate freedom and parliamentary government since these were in keeping with their religious principles.[58]

In Feb.-Mar. 1913 Āzād wrote that since only God enjoyed absolute power, its being wielded by individual leaders or the government amounted to *shirk i.e.* associating others with a divine attribute. Authority should therefore rightly be vested only in the consensus (*ijmā'*) and counsel (*shūrá*) of the *jamā'at*, which should in turn remain true to Islām. In a statement of January 1922 he repeated that as a perfect order of freedom and democracy Islām did not recognize as lawful personal power, nor a paid bureaucracy. Bestowing equal rights on all men and abolishing all national hegemony and racial discrimination, it had made "actions" the touchstone of superiority. In an 'Īd sermon as Imām of a Calcutta mosque he said that although there was no high or low class in its society, Islām did acknowledge economic disparity. Whereas it favoured free circulation of wealth, unlike socialism it did not aim at a complete and unnatural economic uniformity.[59]

Muslims in India

It is interesting that in November 1903, in one of the first articles in *Lisān-al Ṣidq*—the first monthly to be edited by him—Āzād had outlined one of the aims of the magazine as "social reform", which entailed freeing Muslims from their prevalent customs, born of their intermingling with the Hindus. He felt that Akbar's excessive liberalism had caused Muslims to incline greatly, *albeit* imperceptibly, towards Hindu usages, which had begun to surface among them by the nineteenth century. These new-fangled ways had so divorced them from their ancient fountain-head that they were no more recognizable as the early conquerors of India; for instead of their original "Arabian and Iranian traits" they now exhibited "a peculiar Indian colour."[60] However, this early antagonism to Hindu ways, and harping back to the "original Muslim character" is a trait that we find fast replaced in Āzād's later thought by an earnest effort at rapprochement. Faced with the paradox of the Muslim situation in India, Āzād burst into a spurt of poetic idealism in the *Mas'alah,* calling for the birth of a man of vision, capable of *ijtihād,* and steeped in the Qur'ān and *Sunnat*; so that he could accomplish the Herculean task of applying their principles to the present changing conditions of Muslims in India, who had only recently made it their home (*Cf. supra* p. 137). In his Presidential Address to the Congress in March 1940 he denied that Indian Muslims were a political minority, and claimed that he had expressed this conviction even twenty-eight years ago in *al-Hilāl.* For him a minority was not merely a relatively smaller group—rather it should be so small as to be incapable of protecting its interests. He reminded them that they were a vast concourse of eighty to ninety million, not confined to any particular area but unevenly scattered all over the country. Although they comprised only a quarter of the total population and were in a minority in seven provinces, in five they were in a majority. Due to bonds of Islāmic brotherhood and equality they were not weakened by social and racial divisions unlike other communities. He therefore felt that there was no reason for such a vast group to be oppressed by the feeling of being a minority, or apprehensive about their rights and interests in a democratic India; which fundamental mistake had, he felt, created countless misunderstandings.[61]

Language

In the article of November 1903 Āzād had described one of the aims of *Lisān-al Ṣidq* as being the development of Urdu, which he called "our national [*qawmi*] language", bracketing it together with Turkish, Arabic, and Persian as "Islāmic languages." In an article of February next year, he expressed anguish at the refusal of "a few short-sighted Muslims" of Bengal to regard Urdu as their language, or work for its progress; and their determination to employ and develop their mother tongue Bengali instead. He felt that whereas they hoped to strengthen their nationhood (*qawmiyyat*) by guarding their language; they were actually ruining their intellectual life, for Bengali could not serve as an intellectual language for Muslims. He found it strange that Bengali was now being preferred to Urdu, which had been the most commonly used language among Bengali Muslims ever since Persian fell into disuse. He asserted confidently that none could hinder the progress of Urdu which alone deserved to be the intellectual language of all of India, for the times were conducive to its becoming so; despite the fact that earlier Hindus had opposed it, offering Nāgri as a substitute, and now Muslims themselves were ranged against it.[62]

Āzād was of course proved wrong on all counts—Urdu suffered a setback in free India (although it did become the national language of Pakistan). The regional and linguistic nationalism which lay behind the Bengali movement ultimately succeeded in carving out a nation for itself; underlining once more the complex levels of diversity in the Indian subcontinent, and the difficulties in the way of reconciling them. His anguish is reminiscent of Jinnāh's discomfort at the upsurge of caste-based nationalism among the Jāts prior to partition (*supra* p. 114).

In an article of June 1913 Āzād wrote that it was now generally accepted that nations (*qawm*) were for the most part formed and destroyed with the development and decline of their language. He further questioned whether there was, or could be made any arrangement in India for strengthening the foundation of nationhood by means of the "national" language, literature, and history. [It is not clear whether he is here referring to Muslim or to Indian nationhood.] Speaking before the Hindustani Committee in Bihar in 1937 he remarked that since the issue of language was extremely important for a group which called itself a "nation", it was only natural that it should arise in India too. He even suggested that a "nation" must have a uniform language; but appears to contradict himself by stating later that it was not necessary for India to have a single "national" language since it was made up of various geographical regions, each with its own regional language or mother tongue, with which were associated the "national", historical, and social traditions of the region. He believed that one could not rob a people of their language by artificial means; and it would take very long to mould, according to considerations of expediency, their natural sentiments regarding the mother tongue.[63] This appears in stark contrast to his very different stand on Bengali earlier.

Āzād believed that education should be in "one's own language", apparently meaning the mother tongue. He was therefore strictly opposed to the use of English as the medium of instruction, believing it to be an impediment in the birth of a "national mind." Further, by rendering their intellectual life alien to themselves, it would obstruct original thought and true progress among Indians. He also claimed that Urdu, which was born and progressed in India, deserved to be called a "national language" since it had historically proved to be the most widespread Indian language for the past thousand years, having been in use all over the country from the end of the seventeenth century onwards. In the beginning it was called Hindvi, and later by the end of the seventeenth century, both Hindi and Urdu, there being no difference between them—Persianized Urdu was then called Rekhta. The question of script arose only after the revolt of 1857, and now Hindi signified Urdu written in Devanāgri rather than Persian script.[64] Unfortunately, since this speech is incomplete, many questions are left unanswered, but Āzād seems to be suggesting that regional languages must be developed alongside Urdu, which must be granted the status of a national language.

In a statement a decade later in February 1947 Āzād repeated that the mother tongue should be the medium of instruction, while adding that every Indian should learn both Urdu and Devanāgri scripts.[65]

Common Indian Nationhood

In his Presidential Address to the Khilāfat Conference in August 1921 Āzād recalled that in the very first number of *al-Hilāl* he had tried to convince Muslims that according to the *Sharī'at* their real enemy was the British government which was wiping out the whole of the east. He then proceeded to remind them of the example of the Prophet (Pbuh), who while making peace with the people of Madīnah had signed a treaty stating that Muslims would henceforth join with them to form "a single nation" (*ummah wāḥidah*). He inferred from this that it was the religious duty of Indian Muslims to not only nurture ties of true friendship with the Hindus, but also to join with them to form a single "nation"; the motive in both cases being to combat the threat to Islām posed by its enemies.[66]

In his Congress Presidential Address of December 1923 Āzād remarked that the dormant spirit of Indian nationalism (*qawmiyyat*) had been aroused in the field of action and struggle, thus heralding a revolution in that it had marched from the initial period of debate and theorizing into the "life of action." In an article that he wrote in June 1924 soon after the death of C.R. Das, he noted with satisfaction the manner in which all of India, despite its disparities of religion and race, united completely in mourning the loss. He felt this was significant as a measure of the strength of the spirit of "nationalism", and the degree to which it had developed. Paying tribute to Das's patriotism and "nationalism" as being completely free of any taint of divisive sentiments, he felt that in this quality lay the greatest trial of any Indian leader, and without it true patriotism and "nationalism" could never develop in a country like India. He was not surprised at the description of Das as an "idealist" by an Anglo-Indian newspaper, since for those who had passed the remark, the aim of Indian "nationalism" and freedom was nothing more than an impractical ideal.[67]

In his Congress Presidential Address of 1940 Āzād dwelt on the fact that India was home to many races, cultures, and religions which had settled here, the last of these being the Muslims. He believed that their arrival led, according to nature's law, to a merging of two different culture-currents—a new India began to be fashioned by the Hindus and Muslims sharing their precious heritage. In a thousand years of common history they enriched India with their common achievement, every aspect of their life and culture bearing the stamp of their joint endeavour—their languages were different but they grew to use a common language, and their dissimilar manners and customs acted and reacted on each other to produce a new synthesis.[68]

Āzād's manner here is very similar to Sir Sayyad's description of the 'Indianization' of the Muslim settlers, as of the Aryans before them (*supra* pp. 12-13); and in contrast to his earlier stand when he had expressed the need for social reform to correct the customs adopted by Muslims from the Hindus, and lamented the loss of their original Arabic and Persian identity (*supra* p. 155).

On the contrary Āzād now believed that it was neither possible nor desirable to abandon this joint wealth which was the heritage of their common nationality, and revert back to the times when this joint life had not begun. In no uncertain terms he described the desire of the Hindus to recall the life of a thousand years back, or of Muslims to revive the civilization and culture which they had brought from Iran and Central Asia, as unnatural and vain fantasies which should be abandoned at the earliest. He believed significantly that whereas revival may be desirable in religion, in social matters it was "a denial of progress."[69]

We may of course ask how far religion and society could be thus separated in a unified religion such as Islām—we recall that Āzād had himself repeatedly stated that Islām must rule every aspect of a Muslim's life (*supra* pp. 149-50).

Āzād believed that a thousand years of their joint life had gradually and naturally moulded Hindus and Muslims into a common nationality, and the process was now complete and irreversible. Indians should therefore accept this reality and engross themselves in shaping their future destiny, for "no fantasy or artificial scheming" could now break this unity—whether they liked it or not they had become a nation, "united and indivisible."[70]

Religion and Nationality

By 1940 Āzād was convinced that there was no conflict between the two—a Hindu, Muslim, or Christian, even as he followed his particular faith, could say with equal pride that he was an Indian. In a manner reminiscent of Iqbāl (*supra* pp. 83-84) he declared that he was proud to be a Muslim, and unwilling to forego even the smallest part of his wealth—*i.e.* the legacy of Islāmic teachings, traditions, history, arts, and civilization, which in fact it was his duty to protect. The religion and culture of Islām held a special interest for him, and he could brook no interference in these; at the same time its spirit did not come in the way of, rather it guided those other sentiments which were "forced upon" him by the "realities and conditions" of his life. He was proud of being "a part of the indivisible unity that is Indian nationality", and could never surrender his claim to it, since he was an essential and indispensable element which had gone into the building of India, and without which it would be incomplete. When questioned five years later (in October 1945) regarding Gandhi's statement that change of religion did not affect one's nationality, he guardedly replied that it was a very complex issue—while no one had as yet exactly defined nationality, he "personally" thought that "generally speaking" "nationality never changes with the change of religion."[71] This signifies a complete transformation of his earlier views regarding Muslim nationhood—that it was based exclusively on religion, and incompatible with secular nationalism (*supra* p. 131)

Education and National Life

In a statement of February 1947 Āzād explained that he had opted for the education portfolio (in the interim government at the centre) because of his special interest in its problems. He felt that since the present system of education in India "had been shaped by non-nationals, in non-national interests", it "had not led to the development of a national mind"—he regarded its reconstruction as the foundation of a new national life. He was wholly opposed to the idea of communal universities which he felt had been harmful to the country, and hoped that the future would see an end to them. He clarified that although the government was opposed to the establishment of such universities, it would have to continue subsidizing them until strong public opinion prevailed against them, and they were replaced by national universities. Disclosing that the two committees appointed by the government had submitted contrary reports on the question of religious instruction in schools, he felt that if the government decided in favour of offering such instruction, it should be of the best type, for the religious instruction often imparted in India, instead of broadening the outlook and inculcating a spirit of tolerance and goodwill, tended often to produce the opposite result.[72]

Attitude Towards the Hindus

In an undated letter to a Hindu friend, Āzād expressed amazement at the ignorance of the Hindus regarding Islām and Muslims despite a thousand years of close contact. Even while he felt that if this mutual unfamiliarity could somehow be remedied, a large part of their mutual hostility and unsociability would vanish, he lamented that nothing was being done about it. In his Presidential Address to the Khilāfat Conference in August 1921 he said that the Qur'ān had divided all non-Muslims into two categories—hostile, and unaggressive (60:8-9). While Islām forbade friendship and co-operation with the former, by no means did it desist its followers from reconciliation and good treatment with the latter group. In the *Mas'alah* he explained that since so far the Hindus had never displayed hostility towards Islām or Muslims, they belonged to the friendly category of non-believers, and the *Sharī'at* in no way prevented Muslims from kindness and good behaviour towards them.[73] (*Cf.* his earlier advocacy of non-co-operation against the British—*supra* pp. 143-44).

In his Presidential Address of August 1921 Āzād took great pains to explain that Hindu-Muslim concord was not only a political necessity for the *khilāfat* and freedom movements and thus essential for India's deliverance, but it was also a religious duty of Muslims—a realization which he claimed had dawned on him a decade prior to the *khilāfat* movement, when he had set out the objective of *al-Hilāl* as being the promotion of this very concord. He therefore assured the Hindus that Muslims were extending the hand of friendship to them not transitorily in self-defence, or as a political strategy, but rather at the behest of their faith. He emphasized that this view was based on the *Sharī'at*—he was not propounding it in the present in connection with non-co-operation, but had held the same view even twenty years back, and had therefore opposed Aligarh's generally accepted policy of separation.[74]

This obviously belies the view that Āzād "provided a religious justification for limited co-operation with the Hindus", making it "explicitly clear" that the Hindu-Muslim unity for freedom which was in evidence during the *khilāfat* and non-co-operation movements could only be the unity of "two separately organized communities."[75] Far from advocating limited co-operation for freedom, he urged the Muslims to join with their countrymen to form a single nation, as a religious duty (*supra* p. 158). As for the second part of the statement, at least from 1923 onwards Āzād repeatedly urged the Muslims to join the Congress, and desist from organizing themselves separately (*supra* pp. 147-48). While he was prepared to sacrifice *khilāfat* for *swarāj* (even as he refused to accept the former without the latter) in early 1922 (*supra* pp. 152-53), in December the next year he declared that if freedom was possible without Hindu-Muslim unity, he would rather not have such freedom, for that would be the loss of humanity.[76] By 1940 he could confidently assert that the two communities were part of one indivisible nation, even while he repudiated the religious basis of nationality (*supra* pp. 159-60).

In a message issued in December 1921, while reminding the Jamī'at-al 'Ulamā'-i Hind of the need, importance, and religious sanction for Hindu-Muslim unity, Āzād appealed to it's leaders to preserve it since they could best do so. At the same time he reminded Muslims that their success depended on complete agreement with the Hindus, and appealed to them to overlook any oversight on the part of the latter. He also urged them to completely trust Gandhiji and follow his advice, unless he desired anything against Islām, which Āzād was confident he would not. During his Presidential Address to the Jamī'at Tablīgh Ahl-i Ḥadīth in September 1934, he restrained Muslims from trying to reply to the rash and repeated attacks on Islām by groups such as the Ārya Samāj, as well as from interpreting it as an indication of the Hindus' desire to annihilate them, repeating that their adversary was only Christianity and Christians.[77]

Āzād's attitude to the Hindus is very different from, and much more conciliatory than Shibli's, who perceived a threat to Islām (rather than Muslims) not only from the Ārya Samāj and other such Hindu organizations, but also from prejudiced European writers, Christian missionaries, and western atheism. In order to combat these he suggested measures such as the propagation of Islām through extensive missionary work, providing religious education to Muslims, and countering the propaganda against Islām—verbally and in print—but in a polite and refined manner, aiming at reconciliation rather than confrontation (*supra* pp. 36-38).

Divide and Rule

Like most Indians Āzād too perceived the British game of building their success in India by sowing discord among its people. In an undated article he recalled how the session of the Muslim League in Bombay in 1915 had been disrupted by the government's agents because it was suicidal to its interests that the Congress and the League should meet together in one place in an attempt to forge unity. Yet it could not completely foil the purpose of the session, which successfully smashed the myth of Congress-Muslim differences.[78] We recall that in 1943 Jinnāh had also cited this very incident as evidence of the divisive policy of the British government (*supra*, p. 125).

In a conversation with Dr. Sayyad Maḥmūd in early 1922 Āzād perceived the British as trying to appease Muslims in order to woo them away from the national movement, so that it would be weakened and easily quelled. He felt that their strenuous efforts to sow discord between the two major communities would, if successful, irreparably damage the *khilāfat-swarāj* movement, in whose leadership lay Gandhi's real strength. Many years later in his Presidential Address of 1940 he again referred to the British policy of highlighting internal differences in order to consolidate its own power—they created a false picture of India, emphasizing that it was inhabited by two different communities, and therefore no demand could be made in the name of a united nation. Muslims were led to believe that due to their fewer numbers democracy in India would mean Hindu rule, which would jeopardize their very existence; the object being to estrange them from the new political awakening, and the national movement launched by the Congress.[79]

Like Mawlāna Ḥusayn Aḥmad (*infra* p. 201) Āzād too felt that after having first sown dissension among Indians, the British government was directing them to put an end to their communal conflicts as a pre-condition for independence. He accused it of deliberately confounding the communal and political questions in order to convince the world that the former was barring the way to a solution of the latter; even while it used the minorities' problem as a weapon against India's freedom. He believed that once India was free its people would solve the problem forever by mutual agreement.[80]

Hindu-Muslim Problem and Independence

In his Congress Presidential Address of 1923, Āzād lamented that instead of *khilāfat* and *swarāj* Indians were engrossed in *shuddhi*, *sangathan*, and their counter movements;[81] which by arousing frenzied religious bigotry and senseless violence were sure to jeopardize that unity which was essential not only for India's freedom, but for its very survival and progress. Recalling his attempts a decade ago to dispel the political insecurity of Muslims, their distrust of the Congress, and preference for communal organizations; he felt it was now his duty to raise his voice against the flag-bearers of such movements, who claimed to be motivated by an insecurity which was inexplicable in a group three times more populous than the Muslims.[82]

Āzād was strictly opposed to all religious conflict because he felt that although theoretically it could be kept apart from political unity, in practice such distinctions could not hold good. The bitterness caused by the latter would come in the way of breeding that tolerance which was a must for achieving united nationhood (*muttaḥidah qaymiyyat*)—the need of the hour. He emphasized that if the different groups in India desired its freedom they had no choice but to defer all sectarian activities no matter how dear to them, for the country needed neither a Hindu nor a Muslim *sangathan*, but only the Congress—"the cradle of India's united nationhood." He felt it was a pity that both communities were concerned about self-preservation, but not about protecting India.[83]

In this respect Āzād appears to have differed greatly from Shibli and Mawlāna Ḥusayn Aḥmad, who even while they forcefully advocated political co-operation with the Hindus, were equally in favour of simultaneous and independent efforts in the field of religion by Muslims (*supra* pp. 36-38, 52 and 54, and *infra* p. 185). Āzād on the other hand appears more secular in his approach that the two could not go hand in hand, and the latter must be abandoned for the sake of the former.

In his article on C.R. Das, Āzād had written in June 1924 that the greatest obstacle in the way of India's "nationhood" was the complexity and divisiveness of the Hindu-Muslim issue, which at times caused even the greatest patriot to stumble. He felt that only great courage and patriotism could solve India's problem by exalting her people above such lowly sentiments, and thus making them willing to sacrifice everything for her freedom. In his Presidential Address to the All India Khilāfat Conference in December 1925 he cited the example of Syria, which like India was peopled by different races and religions—they had been mutually hostile since centuries, but in the present, for the sake of their country's freedom, they had unanimously adopted the slogan that despite mutual differences, the country belonged to all—he lamented that very few in India were willing to go this far.[84]

In a letter of June 1937 Āzād stressed that in the present atmosphere of distrust there was an urgent need to find a solution to contentious issues—he recalled his own incessant efforts in this direction, and for a rapprochement between Muslims and Hindus, particularly the Congress, since 1920. In the Presidential Address of December 1925 he had made it clear that while the Khilāfat Committee believed in protecting the rights of Muslims and was prepared to demand a fair deal from the Hindus, it was opposed to seeking protection against them from the British. In a statement of February 1940 he repeated that while Muslims had every right to struggle for safeguards, for these they should look to their countrymen rather than the government, or else the roots of British imperialism would be further strengthened (*Cf.* Shibli, *supra* p. 52). On both occasions he emphasized that mutual differences should not be allowed to interfere with their struggle for freedom which was the foremost task, and attainable only through united nationalism (*muttaḥidah qawmiyyat*). In another statement of March 1940 he expressed confidence that indepedence itself would help remove all differences by common consent.[85] (cf. supra p. 163)

In the letter of 1937 Āzād recalled that since 1912 he had been inviting Muslims to participate in the country's political struggle without setting any pre-conditions—he believed it was wrong of them to insist that they should be first given assurances regarding their future rights and interests, for it was disgraceful for eight crore people with a glorious destiny to appeal to others to remove the fear in their hearts before they could stir for the country's freedom. He felt that by admitting that they could not rely on themselves for protecting their interests, they were displaying a cowardice and lack of confidence which would herald the death of collective life. In a statement of March 1942, while claiming that his views regarding the future of Indian Muslims had been unchanged since 1904, he again urged them to strive for independence rather than obstructing it by demanding safeguards etc.[86] We have already commented on the furious debate among Muslim leaders over whether or not safeguards and a solution to the communal tangle should be made a pre-condition for Muslim participation in the freedom struggle (*supra* p. 117).

In a speech at the March 1942 session of the Jamī'at-al 'Ulamā'-i Hind Āzād repeated that neither the British nor constitutional guarantees could save a nation which believed that it could be wiped out—proposals passed in the present would have no value in the future—each group would gain only that which it won by its courage and determination. He therefore urged the Muslims to strengthen themselves—if they were convinced that their rights must be granted, no power on earth could seize them, for numbers were not all, and only the strong survived. For him it was a question of whether Muslims should build their political future on faith and determination, or fear and doubt. In his Congress Presidential Address of 1940 he had added that whereas in the first case they would assuredly march on towards freedom, in the latter situation no safeguard could banish their fears, and they would be compelled to tolerate the presence of a third power, which was contrary to the spirit of Islām.[81]

Āzād's argument here appears a trifle too idealistic and abstract—it is difficult to fathom how mere sentiments (such as faith, courage, and determination) devoid of action, could secure a community's future. While it is true that internal strife would only help the British, he seems to be recommending to the Muslims, unquestioning allegiance and faith in the Congress, and obedience to Gandhi (see pp. 153, 162, 164 and 166-67). Shibli and Mawlāna Ḥusayn Aḥmad's stand in this regard appears more reasonable : while they fully appreciated the efforts of the Congress and encouraged Muslims to co-operate with it, they did not hesitate to criticize those of its policies with which they disagreed, even while they affirmed the need for a separate Muslim political organization (*supra* pp. 52 and 54, and *infra* pp. 185-86 and 201-02).

In a statement of April 1942 Āzād assured the British government of the responsibility, as well as ability of the Congress to find a satisfactory solution to the communal problem once independence was granted (*Cf. supra* p. 163). In his Congress Presidential Address of 1940 he had said that there would be no room in free India for misgivings regarding majority and minority, since its constitution would be democratic and loosely federal, affording internal autonomy to the units and (as he said in a statement of August 1945), freedom to develop according to their needs and wishes, being subject only to certain essential bonds for their common welfare. The free and democratic Indian state would thus be founded not on compulsion, but on the willing co-operation of its principal communities. In another statement of April 1946 he described his vision of India as a socialist nation. [We recall that he had earlier disapproved of the artificial economic uniformity which socialism aspired to impose on society, favouring instead the more moderate Islāmic approach of encouraging free circulation of wealth even while it recognized economic disparities—*supra* p. 155]. He felt further that the old concept of "state sovereignty" would have to be gradually abandoned, so that the sovereign powers of individual states could be merged in a world authority.[88]

The Congress

In a dateless article Āzād described the Congress as representing all Indian communities (*qawm*) and groups. Repeating this in a statement of February 1940, he urged Muslims to muster under its banner for the freedom struggle, assuring them that it would protect their rights. In his Presidential Address of March 1940 he recalled that in keeping with its tradition of working for the interest of the nation as a whole, it had always been in favour of providing constitutional safeguards of their own choice for the minorities. In a statement in July that year he asserted that it was the only political party in India, the others being communal parties whose programme was not confined to political issues. He therefore refused (in June 1945) to accept the Muslim League's suggestion that it was a Hindu communal body, even insisting that the League yield in its traditional claim of being the only representative organization of Muslims, as this would render the Congress a sectarian body.[89]

In a statement of July 1945 Āzād assured his co-religionists that far from being blind to their genuine grievances, the nationalist Muslims in the Congress were as desirous of their well-being in free India as the League—only their methods for achieving this goal were different. In a statement of October 1945 he expressed the conviction that Muslims would come to accept that the principles of the Congress ensured the protection of their future status in India, which could in fact be safe only by treading the path laid down by it. In a statement of April 1946, while reaffirming its commitment to a federated India composed of fully autonomous units, he assured the Muslims that since the centre would have limited powers, they need not fear Hindu domination.[90]

Partition

In various statements in April 1940, July 1945, and April 1946, while describing partition as a scheme of the League, Āzād contested its claim to being the sole representative of Indian Muslims—he also refused to accept its contention that all, or even a majority of Muslims favoured its demand for Pakistan—unless established by a plebiscite. He believed that the right to take such a step could rest only with the Muslims, and the matter should therefore be entrusted to their representatives in the proposed Constituent Assembly, who he was sure would never favour a vivisection of India. He declared in April 1946 (in a manner reminiscent of his 1940 speech— *supra* p. 159-60), that as a Muslim he was not for a moment prepared to give up his right to share in the shaping of the political and economic life of the whole of India; it being cowardice to content himself with a mere fragment of his patrimony, and give up the rest. The scheme of division therefore appeared to him to be a symbol of defeatism—a confession that Indian Muslims could not hold their own in India as a whole, and would be content to withdraw to a corner specially reserved for them. This despite the fact that they were a sufficiently large and important element in Indian life to decisively influence all questions of administration and policy, and were further fortified by being concentrated in certain areas—he felt that in such circumstances the demand for Pakistan lost all force.[91]

In August 1945, while urging Muslims to get rid of the fear complex, Āzād tried to convince them that partition was wholly impracticable, and harmful not only for India as a whole, but for them too—far from benefitting their communal interests, it would create more problems than it solved. Summoning familiar arguments, he reasoned that it would leave behind three and a half crore Muslims scattered in small minorities all over India, rendering them weaker than they were in the present. Made aliens and foreigners overnight, and backward as they were, they would be left to the mercies of what would become an unadulterated Hindu *rāj*. The position of Muslims in Pakistan would also be vulnerable, for nowhere in it would their majority be comparable to that of the Hindus in their state. In fact their slight majority would be offset by the lead enjoyed by non-Muslims in all spheres—and even if Pakistan was overwhelmingly Muslim, it would not solve the problems of Muslims in Hindustan. Finally when its formation appeared inevitable, in June 1947 he was optimistically confident that the partition would be a short-lived one, with those provinces now seeking separation, hurrying back to the Indian union in the near future—for the division existed only on in the map of the country, and not in the hearts of its people.[92]

Notes and References

All references in this chapter unless otherwise specified, are to the works of Mawlāna Abu'l Kalām Āzād.

1. An Urdu weekly which Āzād started in June 1912. It was discontinued in November 1914, but revived from June to December 1927.
2. Prabha Dixit, "Political Objectives of the Khilāfat Movement" and Mushirul Haq, "The Authority of Religion in Indian Muslim Politics", *Communal and Pan-Islamic Trends in Colonial India*, ed. Mushirul Hasan (New Delhi, 1981) pp. 64-65 and 359.
3. Malik Ram, ed., *Khuṭbāt-i Āzād* (New Delhi, 1974) pp. 16-18.
4. *Ibid.*, pp. 18-19; *Mas'alah-i Khilāfat* (New Delhi, 1987) pp. 24-25.
5. Wilfred Cantwell Smith, *Modern Islam in India* (Lahore, 1969) p. 234.
6. Ram, *op. cit.*, p. 110.
7. Ram, *op. cit.*, pp. 19-21; *Mas'alah*, pp. 196-97.
8. Ram, *op. cit.*, pp. 21-26.
9. *Ibid.*, pp. 27-28.
10. *Ibid.*, pp. 31-32.
11. *Mas'alah*, pp. 262-63, 265-67, 270 and 280-82.
12. *Ibid.*, pp. 16, 19, 21-24 and 50.
13. Munshi Mushtāq Aḥmad, *ed.*, *Majmū'ah-i Maḍāmīn Mawlāna Abu'l Kalām Āzād* (Meerut, n.d.) vol. VI, pp. 27-32; Ram, *op. cit.*, p. 130.
14. *Mas'alah*, pp. 26-33, 50, 66 and 266-67.
15. *Mas'alah*, pp. 109-137.
16. *Ibid.*, pp. 314, 316 and 318; Ram, *op. cit.*, pp. 129-133.
17. Ram, *op. cit,* pp. 136-37 and 144.
18. Anwar 'Ārif, ed., *Mawlāna Abu'l Kalām Āzād Ki Taqrīreṇ* (Delhi, 1988) p. 36.
19. *Mas'alah*, pp. 201, 263 and 283.
20. *Ibid.*, pp. 68-69, 73-75, 79, 92-93 and 283-84.
21. *Ibid.*, pp. 33-34, 38-39 and 65-68.
22. *Ibid.*, pp. 12, 83-84, 86, 88-90, 108-09, 118 and 283.
23. *Ibid.*, pp. 186-87, 191-92, 204-212 and 284; Ram, *op. cit.*, pp. 29-30.
24. *Mas'alah*, pp. 141-45 and 150-184.
25. *Ibid.*, pp. 193, 195-97 and 199.
26. Ram, *op. cit.*, pp. 34-35; *Mas'alah*, pp. 219-232, 236-42.
27. *Mas'alah*, pp. 216-19 and 247-257.
28. *Ibid.*, pp. 213-14, 218-19, 246-47 and 284-85.
29. *Ibid.*, pp. 280-82, 285-89, 291 and 293-94.
30. *Ibid.*, pp. 284, 286, 294-97 and 330-35; Mushtāq Aḥmad, ed., *Tāzah Maḍāmīn Abu'l Kalām Āzād* (1921) (Meerut, n.d.) p. 35; Ram, *op. cit*, pp. 48-50.

31. *Mas'alah*, pp. 297-99 and 301-05.
32. 'Abd-al Qawi Dasnawi, *ed., Maḍamīn Lisān-al Ṣidq* (Lucknow, 1967) p. 97.
33. Aziz Ahmad, *Islamic Modernism in India and Pakistan (1857-1964)* (London, 1967) pp. 175-76.
34. Ram, *op cit.*, pp. 108-09.
35. Muhammad Ismā'īl Pānīpati, ed., *Khuṭbāt-i Sir Sayyad*, 2 vols. (Lahore, 1973) vol. I, p. 591.
36. Fayyāz Aḥmad, ed., *Ṣubḥ-i Ummīd* (New Delhi, 1959) vol. I, pp. 144 and 149; M. Aḥmad ed., *Majmū'ah Maḍāmīn*, pp. 39-40, 46-47 and 52.
37. F. Aḥmad, *op. cit.*, pp. 150-52 and 155.
38. *Ibid.*, pp. 151-56.
39. *Ibid.*, pp. 97-98 and 100-01.
40. *Ibid.*, pp. 162, 165-66 and 100-02.
41. Munshi Mushtāq Aḥmad, ed., *Bayān Mawlāna Abu'l Kalām Āzād* (Meerut, n.d.), pp. 45-46; Ram, *op. cit.*, pp. 206-07
42. A.M. Zaidi, ed., *Congress Presidential Addresses (1940-85)* (n.p., 1989) vol. V, pp. 34-35.
43. F. Aḥmad, *op. cit.*, pp. 83 and 85-87.
44. *Ibid.*, pp. 87 and 89; *Mas'alah*, pp. 319-320 and 322.
45. F. Aḥmad, *op. cit.*, pp. 79-82.
46. Ram, *op. cit.*, pp. 110-12, 126-27 and 129; 'Ārif, *op.cit.*, p. 65.
47. *Op. cit.*, pp. 238-39.
48. *Op. cit.*, p. 187.
49. M. Aḥmad, *Tāzah Maḍāmīn*, pp. 14-15, 17, 20-22 and 34.
50. *Ibid.*, pp. 11-12, 14, 16 and 19.
51. Ram, *op. cit.*, pp. 43-45 and 54-55.
52. *Op. cit.*, pp. 238-240.
53. Ram, *op. cit.*, pp. 54-57.
54. *Ibid.*, pp. 45-46 and 54.
55. *Payghāmāt-i Āzād* (Bijnor, n.d.) pp. 4-5, 9 and 16-18.
56. M. Aḥmad, *Bayān*, pp. 37-38, 40, 42 and 45-46.
57. Ram, *op. cit.*, pp. 169, 171 and 228.
58. F. Aḥmad, *op. cit.*, pp. 87, 136 and 145-46; *Mas'alah*, p. 12.
59. F. Aḥmad, *op. cit.*, p. 161; M. Aḥmad, *Bayān*, p. 23; 'Ārif, *op. cit.*, pp. 10-11.
60. Dasnawi, *op. cit.*, pp. 27-28.
61. *Mas'alah*, pp. 317 and 319; Zaidi, *op. cit.*, pp. 31-33.
62. Dasnawi, *op. cit.*, pp. 33-35 and 49-50.
63. F. Aḥmad, *op. cit.*, pp. 115-16; Ram, *op. cit.*, pp. 255 and 267.
64. Ram, *op. cit.*, pp. 266-68.
65. P.N. Chopra, ed., *Maulana Azad: Selected Speeches and Statements (1940-47)* (New Delhi, 1990) pp. 178 and 181.

66. Ram, *op. cit*, pp. 50-52.
67. Ram, *op. cit.*, pp. 159 and 174; 'Aṭīq Ṣiddīqi, ed., *Ā'īnah-i Abu'l Kalām Āzād* (Delhi, 1976) pp. 160 and 162-63.
68. Zaidi, *op. cit.*, pp. 36-37.
69. *Ibid.*, p. 37.
70. *Ibid.*
71. *Ibid.*, pp. 36-37; Chopra, *op. cit.*, p. 110.
72. Chopra, *op. cit.*, pp. 176-77.
73. 'Aqīl Aḥmad Ja'fari, *ed., Mukālimāt-i Abu'l Kalām* (Haydarabad, 1944) p. 206; *Mas'alah*, pp. 299-300; Ram, *op. cit.*, pp. 47-48.
74. *Ibid.*, pp. 46-47, 50 and 53-54.
75. Ali Ashraf, *Khilafat Movement: A Factor in Muslim Separatism*, Hasan, *op. cit.*, p. 77.
76. *Khuṭbāt*, p. 204.
77. *Ibid.*, p. 248; *Payghāmāt*, pp. 14-15.
78. M. Aḥmad, *Majmū'ah Maḍāmīn*, pp. 19 and 23.
79. *Payghāmāt*, p. 16; Zaidi, *op. cit.*, pp. 28-29 and 32.
80. Zaidi, *op. cit.*, pp. 28-29 and 31.
81. The *shuddhi* movement was started by an Ārya Samāji leader Swāmi Shraddhānand in 1922, to convert non-Hindus to Hinduism. The methods and tone of the mission were aggressive, particularly towards Muslims. The leader of the *sangathan* movement was Madan Mohan Mālawiya. It aimed at Hindu solidarity, and at organizing them for social reform. In response the Jamī'at-al 'Ulamā'-i Hind started corresponding programmes of *tablīgh* and *tanẓīm*—Ziya-ul Hasan Faruqi, *The Deoband School and the Demand for Pakistan* (Bombay, 1963) pp. 72-73.
82. Ram, *op. cit.*, pp. 204-07.
83. *Ibid.*, pp. 207-210.
84. *Ibid.*, p. 213; Ṣiddīqi, *op. cit.*, p. 164.
85. Ram, *op. cit.*, pp. 227-28; Ṣiddīqi, *op. cit.*, pp. 179-180; Chopra, *op. cit.*, pp. 1-2 and 23.
86. Ṣiddīqi, *op. cit.*, pp. 181-82; Chopra, *op. cit.*, p. 44.
87. Ṣiddīqi, *op. cit.*, pp. 181-82; Chopra, *op. cit.*, p. 44; Zaidi, *op. cit.*, pp. 34-35; 'Ārif, *op. cit.*, p. 143.
88. Zaidi, *op. cit.*, p. 33; Chopra, *op. cit.*, pp. 47, 99 and 134.
89. M. Aḥmad, *Tāzah Maḍāmīn*, pp. 13-14; Chopra, *op. cit.*, pp. 2, 26 and 72-74; Zaidi, *op. cit.*, pp. 29-30.
90. Chopra, *op. cit.*, pp. 77, 107 and 135.
91. *Ibid.*, pp. 24, 93-94, 132-33 and 136.
92. *Ibid.*, pp. 99-100, 132-34 and 183.

Chapter 6

SAYYAD ḤUSAYN AḤMAD MADANI
(1879-1957)

The Islāmic Caliphate

Besides being a learned religious scholar of great repute, Mawlāna Ḥusayn Aḥmad Madani was also very active politically. In a speech in Delhi in 1921 he reasoned that since politics affected many aspects of a Muslim's life including religion, the political guidance of the *ummat* was obligatory on the *'ulamā'*. In support of this view he quoted a *Ḥadīth* in which the Prophet (Pbuh) has likened the *'ulamā'* of his *ummat* to the prophets of the Bani Isrā'īl (*Cf. infra* p. 173 where the latter have been compared to the Muslim caliphs), who according to another *Ḥadīth* as well as common knowledge, undertook the political guidance of their community.[1]

Mawlāna Ḥusayn Aḥmad's speeches of February and March 1921, delivered in Delhi, Bengal, and Syoharah (U.P.), abound in references to the importance of the caliphate and exhortations to Muslims to strengthen and support it. It is interesting to observe that he employed many of the arguments which were used by Āzād only a year back, in February 1920.

Mawlāna Madani cited the Qur'ān (2:30 and 24:55) as testifying not only to the antiquity, but also the continuity and permanence of the *khilāfat*. [It is however questionable as to how far these verses refer to the institution of the caliphate as it was later understood.] In order to demonstrate the urgency of the need to combat any threat to it, he quoted the *Ḥadīth* that if a Muslim makes a rival claim to the caliphate, he should be killed[2] (*Cf.* Āzād, *supra* p. 138).

Mawlāna Madani cited the historical fact that the Companions tackled the matter of the caliphate before the burial of the Prophet

(Pbuh), as further testifying to its urgency. He also claimed, on the authority of commentaries of the Qur'ān (*tafsīr*) and the verdicts of jurists, that the establishment of the caliphate and the preservation of its power was the most important of the obligations on the *ummat*, and concluded therefore that all Muslims should take care not to fall short of this duty (specially when their enemies were trying to destroy the caliphate); or else they would face a grievous penalty in the hereafter. He described this duty as a *farḍ-i kifāyah* or collective responsibility *i.e.* if any group of Muslims fulfilled it, the rest would be absolved; if not they would all be held responsible.[3] Āzād we recall had designated this as a *farḍ-i 'ayn* (*supra* p. 142).

Mawlāna Ḥusayn Aḥmad vehemently refuted the argument [it was put forward by Sir Sayyad (*supra* p. 29) although the Mawlāna does not mention his name], that since the Prophet (Pbuh) has been reported as saying that the caliphate would last for only thirty years, after this period all commandments relating to it would also be rendered null and void. He believed that the *Ḥadīth* referred only to the period of the four rightly guided (*rāshidūn*) caliphs; and inferred on the basis of the references to Ḥaḍrat Imām Mahdi and Ḥaḍrat 'Īsá as "*khalīfah*" in numerous authentic Traditions, that the Islāmic caliphate would last till doomsday. In support of this view he also cited the *Ḥadīth* in which the prophets of the Bani Isrā'īl, in their capacity as political and religious guides of the community, have been compared to caliphs of the Muslims (*Cf.* Āzād, *supra* p. 139). He also recalled the *Ḥadīth* in which Muslims have been commanded to remain loyal to the caliph, while Allāh would call him to account regarding his lapses. This was for him an assurance that the caliphate, comprising both just and unjust rulers, would forever remain in force for the preservation of Islām and Muslims, and it was binding on them to defend the rights of both.[4]

Mawlāna Madani believed that the Arab caliphate flourished so long as the caliphs showed sympathy for Islām, but God's promise (embodied in 24:55) was reversed when they slackened in upholding the faith. Quoting a *Ḥadīth* according to which the *khilāfat* would remain among the Quraysh only so long as they would strive for the true faith; he believed that accordingly, when they abandoned the *Sharī'at* not only the Quraysh, but all Arabs were deprived of this honour after about five hundred years; and it was bestowed on the Turks for the next five centuries—he even quoted another *Ḥadīth* to confirm this transfer. He refuted the objection [raised among others, by Shibli *supra* p. 44] that their being non-Qurayshites disqualified the Turks for the caliphate, and even went on to say that they had proved themselves more worthy of the honour, and conscientious in discharging their duties, than had the Ummayyad and Abbāsid caliphs.[5] This is comparable to Āzād's slightly different defence of the Turkish caliphate against the same charge (*supra* p. 140).

The Turkish Caliphate

Like Āzād (*supra* pp. 139-40), Mawlāna Ḥusayn Aḥmad emphasized that the Turkish Sultāns had remained true to the caliphal duty of defence and offence for the past five centuries; the difference being that the latter also went on to enumerate their religious services in great detail, specially their valiant protection of Muslim Asia against the military onslaughts of Christian Europe—wherein they had even succeeded in carrying the flag of Islām. He believed that it was for this very reason that Europe wanted to avenge itself by seeing Turkey humiliated. He did not agree with those who reasoned that its survival would not be beneficial to Islām and Muslims, for whom he felt they had shown great consideration. He also countered the argument [presented by Sir Sayyad, *supra* p. 29], that Muslims living outside the territory of the caliphate were not bound by the *Sharī'at* to support it, by saying that those who were politically aware well knew the benefits accruing to world Muslims from the Uthmāṇi caliphate. He went on to reason that even if it did not benefit Indian Muslims, it was obligatory on them to do their duty according to the *Ḥadīth* mentioned earlier. He recalled that they had always been loyal, first to the Arab, and later the Turkish caliphate (*Cf.* Āzād, *supra* pp. 140-41), and believed that in the present when it was being unjustly weakened by Europe, it was their religious duty to help in its survival.[6]

As is obvious, this was the real aim of the Mawlāna, for which the whole of the above argument has been built up. Loss of their political power in India, oppression by the British, pan-Islāmic sympathy, and the perceived European hostility to Turkey and the caliphate drove Indian Muslims to unprecedented loyalty and support for it. These speeches were made in 1921 when the *khilāfat* movement in India was at its peak—Muḥammad 'Ali Jawhar had founded the Khilāfat Conference only two years back. The humiliating treaty of Sevres signed the previous year between the Allies and Turkey, had further inflamed Indian Muslims.

In order to rouse them to come to the aid of the besieged caliphate, Mawlāna Madani tried to bear upon Indian Muslims that it was their religious duty to support Turkey in the war, which it had been forced to join in self-defence [it had entered the First World War on the side of the central powers in 1914]. Quoting the tenth verse of *Sūrah al-Ḥujurāt* which describes all Muslims as brothers, and *Ḥadīth* of similar import, he emphasized that the bond which the *Sharī'at* had established between them was above all artificial worldly connections. He also cited Traditions which likened Muslims to a single organism, so that injury to one part afflicted the others too; and those which called upon them to help to defend the other's honour against his enemy. On the basis of these and other *Ḥadīth* according to which, if unbelievers attacked the Muslims of any area, *jihād* became successively obligatory on all world Muslims in order of their proximity to the attacked area, he concluded that the demands of the *Sharī'at* made it incumbent on all Muslims (including those in India), to participate in the war on Turkey's behalf.[7] Many of these arguments had already been employed by Āzād (*supra* pp. 132, 139-40 and 142).

Mawlāna Madani felt this was more so due to the atrocities being committed against Muslims, and specially women and children during the war. He reminded them of a *Ḥadīth* according to which if a Muslim woman was made captive, it became obligatory on her co-religionists all over the world to free her. He also appealed to Indian Muslims on the authority of the 36th verse of *Sūrah Tawbah* : "Fight the polytheists in groups, as they fight you in groups", urging them that in the present, when the whole Christian world was pitted against Islām and its caliphate, they should help their oppressed brothers. He also reminded them of their duty to oppose rising European influence in Arabia, in the light of a *Ḥadīth* according to which the Prophet (Pbuh) had urged his followers to free the peninsula of non-Muslim power[8] (*Cf.* Āzād, *supra* pp. 134-35 and 141-43).

Mawlāna Ḥusayn Aḥmad reminded the Muslims of India that they had contributed to the ruin of their co-religionists and the caliphate by recruiting themselves in the British-Indian army, which had been active in the wars against Muslims—he advised them that if they desired to be protected from the dire punishment for such action, they must repent sincerely and abstain from it in future.

Citing traditions which warned a Muslim who lifted arms against another, of his loss of faith and God's wrath, he urged the *'ulamā'* to preach extensively against Muslims' serving in the army, since it entailed shedding the blood of their co-religionists. [The All India Khilāfat Conference held at Karachi in July that year passed a resolution pronouncing religious anathema on such Muslims.] He also impressed upon them that it was strictly prohibited to donate or collect subscriptions for such a war, which was being waged against Muslims, Islām, and its caliphate.[9] (*Cf.* Āzād, *supra* pp. 136 and 143).

Mawlāna Ḥusayn Aḥmad disagreed with those who justified these actions on the grounds that the war was a purely political one, and contended that any war between Islām and unbelief (*kufr*) could not but be for upholding the word of God, and therefore religious in nature. He further quoted the British Prime Minister as having referred to the war as a religious crusade, in order to illustrate that Europe also perceived it thus.[10] The stand adopted by him here, of branding all wars between Muslims and non-Muslims as religious, appears impractical. More than two decades later in December 1945 he would accept economic (rather than religious) factors as the prime considerations behind political moves (including European imperialism and the world wars).[11]

We recall that Sir Sayyad on the contrary had regarded the military conflicts between England and Turkey as purely political and secular, and had chided Indian Muslims for supporting the latter against their rulers. He had not only ruled out the possibility and need for *jihād* in India against the British, but had even tried to show that it was opposed to Islāmic precepts, and that verses such as 9:36 were no more relevant and applicable (*supra* pp. 28-30).

Although he espoused the caliphate so vehemently while it lasted, we find Mawlāna Ḥusayn Aḥmad adopting complete silence over the issue after its abolition by the Turkish Grand National Assembly in March 1924, and over the course of action Indian Muslims should adopt with respect to it thereafter. He however continued to appeal to their sentiments of Islāmic unity in order to rouse anti-British feelings among them (*infra* pp. 180-81).

Anti-Britishness

Among the thinkers we have studied so far, for the first time we find in the works of Mawlāna Ḥusayn Aḥmad, bitter antagonism towards the British, and ardent patriotism stemming from the realization of the losses incurred by India due to British rule.

In his speeches of 1921 Mawlāna Ḥusayn Aḥmad tried to bring home to Muslims the disadvantages of British rule—until its advent Indian history had been glorious and effulgent, but it had reduced India (a former exporter of goods) to such straits that it was compelled to import even basic necessities. He tried to jolt them out of their old posture of misplaced loyalty, seeing no reason for fidelity to a tyrannical foreign government which was subsisting on Indian support, yet pushing it into ignominy. He felt that loyalty in such circumstances served only to heighten the pride and racial bigotry of the English, and their insensitivity to Indian demands, making them enforce the harshest laws against Indians to divest them of all religious and political rights and freedom, and insult them in every way possible. The only solution for him was *swarāj,* for destruction awaited all Indians unless they threw off the chains of subservience. His words, replete with expressions such as "our country, our motherland," are laden with patriotic fervour, and betray deep agony for his countrymen.[12]

Mawlāna Madani demolished all the old arguments advanced by the loyalist school in favour of British rule. Whereas Āzād had conceded that the government protected the life and property of its subjects and provided peace and security (*supra* pp. 148-49), the Mawlāna denied it, recalling the countless Indian lives lost on behalf of Britain during the ongoing and previous wars, and due to famine, scarcity and dearness. Also recalling the merciless killing of Indians by British officers such as Gen. Dyer and his like; he attempted to dispel the rosy picture of the government ensuring unprecedented freedom and dutifully guarding India's wealth, as a delusion perpetrated on the people. He also repeatedly drew attention to the fact that in order to develop its own wealth, England was strangulating India's economic life. This was achieved partly by means of an exhorbitant and severe system of taxation which succeeded in siphoning India's wealth into the Royal Treasury and financially ruining its people, particularly Muslims. He lamented that while crores were spent from the Indian treasury on the army (the huge pays of its British officers being many times greater than those of their Indian subordinates), all that they gained in return was widows, orphans, and oppression through unjust laws passed on the pretext of security.[13]

Mawlāna Ḥusayn Aḥmad repeated similar sentiments nearly a quarter of a century later, in the second part of the pamphlet *Pākistān Kya Hay,*[14] written in December 1945. Following the history of Britain's brazen and blatant economic exploitation of India, he felt that one of its consequences was the series of famines, which had left a trail of death and starvation. He lamented that although all high posts were reserved for the British, salaries were drawn from the Indian treasury, and that sixty four per cent of England's industrial produce found a market in India. In the pamphlet *Muslim Līg Kya Hay*[15] written in September the same year, he eloquently and forcefully lamented that besides their ruthless economic exploitation, Indians were deprived of their civil rights in their own country, whose condition had deteriorated from the best to the worst. In two letters of January 1942 and April 1947[16] he repeated that the British policy of enriching their country while they rendered India bankrupt by gaining control of its resources, besides generating mass poverty and unemployment, had ruined its trade and agriculture.

In his speeches of 1921 Mawlāna Madani also protested against the unequal treatment meted out to Indians, and the fact that culprits such as Gen. Dyer, who had the blood of numerous Indians on their hands, were rewarded rather than being penalized. He also recalled how innocent millions had been brutally mown down in 1857, when Indians were merely striving for their right to freedom—yet the government would have them believe its self-righteous claims to care and solicitude for its subjects.[17]

Thus the Mawlāna succeeds in effectively demolishing Sir Sayyad's carefully built up argument in favour of loyalism. It is not difficult to see how effective these strongly worded and passionately expressed sentiments must have been in creating a feeling of nationalism and patriotic fervour among Indian Muslims, and of oneness with the other, similarly aggrieved peoples of the nation. The oft-repeated theme of ruthless exploitation generated a feeling of being wronged against by a common enemy, which no doubt helped to forge a new unity among the varied Indian peoples.

Mawlāna Ḥusayn Aḥmad was quick to point out that Indians—both Hindus and Muslims—had suffered not only worldly, but religious losses too, for crores of the members of both faiths had been converted, while the religiosity of countless others had been severely eroded, leaving them Hindu or Muslim in name only. He perceived western civilization as having destroyed their common heritage of an "eastern morality", and its materialistic perceptions as having obliterated their spiritual tendencies. He astutely remarked that the whole British system of education was deliberately designed to enhance Indian servitude.[18]

In 1945 and a letter of April 1947, in order to jolt Muslims out of their subservience Mawlāna Madani attempted to demonstrate that the British had proved an even greater enemy for them—the former rulers of India—whom they had gradually ruined through deceit and discord, besides turning *dār-al Islām* into *dār-al kufr* (*Cf.* Shibli who regarded India under the British as *dār-al Islām*—*supra* p. 46). Having established themselves firmly, they followed the policy of excluding Muslims from government service and deliberately promoting Hindus, reducing the former to the pit of degradation, and sowing the seeds of hostility between them and the followers of other faiths. They gave free license to the evils forbidden by Islām, enforced un-Islāmic laws, and by abolishing the office of the *qāḍi*, destroyed the special laws for Muslims. He thus concluded that they had suffered the most due to British rule, and that while all non-Muslims were the enemies of Islām and Muslims, the English had proved themselves most bitter in their enmity[19] (*Cf.* Āzād who held that not Hindus, but only Christians were the enemies of Muslims—*supra* p. 162).

In the speeches of 1921 also Mawlāna Ḥusayn Aḥmad had appealed to the anti-British sentiments of Muslims on purely religious grounds too. He repeatedly tried to demonstrate that the religious freedom which was claimed for them was only a delusion, with Muslim government employees not even being permitted to say their prayers. Besides, a faith such as Islām embraced not only rites of worship, but all aspects of life, which under the British were not governed by Islāmic law. Quoting from the Qur'ān to demonstrate at length that it prohibited Muslims from having their disputes settled by unbelievers, he inferred that it was unlawful for them to approach British-Indian courts. Further, whatever little there was of religious freedom could be curtailed by the government wholly at its own pleasure. He also reasoned that it was interfering in their religious matters by preventing them from carrying out their duties related to the caliphate and the guarding of the sanctity of the Holy Places. He also objected to the terms of the treaty of Sevres, which severely encroached upon the military and financial powers of the *khalīfah*, while also laying down that he sever all links with Muslims of other countries.[20]

In 1938, 1945, and 1947, Mawlāna Madani tried to impress upon Muslims that it was their duty to liberate themselves from British slavery, since their subjection was jeopardizing the freedom of other Muslim nations, where British-Indian armies were being deployed. He thus wanted to demonstrate that the British were the greatest enemies of Islām, Muslims, and India (*Cf.* Āzād, *supra* p. 158). In a speech of 1921 and letters of September 1943 and April 1947, he wanted them to realize that Britain had proved itself an enemy of world-Muslims by ruining the glory of Muslim nations. They had disintegrated the Turkish caliphate by compelling its territories to secede. Among other Muslim areas, they had also attacked the Holy Cities, causing rivers of blood to flow, capturing hundreds of women and children, and committing shameful atrocities. Besides this, they had divided Muslim countries among European powers through various treaties (*Cf.* Āzād, *supra* p. 142 *ff.*). He strongly disagreed with those who, being "intoxicated with British wine", quoted a verse of the Qur'ān which describes Christians as being "nearest . . . in love to the believers" (5:82) (Iqbāl was one of them—*supra* p. 59). In the light of the continuous tyranny of the Christian world, he was constrained to believe that it pertained only to a particular age, and could not be interpreted universally.[21] We recall that Sir Sayyad had similarly limited, to their particular historical context, the scope of the verses which enjoined Muslims to wage war against the polytheists (*supra* p. 28-29).

In one of his speeches of 1921 at Delhi, Mawlāna Ḥusayn Aḥmad saw British malevolence towards the Muslims of India and the world in the larger perspective of consistent Christian hostility towards Islām. He recalled the atrocities and oppression perpetrated by the former in the medieval period, and during the lengthy Crusades. He felt that in the preceding century European attacks on Islām had become more concerted and cruel. He recalled the manner in which they had not only incited, but also abetted Turkish territories to rebellion, and then fought unitedly against their common enemy *i.e.* Turkey, resulting in the Russo-Turkish War of 1877, the Greco-Turksih War of 1897, and numerous other military conflicts.[22]

Unfazed by the horrendous miseries inflicted on helpless Muslims, on the contrary Europe and its allies had accused Turkey of tyranny, bloodshed, and war crimes. Mawlāna Ḥusayn Aḥmad accused the British government of being foremost in aggression, as well as in launching false propaganda. By vividly recalling blood-curdling war scenes and gory massacres of Muslims, he wished to impress upon his audience that Europe and Christianity were bitter foes of the east and particularly of Islām, and bent upon destroying it. Many years later he would reiterate that Europe and particularly Britain had caused the greatest injury to Islām by dispossessing Muslims of large areas, where they proceeded forthwith to establish their own power.[23]

Thus the anti-British feeling in the political thought of the Mawlāna is developed at many levels—he regarded them as the worst enemy of India in general and Indian Muslims particularly, as also of the Muslims of the world. He also related this to abiding Christian hostility towards Islām, and on yet another plane, saw the west as constantly encroaching on, and ruining the whole of the east.

Mawlāna Madani felt that the British were so convinced of their imagined superiority that overlooking past history, they regarded all Asian and African nations (*qawm*) who were sailing in the same storm-struck boat, as being beyond the pale of humanity. He therefore, called on Indians to achieve freedom, and thus liberate their other eastern brothers too. He felt that since all Asian "nations" were one, complete sympathy between them was essential.[24]

Jihād

Whereas Sir Sayyad had tried to impress upon Muslims that obedience and loyalty to the British government was their religious duty (*supra* pp. 28-29), Mawlāna Ḥusayn Aḥmad's stand is diametrically opposed. In the speech at Delhi in 1921 he assured his audience that they were not bound by the *Sharī'at* to obey their unjust rulers—in fact it was obligatory on Muslims to oppose them, for according to a *Ḥadīth,* the best form of *jihād* was to speak out fearlessly before a tyrannical ruler. Having established that the British were the greatest enemies of Muslims, he reasoned that it was only by securing freedom from their domination that Indian Muslims could safeguard their religion, and therefore it was their religious duty to struggle for such freedom. He repeated these views in a letter of February 1938. In another dateless letter he reasoned that since the infidels had converted India, a *dār-al Islām*, into *dār-al ḥarb*, it was the duty of every Muslim to try to liberate it from their influence. He therefore did not hesitate to describe such a struggle as a *jihād*, quoting from the *Ḥadīth* and Qur'ān (2:190 and 9:36), exhortations to fight in the way of God; and compared the resultant discomforts to the hardships faced by the Prophets.[25] We recall that Āzād had described not the struggle for India's freedom, but the effort to defend the world-wide Muslim community and its *khalīfah*, as a *jihād* (*supra* pp. 141-42).

In 1921 too, while urging his audience to persevere in the non-co-operation movement, Mawlāna Madani had reminded them of the calm of the Prophets, and the help and great rewards promised by the Qur'ān for suffering in the way of God (9:120). Quoting the verse again in a dateless letter and another of October 1942, he wrote that since the ongoing movement in India against the enemies of Islām—the British—was no less than a *jihād*, its soldiers were *ghāzīs* and *mujāhidīn*. In the pamphlet *Muttaḥidah Qawmiyyat Awr Islām* and a letter of April 1947, he reasoned that since Britain was employing Indian wealth and armies to enslave other Muslim and eastern nations (*qawm*) too, securing deliverance from it became all the more urgent. He therefore described (in a letter of January 1946), participation in the freedom movement as "the religious and human duty of Muslims." Referring to his own involvement in it since 1914, he recalled that earlier he had been a part of the violent, revolutionary party led by Mawlāna Maḥmūd-al Ḥasan, which led to their imprisonment in Malta; but upon his return he came to believe in the policy of non-violence, and participated in the Khilāfat Committee, the Jamī'at-al Ulamā'-i Hind, and the Congress.[26]

In a letter of April 1947 Mawlāna Ḥusayn Aḥmad deduced on the basis of the *Ḥadīth* that if unbelievers attacked a Muslim country its defence became obligatory on its inhabitants, and by degrees on all world Muslims; that in order to liberate India from the domination of unbelievers, its Muslims should employ every possible means of resistance, ranging from civil disobedience to armed *jihād*. He cited numerous references from law books to illustrate his point, and further reasoned that since it was unanimously agreed that fighting the government by violent means was beyond their power, Muslims should adopt peaceful struggle as a religious duty (*Cf.* Āzād, *supra* pp. 148-49 and 153). He also believed that it was not only unavoidable but imperative that they participate in this struggle alongside other Indian "nations", since if they undertook it alone their failure and the resultant political and economic losses were self-evident. Once having achieved their aim, they would all co-operate in building up a new order after independence.[27]

Summing up these points in his Presidential Address to the Jamī'at-al 'Ulamā' in 1945, Mawlāna Madani had added that since the consequences of slavery would affect all alike, Indians should unitedly face the common threat. Any objection we may feel to this mixing of religion and politics is answered by a dateless letter in which he reasoned that politics could not be alienated from Islām, particularly in the present when political and religious problems were closely interrelated (*Cf.* Āzād, *supra* p. 149). He therefore believed that religious and educational institutions could in no way be absolved of the struggle for freedom.[28]

United Nationalism

As a Political Strategy

Since he believed that British exploitation and tyranny had been made possible by Indian disunity, even in 1921 Mawlāna Ḥusayn Aḥmad had appealed for complete agreement between all Indians while keeping religious freedom intact, and had urged the *'ulamā'* to work for the same. He clarified that they needed to be devoted to each other only in national and political matters, without letting their enemies disrupt this concord by bringing religious issues between them. He was convinced that even while remaining staunch Hindus and Muslims, as Indians they could strive unitedly for their rights and freedom. In a letter of July 1931 he wrote that political strategy should be ruled by the prevailing circumstances [we shall see ample evidence of his application of this principle], and the situation in India demanded that Muslims should join hands with others in order to effectively combat the greater enemy, and adopt non-co-operation against it. He proceeded to illustrate from Islāmic history that the Prophet (Pbuh) had joined hands with the Jewish tribe of Bani Ḥārithah in the battle of Khaybar, the non-aligned tribes of Makkah in the battle of Hunayn, and the Khuzā'ah in Hudaybiyah.[29]

In a speech at Bara Hindu Rao in Delhi in early 1938, Mawlāna Madani had said that in the present, nations (*qawm*) were defined by countries. Iqbāl took strong exception to this geographical nationalism, and wrote an article against it, which was published in the *Eḥsān*, Lahore, on 9 March 1938 (*supra* p. 71). This snowballed into a major controversy, with the Mawlāna replying to the Allāmā's criticism, which he later expressed in verse also. Although the seeds of the latter's concept of united nationalism can be seen way back in 1921, he appears to have developed it as a full-fledged theory only after this incident, as a response to Iqbāl's criticism.

Mawlāna Madani was firm in his stand, and clarified in a letter of February 1938 that he had only meant that all the inhabitants of a country, even if they belonged to different faiths and races, were regarded as a single "nation"; just as all natives of India irrespective of their different religious, linguistic, and regional affinities, were regarded elsewhere as a single Indian "nation." He reasoned that the manner in which an alien "nation" was ruining all Indians, made it obligatory on them to get rid of such a government, and the most effective means for this was to achieve complete unity, in the face of which it would be rendered helpless. He felt that for the different elements and faiths that constituted India, there could be no bond of unity except a common nationhood (*muttaḥidah qawmiyyat*) based on country, and this was why the Congress too had, in its very first session in 1885, included its cultivation among its objectives.[30]

In 1938 and after, Mawlāna Ḥusayn Aḥmad repeatedly differentiated between *millat*, which signified a "law" or "religion"; and *qawm*, which denoted merely a group of people united on the basis of race, religion, nation, language, or profession; and clarified that he had deemed the latter, and not the former, to be based on country. He quoted from the Qur'ān to show that its frequent coupling of Prophets and Muslims with an unbelieving nation (*qawm*) established that they were perceived as a single "nation", and that Muslims and others could share in a "common nationhood." He therefore concluded in a dateless letter that on the basis of country, which in European terminology was the ground of the "nation" (which he transliterated into Urdu), Indian Muslims were of the same "nation" as other Indian "nations"; but with respect to religion they were different. On the other hand there were many Muslim "nations" which were of the same race as non-Muslim "nations" such as Rājpūts, Jāts etc. Concluding that Muslims were of the same "nation", as well as different from their compatriots, he believed that there should be no conflict between their identity as Indians and as Muslims. As for the question of precedence, he would grant their "Indianness" the status of the body, and "Islāmiyyat" the rank of the soul—whereas physicality was more important for worldly existence, spirituality enjoyed greater honour.[31]

In the pamphlet *Muttaḥidah Qawmiyyat* written soon after Iqbāl's demise, besides repeating what he had said earlier Mawlāna Madani clarified that "united nationalism" did not imply deserting Islām for irreligiosity as its detractors suggested, its purpose only being to unite Indians for joint action (*Cf. Iqbāl, supra* p. 71*ff.* and *infra* p. 191-93). He envisaged that in such a unity none should oppose the other in religious matters, all the "nations" being free in this respect, and to engage peacefully in the dissemination of their faith, as also to preserve their personal law and culture. He repeated that this had been the aim of the Congress too from the very beginning. He believed that the precedent for forging "united nationalism" with non-Muslims for such purposes as outlined by him had been set by the Holy Prophet (Pbuh) himself, and cited this to counter Iqbāl's view that Islām did not permit Muslims' joining with any non-Muslim "nation" to form a single, united "nation"[32] (*Cf. Iqbāl, supra* pp. 71 and 85-86).

Mawlāna Ḥusayn Aḥmad elaborated that the Prophet (Pbuh) had formed a united "nation" and *millat* comprising Muslims and Jews in Madīnah. The detailed treaty recorded in this connection stipulated that while each group would be free in matters of religion, for other purposes mentioned therein they would be as a united *ummat* against their common enemies. He recalled that the late Mawlāna Anwar Shāh had mentioned this as a precedent in his Presidential Address at the session of the Jamī'at-al 'Ulamā'-i Hind in 1927, also citing the relevant clauses of the treaty. [Āzād we recall, had urged Muslims to follow this precedent way back in 1921—*supra* p. 158.] Mawlāna Madani pointed out that in the treaty this united body of Muslims and Jews was called not a *qawm* but an *ummat*, and that too, of *mu'minūn* or believers, despite the fact that it was partly constituted of non-Muslims. He thus concluded that Islām was flexible enough to permit its adherents to form one "nation" with non-Muslims in order to satisfy mutual needs and confront common enemies.[33]

In 1945 Mawlāna Madani spoke against the tendency to regard Hindus as the irreconcilable foe who could not be befriended, and repeated that Muslims should emulate the Prophet (Pbuh), who in order to combat the greater enemy—the Polytheists of Makkah, effected a treaty with the smaller and weaker foe—the Jews of Madīnah, making them and the Muslims one "nation."[34]

The Mawlāna's concept of nationalism thus appears to be a utilitarian one—he developed it primarily as a political tool against the British. His ideas are also close to those of Shibli, both advocating political unity among Hindus and Muslims alongside complete religious freedom (*supra* pp. 36*ff.* and 52*ff.*). However, when he denies any possibility of conflict between Islām and nationalism he appears to be taking a rather simplistic view of matters, for even such a utilitarian nationalism does imply allegiance to a certain ideology. Later however, he does face the question of a clash of loyalties, specially with religion (*infra* pp. 191-92).

Leadership of Non-Muslims

Apparently responding to criticism from Sayyad Mawdūdi for accepting the *imāmat* or leadership of non-Muslims—he advocated instead, the establishment of Muslim rule in India—Mawlāna Madani asserted in a letter of January 1942 that experience had proved the impossibility of realizing this goal in the present circumstances. Again advocating politics of expediency, he pleaded in favour of adopting the "lesser evil" (which we shall find him mentioning frequently)—since success by violent means was not possible, constitutional struggle must be undertaken, in which there was no option but to act jointly with others. He dismissed Sayyad Mawdūdi's argument that since the *imāmat* of non-Muslims was forbidden for Muslims, they should not follow the Hindus in the freedom struggle, by saying that if this was the case, their participation in all other worldly affairs where non-Muslims were in a commanding position would also be rendered unlawful. A few years earlier also he had expressed surprise that while Muslims vied with each other for participation in other joint organizations, they labelled the Congress, which was struggling for freedom, as prohibited. He felt that while broadly supporting its "composite nationalism", they were free to reject specific proposals which were antithetical to Islām.[35]

In a dateless letter Mawlāna Madani reasoned that while a non-Muslim could not undertake *imāmat* of Muslims in the literal sense of leading their prayers, there was no doubt regarding the acceptability of their guidance in secular matters, as in the war of independence. Regarding verse 28 of *Sūrah Āl-i 'Imrān* ("Let not the believers take for friends or helpers unbelievers rather than believers") which the other group cited forcefully, he held that the friendship and help which it forbade was quite different from joint action. Moreover non-Muslims had been accepted as leaders merely in the strategy of war (as they were in other secular matters), not in the war itself, which was anyway obligatory according to the injunctions of the *Sharī'at*. In order to differentiate between guidance and obedience he cited the instance of the Prophet's (Pbuh) making a polytheist ('Abdullah bin Urayqit) his leader and guide at the time of his *hijrat* to Madīnah—he also referred to it in the letter of January 1942.[36]

In September 1945 Mawlāna Madani wondered if all the furore over his "joining hands" with non-Muslims had anything to do with his membership of the Congress, which had commenced not recently but twenty-five years ago, upon his return from Malta and conversion to non-violence—prior to that he had opposed British power by violent, revolutionary means. He reaffirmed his preparedness to participate in any revolutionary party which attempted sincerely to end or reduce British power in India by non-violent means; but not in any religious or sectarian party of non-Muslims. He saw no reason for the clamour over Hindu-Muslim unity in the freedom struggle, reminding its critics that the two peoples had mingled ever since the advent of Islām in India, and every Muslim mixed with Hindus throughout his life—when the two communities were living in such close proximity, they were bound to be together in all walks of life.[37]

In a letter of April 1947 Mawlāna Madani tried to prove on the basis of *Ḥadīth* that if Muslims did not have the power to resist an enemy, under the principle of adopting the lesser evil it was permissible for them to solicit the aid of other non-Muslims in order to confront the non-believers, since expediency demanded it, and such a war was for a just purpose *i.e.* protecting Muslim interests. He thus inferred that it was not only permissible but necessary for Muslims to engage in joint action with others for India's freedom, due to the importance for them of the issues involved. He also clarified that their participation was not unconditional since they had laid down certain terms for the protection of their rights[38] (for which see *infra* p. 197).

When questioned about the advisability of co-operating with the Hindus who were also enemies of Islām on account of their unbelief, Mawlāna Madani emphasized British malevolence towards Indian and world Muslims. The Hindus on the other hand, he reasoned, had been subjects of Muslims in India for a thousand years or more, and had been promoted and set up against them by the very same English. He therefore tried to convince Muslims that it was their duty to wipe out their deadliest enemy—the British, rather than directing their ire against the Hindu who was far less powerful. He felt that to say that in future he might prove to be a greater enemy, was an imaginary fear based on mere conjecture. Since the Congress aimed at securing freedom from British rule, Muslims participated in it, and the Jamī'at-al 'Ulamā' was acting jointly with it—however this was justifiable only so long as the Congress remained faithful to this goal.[39]

Islām is Not an Exclusive Faith

Mawlāna Ḥusayn Aḥmad refuted those who asserted that Islām and its adherents could not associate with any other system (Iqbāl and Āzād's stand in this respect is comparable—*supra* pp. 71, 86 and 149-50). He reasoned that although Islāmic law had prescribed the course of action in many matters, numerous others which did not interfere with their religion had been left to the liberty and discretion of the believers. He felt it was mistaken to make certain collective commands of the *Sharī'at* an excuse against Islām's uniting with other collective institutions, since it was neither obligatory, nor even permissible for individuals to act on these commandments as long as the government was not in Muslim hands (*Cf. infra* p. 196). He emphasized Islām's flexibility—in spite of knowing others to be on the wrong path, it allowed friendly social, political, and economic relations, and inter-marriage with them, its principles of collective organization being guided by tolerance and even magnanimity. In a letter of July 1931 too he had reasoned that since Islām was a missionary religion it was required to assimilate other nations (*qawm*) rather than drive them away; for intimacy, by mitigating hatred which produced only obduracy and ignorance of the positive qualities of Islām, would attract others towards it. He believed that this was the reason for regarding the treaty of Hudaybiyah as a manifest victory (48:1).[40]

United Nationalism and Islāmic Unity

Apparently responding to Iqbāl's charge that the kind of geographical nationalism which he proposed in India tended to undermine Islāmic unity (*supra* p. 70), Mawlāna Madani asserted in a letter of February 1938 that he and his associates had always not only preached, but acted upon the principle of the unity of the Islāmic *millat* irrespective of race and country, which had even entailed imprisonment and hardships for them. He wrote again of the spiritual bond by means of which Islām united its whole community, and in comparison to which all other connections (it is interesting that here he mentions among others, that of "nation" too), paled in significance. This link was reinforced by Islāmic commandments which enjoined such duties and rights of world Muslims upon each other that differences of race and "nation" were obliterated, and they became as a single entity. Again quoting Traditions which likened them to brothers, and different parts of a single organism, he repeated that this demanded that if a Muslim was oppressed in any part of the world, the obligation of dispelling the injury devolved by degrees on all the Muslims of the world since their strength and honour, as also their king and caliph, was one.[41] We recall that he had expressed much the same sentiments in 1921, to urge Indian Muslims to rise to the aid of the Turkish caliphate (*supra* pp. 174-75).

Describing this unity as pan-Islāmism, Mawlāna Ḥusayn Aḥmad credited it with achieving the phenomenonal military triumphs of Muslims, and the exaltation of Islām over all the religions, races and "nations" of the world. He reasoned that in order to overcome the Muslim "nation" and protect themselves from its world-conquering attacks, the enemies of Islām and particularly the Christian world, which was frustrated and enfeebled by Ottoman Turkish attacks, tried by every means to wipe out this "spirit of pan-Islāmism" (*Cf.* Āzād, *supra* pp. 132-33). After centuries of organized efforts it succeeded in impressing upon them the distinctions of race, country and language, as also the idea that rather than being religious and spiritual, *jihād* should be waged only for one's race and country. By thus wiping out sympathy for the Turks not only among their Christian subjects, but among Muslim "nations" as well, Europe succeeded in weakening the Ottoman caliphate (which at its zenith had begun to threaten European shores), by destroying its very foundations, till even the Turks themselves became disillusioned with it.[41]

Mawlāna Ḥusayn Aḥmad lamented that at this juncture no Muslim had risen to champion Islāmic unity and condemn nationalism based on race, language, etc. Commenting on Iqbāl's objection to territorial nationalism (*supra* pp. 71 and 86), he observed that now that pan-Islāmism (or international Islāmic sympathy) had been destroyed and Muslim countries had become the choice morsel of European nations, they were being told that Islām preaches only unity of the *millat* and could not forge, with any non-Muslim group, a "united nationalism" founded on bonds of country, race, or profession, for to do so would endanger its very existence, and encourage its absorption into other "nations." He found it strange that although Muslims had never been absorbed in the majority in the past despite their small numbers, this apprehension was being voiced in the present, when their numbers had greatly increased. He felt that the very [geographical] nationalism which the west had commended lavishly until the survival of the Islāmic caliphate was now being made out to be anathema, since its growth in India would herald the end of British rule. He felt on the other hand that in order to successfully overwhelm their enemy, Muslims should employ against it those very weapons by which it had destroyed them.[43]

We recall that Iqbāl had opposed territorial nationalism as conflicting with his concept of Islāmic universalism (*supra* p. 66 *ff*). Mawlāna Madani also credited him with the view that Muslim nationhood (*qawmiyyat)* was based only on human dignity and brotherhood, rather than on geographical boundaries, racial unity, or colour; and refuted it on the grounds that this could not be proved from any text of the Qur'ān or *Ḥadīth*. Furthermore it implied that whereas all human beings could be said to comprise a single "nation", those sharing a common country or race could not be thus described. However he appears not to have presented Iqbāl's views faithfully, who had based Muslim nationhood on unity of belief and only "potentially" on the "ideal of a universal humanity" (*supra* pp. 60*ff.* and 66*ff.*). There does not appear to be much difference between them on the second point, for the Mawlāna too agreed that as regards preaching and assimilation, Muslim "nationhood" was based on the brotherhood of man, and this was what gave it a universal character [we recall that Iqbāl had said much the same thing]—he however held that co-operation, sympathy, and true friendship were confined to those within the fold of Islām. He also agreed that while the *Sharī'at* acknowledged the differences between "nations", it also enjoined that all be treated alike as equals and brothers.[44]

We have seen Mawlāna Ḥusayn Aḥmad dwelling at length on the bond that existed between all Muslims (*supra* pp. 188-89). He however held that Islām permitted them to enter into a "united nationalism" with non-Muslims too, on the basis of other bonds such as those of race, country, profession etc.; to rout a common enemy or further common national, political, economic, and other interests; without allowing Islāmic principles to suffer in any way. He was convinced of the undeniable need to do so in India, and felt it was mistaken to regard co-operation with other Indian nations (*qawm*) as forbidden merely on account of their faith. He did not agree with Iqbāl that it was prohibited for Muslims to join with others as a single "nation" on the basis of bonds other than the religious, merely on the grounds that in modern western terminology, nationalism (*qawmiyyat*) was used to denote principles of collective human organization which were often antithetical to religion, and specifically Islām (*supra* pp. 71 and 73-74). He reasoned that the objection must be confined only to that particular usage, and clarified that this connotation of the term "nationalism" was neither commonly present in the minds of the people, nor was the Congress or the Jamī'at-al 'Ulamā' in favour of it. He therefore dismissed the objection as being irrelevant to the debate.[45]

Mawlāna Madani ruled out any possibility of a conflict between religion and such a secular nationalism (*Cf. supra* pp. 184-85), drawing an analogy with the different simultaneous relationships that an individual held with others, whose demands though varied, did not clash. He believed that in like manner it was also possible for a Muslim to participate in a "united nationalism" with non-Muslim organizations, while he also continued to remain a flag-bearer of the unity of the world-wide Islāmic *millat*, fulfilling his duties to each according to the particular agreement and the dictates of religion. He therefore concluded that the Muslims of India could, while living in India and forming a single "Hindustani *qawm*", remain Muslims, preserving their religion, culture, personal law, language, and rights. Alongside this they could also establish religious links with the whole Muslim world, fulfilling all the duties of religious unity enjoined by Islām, for "composite nationalism" did not in any way clash with mutual relations between Muslims. On the basis of the 72nd verse of *Surah al-Anfāl*:

> *"But if they seek*
> *Your aid in religion,*
> *It is your duty*
> *To help them,*
> *Except against a people*

> *With whom you have*
> *A treaty of mutual alliance".*

he even inferred that a Muslim would have to refrain from help and succour to the Islāmic world community if it entailed contravention of any agreement he may have entered into with non-Muslims.[46]

It would do well to keep in mind that this verse was meant to elucidate that the newly formed Islāmic state at Madīnah had no obligations except the purely religious, towards those Muslims who had preferred to stay on in Makkah rather than risk emigration to Madīnah; and even in religious matters they could be helped only if it did not entail contravention of any treaty entered into by the Madīnan state. Later the verse was used to deduce the principle that an Islāmic state has no obligations towards extra-territorial Muslims. The Mawlāna has however applied it to the Indian situation which was quite different in that it comprised a secular polity to which Muslims, like other groups, were a party. He appears in effect to have differentiated between a secular and a religious nationalism, using the word *qawm* for the heterogeneous group united by the former, and *millat* for the world-wide Muslim community bound by the latter. He appears to be employing this verse to argue in favour of precedence for the former in case of a conflict between the two (although he had earlier asserted that they could coexist without clashing, as parallel ideologies—*supra* pp. 184-85). This also appears at variance with his earlier stand, when he had cited numerous texts from the Qur'ān, *Ḥadīth*, and books of law, to emphasize that very world-unity of Islām (and that all world Muslims must *always* come to each other's aid—*supra* pp. 175 and 189), which on the basis of a single verse he now appears to be undermining in favour of a geographical nationalism.

United Nationalism and Religion

As for the notion that nationalism would endanger their religiosity, Mawlāna Ḥusayn Aḥmad believed that the British had planted it in the minds of Indians to turn them against it. In an obvious reference to the leaders of the Muslim League, he wrote that it was strange that on this issue those westernized leaders who followed the English in appearance and dress and betrayed no attachment for religion, were attacking the *'ulamā'* who were steeped in religion, and servants of the faith. He clarified that by "united nationalism" was meant only "joint action", and it certainly did not entail deserting Islām for a system synonymous with atheism, as its opponents claimed.[47]

As for the objection that coexistence with, and proximity to other nations (*qawm*) would make Muslims negligent about religion, and gradually these religious groups (*millat*) would be wiped out, leaving behind irreligiosity as the only common factor between the people of this united "nation" [we recall that these objections had been voiced most eloquently by Iqbāl—*supra* p. 74], Mawlāna Madani felt that it was totally unfounded, and was possible only if firmness of religion, and concern for its preservation were lacking. He felt that the same danger was posed more imminently by the political and economic institutions of the day; intimacy with the English; and most of all by western education; due to which irreligiosity and materialism were daily on the rise among the Indian youth, including educated Muslims. Yet modern education could not be completely shunned, for he felt that the actual reason behind this was unfamiliarity with, and lack of firmness in religion.[48]

Answering another objection raised by Iqbāl (*supra* pp. 72-73), Mawlāna Ḥusayn Aḥmad wrote that it was mistaken to declare "composite nationalism" as prohibited, since as practised in Europe it was opposed to Islām. Drawing an analogy with democracy, he felt that whereas Islām had laid its foundation, Muslims could not now declare it to be forbidden merely because Europe had associated with it many things which were contrary to Islāmic teachings. If, finding religion incompatible with its interpretation of nationalism Europe had bid adieu to the former, or confined it to private life, he did not think it necessary that the progress of Indian Muslims towards "united nationalism" should be accompanied by the same circumstances. He felt further that it was unjustified to weave conjectures on the basis of the conditions prevailing in Europe, since even before the advent of nationalism it had possessed religion in a very minor degree, and no programme for its preservation.[49] He thus differed with Iqbāl on the wisdom of taking the west as an illustration of the results of nationalism. Since he advocated an Islāmic rather than the western concept of nationalism, its experience was immaterial for him.

Muslim Identity

Only on one occasion do we find Mawlāna Ḥusayn Aḥmad dealing explicitly with this important idea which is intimately related to the concept of nationhood. Responding to a query regarding the sneers directed at Muslims in government offices and public places due to their peculiar dress and appearance, and the admissibility of following European ways, he wrote in a dateless letter that the nation (*qawm*) and country which did not guard its distinguishing traits—he called these its "uniform"—very soon lost its identity, and was assimilated into other "nations." He felt that if Muslims, who had settled in India more than a thousand years back, had not guarded their particular "uniform", they would have merged into the indigenous "nation" like those who came before them. They succeeded in maintaining their independent existence in India only because they preserved not only their external peculiarities of dress etc., but also their religion, culture, traditions, language, and architecture, and would continue to do so as long as they kept this in mind.[50] This is in contrast to Āzād's glorification of the merging of Hindu and Muslim identity into a joint Indian nationhood (*supra* pp. 158-59).

This was how Mawlāna Madani interpreted the *Ḥadīth:* "He who imitates a nation becomes one of them"—it defined the need to establish a distinctive Islāmic "uniform", and to lay down one's life for its preservation, regarding it as equivalent to the preservation of the faith and the Muslim "nation." He was strongly opposed to imitating European ways and reasoned that as followers of the Prophet (Pbuh) Muslims should follow him in all matters including appearance, conduct, and culture, and abhor those of the Europeans since they had proved themselves to be his greatest enemies.[51]

It is interesting that Sir Sayyad had used similar imagery in December 1988 while urging Muslim students to faithfully observe the canonical prayers, describing these as their "uniform" *i.e.* the external symbol of their membership of the Islāmic community. Neglecting their prayers was thus tantamount to discarding their uniform, leading to their exclusion from God's army *i.e.* the Muslim "nation."[52]

Muslim Rule and Independence

As we have observed, in a speech of 1921 one of the arguments that Mawlāna Ḥusayn Aḥmad had employed to convince Muslims that it was their religious duty to turn the English out of India, was that it was unlawful for them to take their disputes to the un-Islāmic British-Indian courts. On other occasions too he would appeal to them to overthrow the British on the grounds that the system established by them was wholly against Islāmic principles (*supra*

p. 179). In a letter of April 1947 he again appealed for the overthrow of British authority on the plea that categorical orders of the Qur'ān and *Ḥadīth* proved that far from being content with slavery Islām demanded rule, power, and authority.[53]

However the Mawlāna's detractors and those opposed to joint action with the Congress were quick to point out that the new system proposed to be set up with the co-operation of non-Muslims would not be purely Islāmic either, whereas it was the duty of Muslims to set up a wholly Islāmic order.

In the pamphlet *Muttaḥidah Qawmiyyat* Mawlāna Madani explicated his stand thus: it was imperative to devise means of deliverance from British rule in the face of the devastation caused by it. However if the power to establish a purely Islāmic government was lacking at present, the principle of the "lesser evil" should be followed (*i.e.* a government of all Indians, which provided safeguards for Muslims). He further held that as long they did not have government in their hands, it was neither obligatory, nor even permissible for Muslims to act on the collective commandments of the *Sharī'at* (such as those regarding the penal code), which hinged on Islāmic rule, and were therefore not addressed to Muslim individuals, but rulers. He believed that in such circumstances the duty of individuals was only to strive as much as was in their power to establish an Islāmic government. He also made the significant concession that until they succeeded in doing so, they should take such steps as were most beneficial for the community.[54]

In a letter of January 1942 Mawlāna Madani wrote that while every Muslim desired Islāmic rule (just as adherents of other faiths wanted the government of their own religion), Sayyad Mawdūdi's view that they should strive to establish it in India was "incomprehensible", since prevailing conditions precluded the possibility of its realization. He believed that the dying out of the six hundred-year-old Muslim rule in India, resulting in its enslavement at foreign hands, bore out the unfavourableness of the circumstances. Perhaps in a bid to further demonstrate the impracticability of the ideal, he pointed out that Muslims in other parts of the world were also enslaved, and even where they were free, the divine government prescribed by Sayyad Mawdūdi was non-existent. He reasoned that the attainment of such a goal was all the more difficult (and well-nigh impossible) particularly for Indian Muslims due to their peculiar situation, surrounded as they were by an unjust Christian government on the one hand, and an overwhelming non-Muslim majority on the other, with the former fanning the differences between them and the latter. Besides their helplessness, penury, and lack of command over violent means, the total failure of the efforts of the *'ulamā'* of former times in this direction, was for him further proof of its impracticability.[55]

Appealing for realism in politics, Mawlāna Madani pleaded that it could not rely solely on philosophy, but must also respect historical truths and practical constraints which compelled one to turn to the policy of "the lesser evil", for to be blind to prevailing conditions heralded death and suicide. He repeated that since the present circumstances in India (which was *dār-al ḥarb*), were not conducive to the establishment of divine government, the enforcement of the articles of Islāmic law was not obligatory on Muslims. In support of his view he cited the fact that even the most binding Islāmic commandments were subject to changes according to altered circumstances, and many forbidden things were permitted in extraordinary conditions. He also felt that the manner in which the Prophet (Pbuh) had adapted his political strategy to the prevailing circumstances should enlighten and guide Muslims: in Madīnah he made a pact with its Jewish tribes, and warred against the polytheists of Makkah. Later when circumstances so demanded, he did not hesitate to take on the former, and in Hudaybiyah, made peace with the latter[56] (*Cf. supra* pp. 183 and 185).

The hallmark of the Mawlāna's political philosophy thus appears to be expediency and realism rather than uncompromising idealism. However his philosophy can be distorted into one of pure convenience and political opportunism—similar arguments can be applied against his theory of the necessity of *jihād* against the British—that it was impractical in the prevailing circumstances due to the weakness of Muslims etc.; or can be used by hypocrites as an excuse to plead their inability to fulfil none but the most basic religious obligations. The comparison he draws with relaxation of rules in extraordinary circumstances does not seem to apply, since in that case concessions are being prescribed by the law itself; whereas he is recommending that believers may be forced by circumstances to fall short of the ideal. Had he altogether denied the need or obligation to establish a Muslim state it would have simplified matters enormously, but the fact that he does not, compels him to walk a tight-rope as it were.

Similarly, although it is true that as a statesman the Prophet (Pbuh) formulated his political strategy according to the demands of the situation, it is also an undeniable fact that in pursuit of truth and justice he struggled against heavy odds on numerous occasions. Islām thus appears to demand a delicate balance between worldly sagacity and a blind commitment to the faith. The Mawlāna's comparison of the desire for Islāmic rule with the ambitions of hegemony harboured by other groups is also a little incongruous, for Islām desires power not merely for its own sake, but so that it may establish its own true and just system. However, as we shall presently see, perhaps he is not as averse to the idea of Muslim rule as he appears, being opposed only to any attempt to implement it immediately. His political theory being an evolutionary one, the objectives he is advocating are not an end in themselves, but only a means to an end, which may not be very different from what Sayyad Mawdūdi had in mind, only that his method of arriving at it is very different.

Regarding the question of whether or not Muslims should make their support to the Hindus in the struggle for independence conditional upon the fulfilment of their demands such as safeguards, Mawlāna Ḥusayn Aḥmad wrote in a letter of April 1947 that it was more urgent to first ward off injury rather than secure benefits. He therefore held that the present circumstances urgently demanded that Muslims join hands with others to turn the English out of India—the question of demanding rights and consolidating their future position were issues which they could settle later with their fellow-countrymen. He thus envisioned the co-operation of the various Indian nations (*qawm*) in the peaceful struggle against the British, and later their participation in building the new post-independence order. For the present, he justified the co-operation of Muslims with unbelievers on the condition that in the future they would play an influential role in governance; their personal law, religious institutions, and culture would be preserved; and that Muslim majority governments would be formed in at least five provinces, which would be independent in internal educational, economic, cultural, and social matters[57] (*Cf.* Āzād, *supra* pp. 165-66).

Mawlāna Ḥusayn Aḥmad felt that the joint order to be set up after independence was the "lesser evil" as compared to the present arrangement. He envisioned a democratic government in India, whose elected executive may or may not be a Muslim. Admitting the lower proportion of Muslims in the central government, he proposed safeguards in the constitution to ensure the protection of their religious, political, and economic rights, particularly in provinces where they were in a minority. He envisaged a loosely federal rather than unitary political structure, with the centre enjoying jurisdiction over very limited subjects, while all other internal matters would fall under the purview of the provincial governments, as this would provide freedom for the interplay of Islāmic forces. He felt that even while remaining part of such a union, if Muslims so desired, they could implement Islāmic ideals in social, cultural, and economic matters—to the extent that collaboration with other "nations" permitted it[58]—the inclusion of this condition is interesting.

While Mawlāna Madani conceded that this joint arrangement could not be wholly true to Islāmic ideals, he felt it depended on the missionary work undertaken by the Muslims (who would comprise an important and effective element in it), as to how far they could mould the future system on Islāmic lines. While he accepted as an undisputed truth that only Islāmic laws ensured true peace and security for the world, and that their absolute authority could not be established in the joint government of free India, he believed that it was the intellectual and practical duty of Muslims to make other "nations" concede this status of Islāmic law. He made the significant observation that the "lesser evil" could not be the final goal, and far from being closed by India's independence, the ways of endeavour and action would continue to remain open to Muslims.[59]

Thus independence for the Mawlāna was perhaps an intermediate step to a final goal which he did not outline very clearly, although here we do find a crucial hint to his future plans and the means by which he proposes to arrive at an Islāmic, or in the beginning a quasi-Islāmic order. However the theory appears a little unrealistic and even naive, for political moves are unlikely to be influenced by missionary work—as he had himself admitted two years back, they were motivated more by economic than other factors (*supra* p. 176). We recall that Iqbāl had also proposed safeguards and a federal structure for free India; as for Āzād, while he was in favour of the latter, his stand regarding the former is a little ambiguous (*supra* pp. 81-83 and 165-66).

Mawlāna Ḥusayn Aḥmad felt that since education would be under the jurisdiction of the provincial government, the Muslims in the majority provinces would not face any problems on that score. Elsewhere too, they could either arrange for their religious education themselves, or demand its protection by the government. He believed (unlike Sir Sayyad, *supra* p. 18) that merely the fact of acquiring education in the company of non-Muslims would not endanger their nationhood if the system and syllabus of such education was not opposed to their national (*qawmi*) and *milli* temper. Since it was impossible to avoid co-operation with non-Muslims in all walks of life, in such a situation the propagation of purely Islāmic culture among Muslims, and the repulsion of non-Islāmic influences could be achieved through the activities of voluntary reformative institutions. As for the apprehension that the foreign policy of free India might clash with Islāmic considerations, he hoped that the large number of Muslims in the country; their "independent governments" in various provinces; the crucial geographical location of these; their relations with neighbouring Muslim countries; and the "national" religious and political unity of Muslims [apparently at the international level], would serve as guarantees against the possibility.[60]

Hindu-Muslim Relations

In a letter of July 1931 Mawlāna Ḥusayn Aḥmad wrote that history proved that when Muslims first came to India there was great intimacy between them and the natives, which led to a large number of conversions. He felt that later in self-defence, the Brahmans let loose a propaganda of hatred against the Muslims since the peaceful tide of Islām threatened their hegemony—they were successful, and this mentality soon spread. Whereas the early Muslim rulers combated all opposition by the use of force, Mawlāna Madani credited the Mughal emperors, and particularly Akbar, with having first attempted to root out this attitude—he not only captured individual hearts, but rendered hollow the very roots of the Hindu mentality. Betraying great admiration for this monarch, he felt that if Akbar's policy had been consistently followed, the stratagem of the Brahmans would have failed, and Muslims would have been in a majority in India—but unfortunately he erred in his interpretation of Islām, which turned Muslims against him[61](*Cf.* Shibli, *supra* p. 49).

In the above letter and a speech of 1945 Mawlāna Ḥusayn Aḥmad appealed for good relations with the Hindus on the plea that though non-Muslims, all the rights of neighbours enjoined by Islām were due to them. In a language and manner strongly reminiscent of

Sir Sayyad (*supra* p. 10), he emphasized that most Muslims were native converts and even the blood of those of foreign origin had mingled with Indians through marriage. Besides these old bonds of kinship, in the present too they shared intimate relations, had much in common, and needed each other. He reminded Muslims that ten crore of them could not leave India to settle elsewhere—they were its inhabitants, had been born there, and had to live there; and therefore they would have to be tolerant towards each other, for without amity it was impossible to coexist in India.[62]

Divide and Rule

Mawlāna Madani felt in 1931 that having realized that the best way to fulfil its imperial ambitions was by sowing discord between the different Indian nations (*qawm*), the British government continued to follow this policy to the present day, and its success in India could be attributed to it. In various writings and speeches of 1945 he repeatedly asserted, on the authority of British historians themselves, that Theodore Beck's (a close associate of Sir Sayyad and Principal of the Aligarh College from 1883 to 1893) refrain about Hindu-Muslim hostility was entirely mistaken, for they had lived in concord for centuries before the advent of the British, who for the perpetuation of their own rule sowed discord between them (through their scheme of education, among other things), which therefore could not be attributed to religious differences.[63]

Mawlāna Ḥusayn Aḥmad wrote that Britain had used the same technique of divide and rule to combat Indian nationalism (*jazbah-i qawmiyyat*), which posed the greatest threat to its power, specially since the formation of the Congress. He felt that three successive Principals of the Aligarh College, Beck, Morrison, and Archibald had been most active in turning Indians, and particularly Muslims, against "nationalism" by spreading vicious propaganda against it. He felt that even an intrepid and intelligent person like Sir Sayyad who had said much in favour of "united nationalism" (and the Mawlāna quoted him extensively), was misled by Beck and his associates. He quoted Shibli in support of this view, who appears to have expressed a similar opinion, albeit in very couched language in his article "Musalmānoṇ ki Political Karwat."[64] The Mawlāna felt that not only Sir Sayyad but other Muslim politicians such as Iqbāl too were beguiled by British tactics. They spread hatred among the people in their attempts to prove that Muslims could not share a "common nationhood" with others, and nor should they participate in the freedom struggle; without realizing that they were thus rendering a great service to the British.[65]

In 1938 and 1945 Mawlānā Madani felt that in a similar manner the British had consistently maligned the Congress since no matter how slow its struggle, it spelt doom for them. He claimed on the authority of Sayyad Ṭufayl Aḥmad's *Musalmānoṇ ka Rawshan Mustaqbil* that the efforts of Beck and his successors left a deep impression not only on Sir Sayyad and others of the Aligarh College, but produced sectarian hatred and disenchantment, not only with the Congress but all Hindus, among educated Muslims in general. Beck had tried to convince them that Anglo-Muslim unity was possible, but not Hindu-Muslim amity : since Indians were sharply divided over religious issues, they could never unite and govern themselves democratically.[66]

Between 1938 and April 1947 Mawlānā Ḥusayn Aḥmad expressed the view that the revival of the issue of Hindi and Urdu by making the former the official language in U.P. in 1900; the *shuddhi* and *sangathan* movements (see *supra* p. 171, note 81); the formation under British patronage of the Muslim League and the Hindu Mahasabha in 1906, and their being nurtured to the present day; were all a part of British efforts against the Congress. He felt that the fact that Archibald had taken a keen interest in the presentation of the Simla Deputation, and the League continued to enjoy the patronage of the Viceroy and other British officers, bore this out. He believed that it was in keeping with the policy of divide and rule that whenever the struggle for independence gained momentum the British kindled sectarian quarrels at different places, for which the League and the Mahāsabha served as convenient instruments. Then they proclaimed to the world that despite their desire to transfer power they were compelled to stay on in India in order to maintain peace, and protect the Muslim minority which would otherwise be annihilated by the majority (which incidentally was also the refrain of the League). He therefore appealed in 1945 to all political parties, that since Britain was making their differences an excuse for their subjugation, they should agree upon a common solution to India's constitutional problem.[67]

The Congress, the Jamī'at and the League

Between 1938 and 1947 Mawlānā Madani strongly defended the Congress as an association of all Indians, that worked without discrimination for their common good, which he felt was borne out by the fact that among its Presidents had been numerous Muslims, Christians, and Parsis. He unhesitatingly attributed to its ceaseless efforts, the success achieved against the British. He reassured the Muslims that there was nothing in the "united nationalism" which the Congress desired to create in India that might adversely affect their religion, culture, or personal law. He felt that since the Jamī'at-al 'Ulamā' and the Congress were marching along the same road towards a common goal, it was not surprising that they should act jointly. He asserted that far from blindly following the Congress, as an independent organization the Jamī'at had opposed it whenever it was perceived to be going against Islāmic principles. While continuing to take active interest in Muslim politics outside India, on religious issues such as countering the *shuddhi* movement it had worked independently of the former. He felt that rather than making the misdoings of a few prejudiced individuals in it an excuse for disassociating with the Congress as a whole, they should be criticized, as was being done by the Jamī'at.[68]

Mawlāna Ḥusayn Aḥmad's attitude towards the Muslim League was highly disparaging and critical, specially between 1945 and 1947. He alleged that it was born out of the favours of the English, and quoted Shibli to the effect that the pro-British and anti-Hindu spirit behind its inception was still at work within it (see *supra* p. 52). He charged it with spreading hatred against the Hindus and the Congress by deceiving the Muslims into believing that the twin danger posed them a great threat, even while it deliberately overlooked the harm caused by the British. He felt that far from struggling for India's freedom (except in 1914 and 1919), by acting as an impediment in its way the League was rendering a great service to British imperialism. He accused Jinnāh of not desiring freedom, and was strongly critical of his policy of avoiding "direct action" against the British on the plea that it was against Islāmic interests. The Mawlāna believed that mere threats and constitutional protests were insufficient, as was evident from the government's persistent indifference to the demands of the League.[69]

Mawlāna Madani accused the leaders of the League of falsely claiming to be the sole representative of Muslims, while they were not only unacquainted with, but opposed to religion. He recalled that while the Jamī'at had agreed to co-operate with the League in 1936-37 on the understanding that its opinion would be followed in religious matters, the League had deliberately flouted Islām in the matter of the Sharda Bill, Khula' Bill, Qāḍi Bill etc. He also blamed it for spreading hatred and triggering off a spate of sectarian riots through provocative speeches and writings, ever since it adopted the resolution of direct action on 16 August 1946, and declared *jihād* thereafter. At the same time he hastened to clarify that while it regarded all Muslims as brothers and bore no hostility against the League, the Jamī'at was forced to maintain a distance from it for the reasons mentioned above.[70]

Pakistan

In 1945 Mawlāna Ḥusayn Aḥmad denied any connection between the demand for Pakistan and the alleged atrocities committed by the Congress governments. Calling the latter a lie forged to arouse the passions of the masses, and dismissing the Pīrpūr Report (*supra* p. 103) as carrying no weight, he challenged the League to prove its allegations against the Congress. He also pointed out that whereas these governments had come to power towards the end of 1936, the demand had first been made in 1930, and in 1933 Chawdhry Raḥmat 'Ali of Cambridge had even coined the name of the proposed province (see *supra* p. 92, note 104). He on the other hand described the idea of Pakistan as a brainchild of the Tories, which they had planted among the Muslim delegates to the second Round Table Conference in 1931 (in return for promised support to them against the Hindus), and the Muslim students of Cambridge and Oxford, in order to continue their hold over India.[71] (Professor Ziya-ul Hasan Faruqi[72] and Wilfred Cantwell Smith[73] have also documented evidence of Britain's undue interest in the scheme in 1932 and 1933, at a time when the Muslim response to it was not even lukewarm).

Mawlāna Madani believed that the strategy of the British had been exposed in 1931 after the leakage to the Press, of a letter of one Plowden, a judge of the United Provinces, in which he had favoured a division of India and subsequent British control over, and trade links with the Muslim part, since the Hindus had completely turned against them. By thus perpetually setting off one against the other they would also ensure their prolonged presence in the subcontinent as peacekeepers. The Mawlāna was thus convinced that the issue of partition had wholly been created by the British, and therefore they were exerting themselves so strongly in its favour—the extraordinary support and patronage extended by them to the League being for him further evidence of this, and of a secret agreement between the two parties. He felt that having firmly resolved to partition India to serve their own interests, the British were deceiving Indians, and particularly Muslims, who were once more being caught in the snare of the old British policy of divide and rule. He felt that Jinnāh particularly was facilitating their plans, and as evidence of this the Mawlāna quoted a statement made by him on 29 February 1944 [which we have been unable to trace], to the effect that while India would be internally free, military and foreign policy control of the British would be essential as long as the two parts did not coexist in peace[74] (*Cf.* Jinnāh, *supra* p. 125).

Mawlāna Madani felt that at a time when the world was gradually abandoning the absurd political policy of division and separation, and attempts were being made to bring the nations (*qawm*) of the world closer to form an international federation; the demand for separation on the basis of culture and race [it is interesting that he does not include religion], was not only absurd, but ruinous. He felt further that far from being a solution to their ills, the idea of Pakistan would prove to be detrimental for Muslims of both the majority and minority provinces. He feared that after having secured supposed freedom from the Hindus, the governments of the proposed states of Bengal and Panjab would, being weak, again succumb to the kind of foreign subjugation under which they were at present groaning. He therefore felt that merely on the grounds of what they perceived to be Hindu narrow-mindedness, Muslims should not take such a step. Accordingly he appealed to Muslims not to view everything only in the light of an anti-Hindu feeling, and to so reform the *millat* that it became a living and vibrant "nation." Rather than separating to become enslaved, they should unite with the Hindus, thereby not only keeping intact their own freedom, but also benefitting from the resources of a united India. He was also quick to point out that if Jinnāh's contention that Muslims and Hindus could never peacefully coexist in a united India was accepted, then Pakistan too could never remain peaceful, since its forty per cent Hindu population would always be in conflict with the Muslim government and people, specially because they were educated, wealthy landowners, and better organized than the poor and debt-ridden Muslim peasantry[75] (*Cf. supra* p. 111).

In a speech of 19 September 1945 Mawlāna Ḥusayn Aḥmad opposed the scheme of Pakistan on the grounds that it would limit the right of Islāmic missionary activity to a particular area. He wanted to bridge the gulf of hatred being created by the protagonists of the scheme, since the propagation of hatred towards those very non-Muslims who were the field of action for this missionary work would only cause this raw material to be wasted, which was against the message of the Prophet (Pbuh). While crediting the missionary work of the *'ulamā'* with bringing about an increase in the number of Muslims, he emphasized that the preaching and progress of Islām required an atmosphere of compassion and justice. (*Cf. supra* p. 188).

In 1945 Mawlāna Ḥusayn Aḥmad felt that the leaders of the League were deceiving Muslims when some of them claimed that an Islāmic government based on the *Sharī'at* and the administration of the Pious Caliphs would be established in Pakistan. Claiming that if assured of this the members of the Jamī'at-al 'Ulamā' would be the first to respond to their call; he commented on the incompatibility of such promises for the revival of religion with those whose lives were far removed from religiosity. He held that elsewhere the same leaders had made it amply clear that the government of Pakistan would not be religious (by their own admission this was possible only if either all the people belonged to the same faith, or there was enough armed power to keep the others in submission), but wholly democratic, secular, and socialist (*Cf.* Jinnāh, *supra* p. 119*ff.*). Since he felt that the confusion had deliberately been created in order to mislead the Muslim masses and gain their sympathy, he sought to enlighten those who were labouring under the delusion perpetrated by the League—that the formation of Pakistan would facilitate the establishment of an Islāmic government.[77]

In a letter of April 1947 Mawlāna Madani reasoned that the presence of a forty per cent-strong and organized non-Muslim minority precluded such a possibility. The League leaders had clarified that there would be a joint system of government in Pakistan, with both Muslims and others participating in it with equal rights and powers, albeit in different proportions. He believed that a shared system of government could not be described as Islāmic or divine—the difference in numerical proportion of both groups could not alter its joint character. He reasoned that since in internal matters provinces would enjoy as much autonomy in a united federation as under two centres of power, even while remaining a part of the former in India; in social, cultural, and economic matters Muslims could implement Islāmic principles to the extent that collaboration with other nations (*qawm*) permitted it[78] (*Cf. supra* pp. 197-98).

Notes and References

All references in this chapter unless otherwise specified, are to the works of Sayyad Ḥusayn Aḥmad Madani.

1. *Taqrīr Jalsah Syohārah-o Khuṭbah-i Ṣadārat, Taqrīr Jalsah Dihli* (n.p, n.d) p. 64.
2. *Ibid.*, pp. 3-4 and 38-40.
3. *Ibid.*
4. *Ibid.*, pp. 4-6.
5. *Ibid.*, pp. 6, 10-12 and 40-43.
6. *Ibid.*, pp. 8-9, 12-14 and 41-43.
7. *Ibid.*, pp. 15-17.
8. *Ibid.*, pp. 43-44 and 47-48.
9. *Ibid.*, pp. 45-47.
10. *Ibid.*, p. 47.
11. *Pākistān Kya Hay,* 2 vols (Delhi, 1946) vol. I, pp. 3-4 and 6.
12. *Taqrīr*, pp. 26, 31 and 55-56.
13. *Ibid.*, pp. 28-29, 51-52 and 54-57.
14. *Ibid.*, pp. 4-7.
15. *Ibid.*, pp. 26-28.
16. Najm-al Dīn Iṣlāḥi, ed., *Maktūbāt-i Shaykh-al Islām*, 3 vols. (Deoband, 1371 A.H.) vol. I, p. 397, vol. II, p. 128.
17. *Taqrīr*, pp. 53 and 80.
18. *Ibid.*, p. 30.
19. *Muslim Līg Kya Hay* (Delhi, 1945) pp. 28-29; *Maktūbāt* II, pp. 128-130.
20. *Taqrīr*, pp. 26-29, 48-50 and 81.
21. *Ibid.*, pp. 17-18; *Muslim Līg Kya Hay*, pp. 28-29; *Maktūbāt* I, pp. 345-46; *Maktūbāt* II, pp. 130-31; *Muttaḥidah Qawmiyyat Awr Islām* (New Delhi, *n.d.*) pp. 68-69; *Khuṭbah-i Ṣadārat*: *Jamī'at-al 'Ulamā'-i Hind Ka Ijlās-i Sahāranpur,* May 1945 (Delhi, 1945) p. 35.
22. *Taqrīr*, pp. 65-69 and 73-79.
23. *Ibid.*, *Muttaḥidah Qawmiyyat*, p. 70.
24. *Taqrīr*, pp. 32 and 58.
25. *Ibid.*, pp. 82-83; *Nazaryah-i Qawmiyyat Par Mawlāna Ḥusayn Aḥmad Madani Awr Allāmah Iqbāl Ki 'Ālimānah Khaṭ-o Kitābat* (Lahore, n.d.) pp. 43-44; *Maktūbāt* I, pp. 199-200 and 325-26.
26. *Taqrīr*, p. 60; *Maktūbāt* I, pp. 325-26, 349-350 and 357; *Maktūbāt* II, pp. 118-19; *Muttaḥidah Qawmiyyat*, pp. 68-70.
27. *Maktūbāt* II, pp. 116-17; *Muttaḥidah Qawmiyyat*, p. 70.
28. *Khuṭbah-i Ṣadārat*, pp. 20 ff., 27-28 and 35; *Maktūbāt* I, p. 334.

29. *Taqrīr*, pp. 24-25 and 60; *Maktūbāt* I, pp. 147-48.
30. *Nazaryah-i Qawmiyyat*, pp. 19-21 and 24-28; *Muttaḥidah Qawmiyyat*, pp. 7-8.
31. *Nazaryah-i Qawmiyyat*, pp. 22-24; *Muttaḥidah Qawmiyyat*, pp. 10-15, 17-19, 21-23 and 26-28; *Maktūbāt* II, pp. 375-77; *Pākistān Kya Hay* I, p. 11.
32. *Muttaḥidah Qawmiyyat*, pp. 41, 48, 51-52 and 59-60.
33. *Ibid.*, pp. 42 and 44-49.
34. *Khuṭbah-i Ṣadārat*, p. 38.
35. *Muttaḥidah Qawmiyyat*, pp. 40-41; *Maktūbāt* I, pp. 396-98.
36. *Maktūbāt* I, pp. 394-400.
37. *Muslim Līg Kya Hay*, pp. 6 and 8-9.
38. *Maktūbāt* II, pp. 125 and 127-28.
39. *Ibid.*, pp. 131-32.
40. *Muttaḥidah Qawmiyyat*, pp. 49-51 and 63; *Maktūbāt* I, p. 146,
41. *Nazaryah-i Qawmiyyat*, p. 44; *Muttaḥidah Qawmiyyat*, pp. 30-32.
42. *Muttaḥidah Qawmiyyat*, pp. 34-35.
43. *Ibid.*, pp. 35-38.
44. *Ibid.*, pp. 32-34; *Nazaryah-i Qawmiyyat*, pp. 25-26.
45. *Muttaḥidah Qawmiyyat*, pp. 38-40.
46. *Ibid.*, pp. 64-65.
47. *Ibid.*, pp. 60 and 72.
48. *Ibid.*, pp. 60-62.
49. *Ibid.*, pp. 58 and 61.
50. *Maktūbāt* II, pp. 143-44.
51. *Ibid.*, pp. 146 and 148-49.
52. Muḥammad Ismā'īl Panīpati, *ed.*, *Khuṭbāt-i Sir Sayyad*, 2 vols. (Lahore, 1973) vol. II, p. 75.
53. *Taqrīr*, pp. 48-49; *Maktūbāt* II, pp. 115-16.
54. *Muttaḥidah Qawmiyyat*, pp. 63 and 70.
55. *Maktūbāt* I, pp. 395-96.
56. *Ibid.*, pp. 396 and 399-400.
57. *Maktūbāt* II, pp. 127-28, 131-32 and 140.
58. *Ibid.*, pp. 117 and 120.
59. *Ibid.*, pp. 117 and 119.
60. *Ibid.*, pp. 118-19.
61. *Maktūbāt* I, pp. 141-44.
62. *Ibid.*, p. 148; *Khuṭbah-i Ṣadārat*, pp. 28 and 37.
63. *Khuṭbah-i Ṣadārat*, p. 37; *Pākistān Kya Hay* I, pp. 16 and 29-30; *Muslim Līg Kya Hay*, p. 32.
64. Sayyad Sulaymān Nadwi and Mas'ūd 'Ali Nadwi, ed., *Maqālāt-i Shibli*, 8 vols. (A'zamgarh, 1932-65) vol. VIII, p. 155.
65. *Pākistān Kya Hay* I, pp. 8-10; *Muttaḥidah Qawmiyyat*, pp. 70-72 and 74-76; *Nazaryah-i Qawmiyyat*, pp. 28-29.

66. *Nazaryah-i Qawmiyyat*, pp. 29-30; *Muslim Līg Kya Hay*, pp. 29-31 and 33; *Khuṭbah-i Ṣadārat*, p. 33.
67. *Nazaryah-i Qawmiyyat*, p. 30; *Muslim Līg Kya Hay*, pp. 13, 15, 24 and 34-35; *Khuṭbah-i Ṣadārat*, pp. 33 and 40-41; *Maktūbāt* I, pp. 396-97; *Makṭūbāt* II, pp. 132-33.
68. *Khuṭbah- Ṣadārat*, pp. 25, 28 and 31-33; *Maktūbāt* I, pp. 139, 141 and 399; *Muttaḥidah Qawmiyyat*, p. 56.
69. *Maktūbāt* II, pp. 133-34; *Muslim Līg Kya Hay*, pp. 13, 15, 24 and 36-37.
70. *Ibid.*, p. 134; *Ibid.*, pp. 38-39.
71. *Pākistān Kya Hay* I, pp. 13 and 18-21.
72. Ziya-ul Hasan Faruqi, *The Deoband School and the Demand for Pakistan* (Bombay, 1963) p. 110.
73. Wilfred Cantwell Smith, *Modern Islam in India* (Lahore, 1969) p. 308.
74. *Pākistān Kya Hay* I, pp. 15-16 and 21-22; *Maktūbāt* II, p. 139.
75. *Pākistān Kya Hay* I, pp. 3, 31 and 38-39.
76. Faruqi, *op. cit.*, pp. 116-17.
77. *Khuṭbah-i Ṣadārat*, p. 39; *Pākistān Kya Hay* II, pp. 8-13.
78. *Maktūbāt* II, pp. 120-21.

Chapter 7

SAYYAD ABU'L A'LÁ MAWDŪDI
(1903-1979)

Islāmic Nationhood

Sayyad Mawdūdi's early views regarding the subject echo Iqbāl's—not only conceptually but verbally too. In an article which appeared in the *Tarjumān-al Qur'ān*[1] in Nov.-Dec. 1933, he wrote that Islām had built a new nationality (*qawmiyyat*) on purely spiritual and intellectual, rather than material and earthly foundations (*Cf.* Iqbāl, *supra* pp. 60-61). Like Mawlāna Āzād and Ḥusayn Aḥmad (*supra* pp. 131-32, 175 and 189), he believed that all world Muslims must co-operate, and share their joys and sorrows. In this connection he quoted numerous and familiar *Ḥadıth* to the effect that Muslims, who had equal rights and duties with respect to each other, were like the firmly cemented bricks of a single wall; or an organism which participates in the suffering of each of its constituent parts. This organism of the Islāmic *millat* had been described by the Prophet (Pbuh) as the *jamā'at* or *ummat*.[2]

At this point it would be pertinent to recall that in 1937 Iqbāl wrote to Sayyad Mawdūdi to shift to Panjab, and co-operate with him in research work for the reconstruction and codification of Islāmic jurisprudence. The two met twice, and it was decided that the Mawlāna should move to Panjab and direct an institution of Islāmic research, Dār-al Islām. In March 1938 he left Haydarabad (where he had shifted from Delhi in 1929) and settled in Panjab, but Iqbāl died next month. It is around this period that we notice a marked change in his religio-political thought.

By April 1939 Sayyad Mawdūdi's views regarding Muslim nationhood had undergone somewhat of a revolution—he now asserted that Muslims were not a nation (*qawm*) at all, and nor had they been described as such in the Qur'ān or *Ḥadīth*. Rather they had been called a party (*ḥizb*, the other words of similar import used for them being *ummat* and *jamā'at*)—"an international party" with the aim that its principles should rule the world. He reiterated that the conventional "racial" basis of "nationality" was fundamentally opposed to the Islāmic conception of society, founded only on common principles and modes of thought. In fact its very beginnings in emigration implied a severance of all familial and material connections (*Cf.* Iqbāl, *supra* pp. 60-61 and 70). However, he reasoned, this international "party" of Islām gradually became transformed into a "nation" due to social uniformity and racial bonds created by inter-marriage and common historical traditions. Ultimately it forgot its origins and the basis of its unity, and adopted "the ignorant concept of nationalism" from non-Muslims, which error, he believed, needed to be rectified.[3]

Sayyad Mawdūdi reasoned that since Islāmic "nationhood" was rational, it was by its very nature open to expansion, unlike static racial "nationalities." It was thus prepared to absorb all of mankind, and build a "world nationality" on an ideological foundation and cultural unity (*Cf.* Iqbāl, *supra* pp. 61 and 66-67). Yet, he insisted, in spite of becoming a "nationality" it actually remains a party (*jamā'at*), for the basis of inclusion in it is not birth but fidelity to its ideology. "Muslim" was thus not a title bestowed by birth, but an adjective earned and lost by actions.[4] This definition of a Muslim acquires great significance in his later thought.

Islāmic and Secular Nationhood

Sayyad Mawdūdi's stand regarding patriotism betrays some ambiguity : whereas he held in 1933 that Islām did not restrain one from service to one's country (although he rejected as unreliable, the saying attributed to the Prophet [Pbuh] that "patriotism is a part of faith"); at the same time he undermined the very basis of patriotism by declaring that a Muslim could become a loyal citizen of any other country, and fight as valiantly for it as for his own, there being no difference between the Muslims of two countries. Many years later in a speech in May 1947 he would repeat that Islām did not object to nationality (*qawmiyyat*), patriotism, and the desire for national (*qawmi*) freedom, provided these were free of prejudice and blind favouritism—the abominable traits of nationalism (*qawm parasti*), which he described as selfishness at a "national" level. [*Cf.* Iqbāl, *supra* pp. 70-71.] In 1933 he had also inferred from the Qur'ān (4:89) that in case of a conflict between religion and patriotism, the true Muslim must forsake the latter by emigration. He reasoned that this supreme loyalty to the faith was essential for the survival of Islāmic nationhood (*qawmiyyat*) : unless its constituent elements overlooked their different origins, the whole edifice would crumble. He therefore concluded that since Islāmic "nationhood" could not coexist with other "nationalities" of race, country, and language, a Muslim must sever all bonds of land and blood[5]; which contradicts his earlier admission of patriotism.

Sayyad Mawdūdi's conviction that Islāmic and geographical "nationalism" were mutually exclusive was based on the perception that they bred feelings of identity ("oneness") and alienation ("otherness") with two different groups *i.e.* co-religionists and fellow-countrymen respectively. He was convinced that the birth of geographical "nationalism" among Muslims would necessarily herald the extinction of Islāmic "nationhood" and therefore unity; and that this was borne out by their history (*Cf.* Iqbāl, *supra* p. 70 *ff.*). He therefore held that whereas in their capacity as human beings Islām urged Muslims to be tolerant and friendly towards all non-Muslims (if these were not enemies of Islām), and permitted them to co-operate for common aims; since the two groups were different with regard to religion, no worldly collaboration could ever unite them so as to make them one nation (*qawm*).[6]

This view is thus the very reverse of what Mawlāna Ḥusayn Aḥmad Madani espoused (*supra* p. 183 *ff.*). We recall that Sir Sayyad had also differentiated between relationships on the human and the religious plane, but had employed it to reason in favour of friendly relations with non-Muslims (*supra* pp. 10-11).

In another article which appeared in the *Tarjumān* in 1939 Sayyad Mawdūdi wrote that Islām and nationalism could not co-exist since they were diametrically opposed in their spirit and aims. Islām invites mankind to a world-state based on a certain creed, and on equality untainted by any trace of racial and national prejudices. Nationalism on the other hand divides men—its ultimate goal is a national state in which members of other nationalities cannot participate as equals. By implying not only love for one's nation but also hostility towards others, it had inflated the noble sentiment of patriotism to make it ugly. He felt that the principles of western nationalism had struck a vital blow at the foundations of divine law by replacing moral sanctions with material power and beastly force. Since nationalism was not regulated by any spiritual code, it exceeds its limits to assume the form of imperialism and racial hatred leading to war: he extensively cited modern western writers and Hitler's fanaticism to prove his point.[7]

In May 1947 Sayyad Mawdūdi would reiterate that Islāmic society was based on the principle of humanity which did not negate nationality (*qawmiyyat*) but confined it to its natural limits; it thus accommodates national love and freedom but not prejudice and selfishness. It demanded that each individual should be a member of the whole world rather than of any one country; and all nations (*qawm*) should manage their affairs themselves, in a spirit of co-operation rather than competition.[8] His views here are strikingly similar to Iqbāl's (*supra* pp. 61, 66-67, 70 and 73-74). As Kenneth Cragg has truly remarked, he appears to be "a better disciple of the universalism of Iqbāl than many of those who freely invoke his name."[9]

In 1939 Sayyad Mawdūdi had employed Turkey's example to illustrate that nationalism was incompatible with Islām. He called it a "religion" which set itself up against the law of God, aiming to usurp it from all departments of human life—a Muslim must therefore choose between the two. He felt that the world was rushing towards nationalism because it did not possess a moral teaching to regulate individual and social behaviour. Muslims should therefore present divine law as a remedy to the world, rather than themselves following the misguided.[10] Here again one can detect echoes of Iqbāl (*supra* pp. 70-73 and 85-86).

Nationalism

Nationalism in India

In 1938 Sayyad Mawdūdi asserted that India's problem was not communal but international (*Cf.* Iqbāl, *supra* p. 78). He did not agree with the nationalists that the mutual differences among its religious groups were a product of the British policy of divide and rule (See Madani, p. 200), and felt rather that whereas genuine differences had already existed, the English had only tried to draw political mileage out of these. In an article of 1939 he echoed Iqbāl's view (*supra* p. 78) that the differences between its "cultural nationalities" were more deep-rooted than among those of Europe. He asserted that not only was there nothing in common between them, but they were even mutually repulsive and antagonistic. Differentiating between "cultural" and "political nationality", he felt that whereas India possessed the latter (in being bound by a single political system), even when coupled with a common desire for freedom and shared hardships, it was insufficient to enkindle the sentiment of nationalism, which could only be born of the former.[11]

Defining "cultural nationality" as identity of religion and thought leading to intimate social relations including inter-marriage, which in turn bred common historical traditions making the people a single organic whole; Sayyad Mawdūdi felt it was non-existent in India. [We recall that Iqbāl too had spoken of the impossibility of India's "cultural units" and "cultural entities" ever evolving a united nationalism—*supra* p. 79]. He reasoned that in India a new nationality could be formed either by the culture of one nation absorbing that of the others; or through the evolution of a composite culture by the mutual interaction of the different nationalities. He ruled out the first possibility since the resultant nationalism would be that of a particular group rather than Indian; and the second because it could not be achieved in a day or two by artificial means—indeed he felt, often the transformation did not take place even after centuries of close contact between what had become permanent nationalities, for it demanded that their moral system and mental temperaments should resemble closely.[12]

Sayyad Mawdūdi felt that Indian political leaders were mistaken in thinking that in order to get rid of foreign domination it was necessary to create a common Indian nationality by the second method, for he felt that all groups conscious of their individuality would resist this kind of nation building (*Cf.* Iqbāl, *supra* pp. 78-79). Since the process was a long one it would further delay freedom, and if sought to be achieved by artificial pressure, it would bring about moral degeneration by causing the old value system to disintegrate, while a new one would be very long in the making. Unlike the nationalists he felt that for political and economic progress India needed not unitary but federal principles : that the individuality of each group and the right to its preservation be recognized, besides allowing it sovereign control over its "national subjects"; even while they agreed on joint action for common interests.[13]

We recall that Iqbāl had also opposed the nationalist's ideal of a "unitary" India as not only unattainable, but undesirable too; and had championed federalism, the retention of communal individuality, and co-operation for common interests (*supra* pp. 78*ff.* and 81*ff.*).

However in this and another article of the same period Sayyad Mawdūdi clearly distanced himself from Iqbāl's political views by criticizing, as misled from the Islāmic point of view, both "nationalist Muslims" and "Muslim nationalists"; who claimed to champion Indian nationalism, and Islām in India respectively. Differentiating himself clearly from the second group, he believed that they were concerned not with the revival of Islām but of the Muslim "nation", only because of the accident of their birth in it—he criticized those Muslim leaders from the time of Sir Sayyad to the present, who had mistakenly equated the two, or given precedence to the latter. This had led them to "Muslim nationalism" *i.e.* the effort to make the Muslim nation ascendant by improving its educational, economic, and political condition, irrespective of whether this was done within or outside the bounds of Islām—he felt they would be satisfied even with a "Muslim" rule built on un-Islāmic foundations. [His definition of a "Muslim"—*supra* p. 210 is relevant in this context.] He reasoned that since Islāmic ideology—which a Muslim must uphold in every concern of life in order to keep his faith intact—was antithetical to nationalism, he must constantly oppose it; and the phrase "Muslim nationalist" was thus a contradiction in terms.[14] Iqbāl, we recall, had similarly denied the validity of the term "Indian Muslim" (*supra* p. 60).

Nationalism and Mawlāna Ḥusyan Aḥmad

In 1933 Sayyad Mawdūdi had objected to Mawlāna Madani's definition of *qawm* as merely a "group" (*supra* p. 184), as being anachronistic since it was based on the Qur'ān and the Arabic lexicon. He felt that this ancient meaning was irrelevant to the current debate involving a totally different and modern sense of the word "nation", and challenged anyone to claim that it was in this modern sense that the Qur'ān admitted the merging of Muslims and others in a single nationhood (*qawmiyyat*). He similarly argued that the so-called united *ummat* which Mawlāna Ḥusayn Aḥmad claimed the Prophet (Pbuh) had formed with the Jews of Madinah (*supra* p. 185) was merely a military alliance which lasted for barely a couple of years. It had nothing in common with the united nationhood (*muttaḥidah qawmiyyat*) of the present, and nor could it be cited as a precedent in favour of the latter. He felt that undue emphasis was being laid on the words *ummah wāḥidah* [see Āzād, *supra* p. 158], whereas according to the dictionary *ummah* signified merely a group bound by time, place, religion etc. [we recall that Mawlāna Ḥusayn Aḥmad had defined *qawm* thus—*supra* p. 184], and even two "nations" united temporarily for a common purpose may be thus described.[15]

Sayyad Mawdūdi dismissed as flawed reasoning, Mawlāna Madani's contention that since Muslims participated unhesitatingly in other organizations formed for common ends, there was no reason for their abstinence from the Congress (*supra* p. 186). He believed on the contrary that Muslims should not take part in any such organization unless their powers had been clearly differentiated from those of the *Sharī'at*. He reasoned that the Congress was struggling to establish a legislature which would have the discretion to enforce, abrogate, or alter the *Sharī'at*, thus giving the non-Muslim majority the power to influence the life of Muslims. He was against the idea of the different Indian nations (*qawm*) joining to form one "nation", since it would entail giving precedence to nationality (*wataniyyat*) over religion: for the sake of homogeneity they would have to forsake those elements of their identity which tended to nurture their sense of separate nationality (*qawmiyyat*) (*Cf.* Iqbāl, *supra* pp. 74 and 85-86). This he felt was the "nationalism" which the Congress and its leaders wanted to build, which was very different from Mawlāna Madani's concept of "united nationalism", that he was mistakenly ascribing to the Congress[16] (see *supra* p. 191).

Muslim Culture

In a dateless article Sayyad Mawdūdi assigned a decisive place to the language and script of a "nation" in the survival and death of its culture and "nationality." He even felt that in order to transform a "nation" it was sufficient to merely alter its language and script : cut off from their past, its future generations would gradually develop a new national (*qawmi*) identity. He therefore protested against the efforts of the "nationalists" in India to replace its various languages by a single one, as part of their efforts to create a united "nation." He did not believe their claim that since this "national" language was "Hindustani", both Urdu and Hindi in Persian and Devanāgri scripts respectively would be afforded equal opportunity for development. He alleged that in practice even commonly used Persian and Arabic words which had for long been a part of the common heritage of Hindustani were being replaced by unfamiliar Hindi and Sanskritized words, and proceeded to give a list of the same.[17]

In an article first published in *al-Ma'ārif* in 1929 and later reprinted in the *Tarjumān-al Qur'ān* in January 1940, Sayyad Mawdūdi wrote that the dress of a "nation" was an expression of its "spirit", and had deep roots in its culture and civilization. Together with dress he included language and script as factors which established its individuality and therefore its "nationality", and which if destroyed, would herald its gradual effacement and ultimate absorption into other "nations." He thus explained the extinction of many previous "nations" by the loss of their individuality, caused by imitation of others in what he called "these props of nationality." According to him Islām demands that the dress of Muslims should be free of "un-Islāmic signs" *i.e.* specific symbols of polytheism associated with a particular religious group. While it did not specify any particular dress, it stipulated that they should adopt some distinctive traits in their dress in order to differentiate them from non-Muslims, make them recognizable to each other, and to strengthen their collective life.[18]

In this article and another published in 1939 Sayyad Mawdūdi wrote that the adoption of western dress by Muslims was against the commands of the Prophet (Pbuh) who had repeatedly restrained them from the imitation of non-Muslims, as being detrimental to their collective unity (*Cf.* Madani, *supra* pp. 193-94). Not only this, he reasoned that Islām was against the wholesale imitation of any "nation" by another, since marks of culture such as language and dress served as distinguishing traits for the different tribes and nationalities which existed among mankind despite its common origin. Although it did not approve the exaggeration of nationality (*i.e.* nationalism), Islām was also against altogether destroying the individuality of "nations." Its internationalism thus aimed not at complete uniformity, but a concord which would wipe out misunderstandings, and inspire co-operation and brotherhood. He also clarified that while Islām frowns upon wholesale imitation, it not only legitimizes, but encourages natural cultural reciprocity between friendly "nations" without disturbing the identity of either.[19]

However the views expressed herein seem to be belied by an

article of 1938 in which Sayyad Mawdūdi had written that Muslim culture was not equivalent to the external manifestations of civilization *i.e.* manners, dress, food, music etc., and denoted rather the mode of thought and principles of life which were derived from the Qur'ān, irrespective of external variations. He clarified that Muslims were concerned with seeing to it that their culture did not deviate from this Qur'ānic path : they were thus not concerned with preserving chaste Urdu, but with keeping the mind which expressed itself in it, a truly Islāmic one.[20]

Education

Sayyad Mawdūdi realized the importance of education for preserving identity. Towards the end of 1937 he wrote that like others, the survival and progress of the Islāmic civilization also depended on two factors : an Islāmic system of education; and the political power to practically establish its true culture and peculiar social organization. He felt that the greatest loss caused by British subjugation was that Muslims had been deprived of both these means of keeping alive their civilization.[21]

Sayyad Mawdūdi believed in October 1934 that the benefits of modern education could not compensate the great damage it had done to the religion and culture of Indian Muslims. In an article of September 1936 he clarified that while western sciences and arts were beneficial *per se*, Islām was opposed to their fundamental hypotheses according to which westerners had moulded the facts of knowledge. Islām possessed its own intuitional framework which was the very antithesis of these, and Muslims had strayed from it by adopting western intuitional moulds together with the facts of knowledge. In another article of the same period he wrote that in its total alienation from any concept of divinity, the spirit of modern education and culture was contrary to that of Islām. He therefore felt (in August 1936) that if it was propagated as such among the younger generation of Muslims, they would soon be lost to their faith.[22]

Sayyad Mawdūdi totally disagreed with Sir Sayyad's method of teaching the Qur'ān and *Ḥadīth* alongside this new education, for he felt that such artificial grafting of contrary and incompatible elements was futile. He reasoned that this divorce of religious and secular was essentially un-Islāmic, and would nurture the same attitude in the students who, in being unable to reconcile the two, would not be complete Muslims. He described its products as non-Muslim in philosophy, sciences, law etc., with their Islām being confined only to some beliefs and religious customs.[23]

Islāmic Education

Sayyad Mawdūdi was convinced that in order to keep alive the culture and independent national (*qawmi*) identity of Muslims, it was essential to revolutionize their education on a pattern which he outlined in two articles of August and September 1936. He believed that the basic idea behind the modern educational policy of Muslims should be to teach the secular sciences from the religious viewpoint, so that the student's world view was not bereft of God, and religion became his whole life, rather than merely an appendix or supplement to it. To achieve this, in the new system the individuality of religious and worldly sciences would be abolished to make them one. (There would thus be no need to teach theology [*dīnyāt*] as a separate subject, since the whole course would be transformed into one of theology. He repeated these views in a speech at the Nadwah-al 'Ulamā' in January 1941.) He believed this was the only way to create Muslim philosophers, scientists, economists etc., who would solve questions of life and the universe from an Islāmic angle, help the progressive elements and resources of modern civilization to serve Islām, and formulate Islāmic thought afresh according to the contemporary spirit, so that Islām once more became the leader in every field of knowledge, as it was meant to be. However this necessitated weeding out the western viewpoint permeating all fields of knowledge, and compiling them afresh in the intuitional mould of Islām. In December 1937 he wrote that this task would be undertaken by a group specially trained for the purpose, in both streams of knowledge[24] (*Cf. infra* p. 229).

In 1936 Sayyad Mawdūdi had also envisioned the setting up of a permanent department for independent research on fresh lines in Islāmic sciences for the award of doctoral degrees, which would prepare scholars who would lead not only Muslims but the whole world in thought and vision. He advocated that a new syllabus be formulated for teaching the Islāmic sciences (including the Qur'ān) on modern lines rather than from the old books. He felt further that each of the Islāmic subjects should be taught with its modern counterpart: thus Islāmic law with Law, Islāmic philosophy with Philosophy etc. He also believed that Islāmic history, which was meant to acquaint the student with the source of his nationality (*qawmiyyat*), should be taught only upto the period of the Prophet (Pbuh) and his Companions. He felt that teachers of Islāmic sciences should know both English and Arabic. Further, since sufficient material for the syllabus was not at present available in either English, Urdu, or Arabic, rather than confining this type of education to any one language, flexibility should be adopted. In 1941 he would stipulate that its student must know his mother tongue, Arabic, and one European language[25]—interestingly this would not necessarily include Urdu.

The Aligarh University

Sayyad Mawdūdi felt in August 1936 that whereas the Aligarh movement had to a certain extent improved the worldly life of Muslims, it had injured their religion more, turning them into "Anglo-Muḥammadans." It had sold them to Europe's materialistic culture for the price of a few posts and titles for those calling themselves Muslims. Whereas the university had been founded so that Muslims could preserve their identity even while benefitting from modern sciences; he felt that the fact that it lacked Islāmic character as did its students, proved that it had failed in its aims. In order to make it a truly Muslim university, rather than adopting western arts and sciences as they are, they must be critically appraised from an Islāmic viewpoint, so as to abandon their defects.[26]

Sayyad Mawdūdi wrote in September 1936 that in order to preserve Islāmic culture, Muslims should check the increasing inclination of their youth towards westernization; and completely eradicate it from the university, where a practical manifestation of a living Islāmic atmosphere must be created and inculcated in the students, for no culture could survive only theoretically. He felt that since this to a large extent depended on the teachers' being possessed of the Islāmic spirit, atheists and westernized teachers should be weeded out : it was insufficient only to retain a few Mawlwis to teach *dīnyāt* when the other teachers were non-Muslims or Muslim only in name. At the same time they should have the aptitude to divest the facts of western sciences from their intuitional base, and compile them according to Islāmic principles. He was convinced that such people well-versed in both streams of knowledge were not very hard to come by.[27]

Sayyad Mawdūdi reasoned that Arabic should be made

compulsory in the University as the language of Islāmic culture, and the only means of direct access to its sources—the Qur'ān and *Sunnat*, so that modern educated Muslims could interpret Islām and its issues rightly and independently. He felt that without it they would remain unacquainted with Islām, and champions of western concepts of morals, society, and law. If such Muslims represented their community in the Indian legislatures of the future, its laws would further alienate Muslims from Islāmic principles. He was therefore convinced that the question of Arabic was not merely one of language, but was related to the fundamental aim of the university.[28]

The Struggle for Independence

Muslim Participation

Sayyad Mawdūdi's early statements about this subject display a certain vacillation—his somewhat half-hearted expressions regarding the evils of foreign domination and the need for Muslims to contribute to the struggle for freedom, are nearly always accompanied by certain qualifications which raise doubts about his actual views regarding the issue.

An article which Sayyad Mawdūdi wrote around 1935-36 is typical of this attitude. He admitted that since British subjugation was adversely affecting all alike, to strive together to obtain freedom from it was in every way reasonable, and co-operation with the Congress thus "appeared" not only justified, but essential. Yet he also warned that this would expose Muslims to its atheistic thought and un-Islāmic ways. While it was not only essential but obligatory for a Muslim to fight against British subjugation, his viewpoint in opposing it was absolutely different from that of a nationalist, in that it was not based on any feeling of aliens *versus* countrymen (for such categories were non-existent for him). Rather he opposed them because they were unrighteous, and running an unlawful and unjust government. Therefore, he reasoned, while it was the duty of Muslims to break the bonds of British servility, it was not permissible for them to help in the establishment of a government based on the same principles as the British government, irrespective of whether it was native or foreign—they should aim at replacing evil by good, not by a greater evil.[29]

In another article of the same period there appears to be some confusion, stemming from Sayyad Mawdūdi's recognition of the twin status of Muslims in India. At first he writes that as Indians, the prosperity of Muslims as of all other nations (*qawm*) depended on India's freedom, but as Muslims their problem of the threatened disintegration of Islāmic nationhood (*qawmiyyat*) in India was peculiar. He however goes on to say that the solution of this problem also depended on their liberation, but again there was a catch—those who desired freedom purely as Indians were desirous of wiping out "national" differences in India. He therefore believed that Muslims should be led by a group which was ready for common action with other "nations" for India's freedom, but not at the cost of religious considerations. While (as Indians) he affirmed their unity of aims with the Congress and the need to co-operate for these, in the same breath he desired that Muslims be excused from participation in the Congress for the present, due to lack of the ability to defend their interests as Muslims.[30]

Sayyad Mawdūdi stated rather cryptically that without removing those weaknesses due to which they were unable to influence India's political development as Muslims, it would be alike ruinous for them both to participate in, and abstain from, the freedom struggle. However elsewhere he stated that they should distance themselves from the struggle for the time being, and concentrate on generating in themselves that strength which was necessary for participation in it. (For this they should be educated about Islām, and made practically obedient to its commandments.) He believed that neither should India's political development be suspended till such a time, nor would it suffer due to their non-participation, and if they were not opposed during this period, they should also not obstruct others.[31]

Towards the end of 1937 Sayyad Mawdūdi wrote that Muslims were prepared to sacrifice their lives for the country (*watan*), but not to destroy their nationality (*qawmiyyat*) and culture. In 1938 he claimed that Muslims were even more desirous of freedom than others, because their religion teaches them to detest a system founded on materialism and tyranny; and because the British had seized power from them, and ruined them the most. In another article published in Oct.-Dec. 1938 he affirmed that he was not against friendship and co-operation between Muslims and others, nor did he want to turn them against India's freedom merely due to the fear that the Hindu majority would destroy them; but the question was on what conditions they were to unite. He claimed that they were prepared for unity if their survival was assured, but the Hindus were obsessed with "national imperialism." He affirmed that Muslims desired good relations and co-operation for India's betterment, but while keeping alive their "national type."[32]

Complete Freedom

In 1935-36 Sayyad Mawdūdi wrote that Muslims should fight for that freedom which was compatible with the religious status of Indians *i.e.* whereas religious issues should not come in the way of common national (*qawmi*) interests, each group should have the power to tackle its religious matters independently of others. He believed that the objective of Muslims was not only freedom, but such freedom as not only established Islām in India, but gave it power and honour. He believed—in contrast to his frequent espousal of independence during the same period—that if it meant the transfer of government from English to Indian non-Muslims, such freedom was accursed, and striving for it was forbidden for Muslims. Rather, if they wished to remain Muslims and to see Islām surviving in India, they should be prepared for a war unto death in order to turn the direction of the freedom movement from the government of *kufr* to that of truth.[33]

Freedom was thus not an end in itself, but a means to making India a *dār-al Islām* or at least *shibh* [like] *dar-al Islām i.e.* in it Muslims should have an influential enough share in governance to enable them to organize themselves on Islāmic principles; arrange for Islāmic education and upbringing for their children; and enforce Islāmic commands and necessary reforms in their nation (*qawm*). They should so influence the rebuilding of the country that it was not against their principles, and nor was its political strength ever employed against Muslim "nations" of the world. Reiterating these objectives in an article written towards the end of 1937, Sayyad Mawdūdi repeated that he did not regard as truly national (*watani*) and desirable, any freedom or government in which Muslims did not have these powers alongside the freedom of the country as a whole. In the Preface to the first part of *Musalmān Awr Mawjūdah Siyāsi Kashmakash* (dated 4 November 1937), he repeated that whereas those who were primarily or only Indians desired independence as an end in itself; for those who were first and only Muslims, it was desirable only as a means towards arresting their declining Islāmic power, to once again see the Muslims of India as a self-governing "nation."[34]

In 1938 Sayyad Mawdūdi repeated that Muslims demanded active, not passive freedom, so that they should have their government, and thereby their education and culture in their own hands—if not, it was alike for them whether the government was run by foreign or native unbelievers. He reasoned that when a country was inhabited by various groups with major differences between them, it was mistaken to regard them as one, and the freedom of the country as equally the freedom of all, since it was possible that one group would reap its advantages while depriving the others. He therefore felt it was a delusion to style the struggle to replace foreign domination by domestic, as a "war of independence" in which all were duty-bound to participate. For him it was only a prelude to true independence, which was equivalent to self-government—if any group was denied this, it was in reality still enslaved. He believed that a purely democratic government spelt not freedom for the minorities, but their subjection to a majority government.[35]

The Freedom Struggle and Single Nationhood

In 1935-36 and again in 1938, Sayyad Mawdūdi wrote that the Congress believed that in order to liberate India it was necessary to wipe out its different nationalities (*qawmiyyat*) and make it one "nation." They therefore denied and attacked Islāmic "nationalism" as a hurdle in their path, branding the Muslims' feeling of "nationhood" as communalism, and engaging in propaganda against it; whereas those Muslims who adopted Hindu ways were called nationalists (*qawm parast*). Those who thought on these lines were willing to concede freedom only in personal religion and were opposed to organized religion and the separate identity which it necessarily bestows on its followers; whereas for Muslims accepting this path meant sacrificing their very status as Muslims. Contrary to his espousal of the cause of freedom elsewhere in the same article (*supra* p. 221), he now concludes that the kind of freedom desired by nationalists was even more accursed for Muslims than British subjection, since it posed a greater threat to their "nationhood."[36]

Towards the end of 1937 and again in 1938 Sayyad Mawdūdi wrote that for Muslims the actual problem was to repair the losses caused to their "nationhood" and culture by British rule. But the "nationalistic" banner under which the war of independence was being waged did not help them to achieve their national (*qawmi*) goal. Rather, through it the Hindus desired to carry these losses to their natural conclusion—they wanted Muslims to forgo the concept of Islāmic "nationhood", and merge their weak identity in the common Indian "nationhood." Since they desired to organize the collective life of all of India according to their own views of culture and civilization (which were antithetical to Islāmic principles), for Muslims participating in their movement would mean completing the process set in motion by British imperialism, by themselves annihilating their own "nationality" and culture. Refuting the "nationalists'" charge of being pro-imperialism, he alleged that they were the ones delaying freedom by adopting for it such means as were unacceptable to one-fourth of the population[37] (*Cf.* Jinnāh, *supra* pp. 116-17).

In Oct.-Dec. 1938, while asserting that Muslims were an independent nation (*qawm*), Sayyad Mawdūdi perceived fundamental differences between them and Hindus, which precluded the possibility of their uniting on all fronts. Whereas he was earlier willing to co-operate fully on common issues (*supra* p. 221), he now perceived differences of detail even in these, such as in the matter of education. Since the status of his co-religionists as Indians and as Muslims was inseparable, he felt that the ways of the two communities were parallel, and although they could cross occasionally, could never unite completely.[38]

Democracy

Sayyad Mawdūdi wrote in an undated article that if in a country of many "nations" and cultures political power was centralized in the hands of one "nation", it was imperative that it would determine the character of the single "nationhood" which it desired for the whole country. The share of the culture and "nationality" of other "nations" in it would become gradually fainter, until it was wholly assimilated. The manner in which the Congress had "begun shaping the India of the future" after coming to power in the provinces had further convinced him that there was no scope in it for Muslim culture and "nationhood." In an undated article of the same period he wrote that injustice lay concealed in the very nature of the future system if it was to be one of false democracy in which Muslims would be subjugated by the Hindus only due to their population ratio.[39]

Sayyad Mawdūdi clarified in an article which appeared towards the end of 1938 that Muslims were not opposed to democracy *per se*, but to democracy coupled with single "nationhood", for they believed that the latter neither existed in India, and nor could it be built in future. In the same year he reasoned that democracy could succeed only where differences were those of opinion, rather than national (*qawmi*) variations of religions, race, language etc. In the former instance "majority" and "minority" were not permanent but fluid terms, subject to reversal. In the latter, democracy would mean the perpetual rule and tyranny of the majority, and could therefore never be truly implemented. He cited historical evidence to show that merely by forming one "nation-state", two different "nations" could not become one.[40]

Constitutional Guarantees

In 1936 and 1938 Sayyad Mawdūdi expressed his lack of faith in constitutional guarantees and fundamental rights respectively, as means for ensuring the life of a "nation" if its own strength was not behind these (*Cf.* Āzād, *supra* pp. 165-66). He reasoned that since in a democracy their enforcement depended on the will of the majority, the whole life (culture, society, and religious laws) of the minority would be open to its high-handed interference—by controlling the educational system it could even try to wipe out the latter's "nationality." He inferred from Europe's example that nowhere had fundamental rights protected religious, racial, and linguistic minorities from the tyranny of the majority. He therefore concluded that the Muslims of a future free India would be as helplessly in the power of the Hindus as of the British at present.[41]

Sayyad Mawdūdi felt that the religious freedom guaranteed by the Congress resolutions on fundamental rights (passed in 1937 and '938), ruled out only forceful prevention of religious observances; not the creation of such conditions (through education etc.), that future generations of Muslims would gradually abandon religious practices of their own accord. Similarly, the right to preservation of culture, language, and script did not preclude making Hindi the national language; nor the implementation of a system of education which, by being bereft of the cultural traits of the minorities, would ensure a natural death for these. He reasoned that such (superficial) freedom and rights had been available under the British also, but had failed to invigorate the language and culture of Muslims, which was possible only under their own "national government."[42]

Solutions

Between 1935 and 1937 Sayyad Mawdūdi proposed the

establishment of "a state within a state" (which he did not define very clearly), in order to preserve the "national life" of Muslims. He felt that without such a central power, living under a non-Muslim system of government would weaken, and ultimately destroy their status as a Muslim "nation." He did not agree with those who believed that such a state could be achieved after independence; for the course of the revolution could be influenced only while it was actually in progress. He felt that other Indian "nations" could also acquire similar autonomy, and such an arrangement would not obstruct their mutual co-operation for common interests (*Cf. supra* p. 224), nor the working of India's common national government, unless they were aggressive towards each other. He clarified that he desired not anarchy or civil war, but only that Muslims be allowed to organize themselves according to their own principles; and were strong enough to ensure that India's political and cultural development too did not go against these. Later, towards the end of 1938 he proposed three alternative kinds of federations for India: an international federation or a state of federated nations based on cultural autonomy; redistribution of population according to cultural regions (*Cf.* Iqbāl, *supra* p. 82); and partition, and participation of the two units in a confederacy.[43]

Sovereignty of God

Later, sometime after April 1939, Sayyad Mawdūdi completely changed his stand regarding the Muslim attitude to the freedom struggle. In the Preface to the third and final part of *Siyāsi Kashmakash*,[44] while he admitted that the great difference between it and the first two volumes might seem like self-contradiction and a *volte-face* on his part, he tried to justify it on the grounds that while the first two volumes constituted an effort to revive the Islāmic movement, the third was a post-revival attempt to create an altogether new movement : the difference in aims necessitated the variation in approach. He claimed that earlier, instead of delineating the ultimate Islāmic ideal, he had confined his discussion to the actual conditions; and placed before Muslims the lesser goal of *shibh dār-al Islām*, so that the loftiness and unattainability of the former might not demoralize them. [Yet he would later criticize all kinds of compromise and gradualism in politics as advocated by Mawlāna Ḥusayn Aḥmad and others—*infra* p. 227*ff.*]. Now that this strategy had fulfilled its purpose, he felt he should motivate Muslims towards their real goal as outlined in Islāmic social and political concepts; the protection of their individuality being only a means to this greater end.

In a booklet published in 1944 Sayyad Mawdūdi wrote that as a Muslim he was not interested in freeing India, since it implied merely replacing the false deity of imperialism by that of democracy. He now held that as followers of a world-wide ideological movement, Muslims could not be called a national (*qawmi*) minority, and desired neither safeguards as such, nor "national" government as a majority. Since their only aim was the replacement of all other sovereignty by that of God, they were politically opposed neither to the Hindus nor the British; rather those who accepted their aim were their friends, and those who refused, their enemies. He dismissed all other Muslim organizations as being misguided in being obsessed with freedom from either Hindu or British imperialism, whereas according to Islāmic standards true salvation lay in deliverance from the rule of "those other than God." This was the message of the Prophets, and should be the sole aim of those organizations which had adopted un-Islāmic aims and methods.[45]

Sayyad Mawdūdi did not accept the *'ulamā's* plea that since divine government was unattainable in the present circumstances, Muslims should co-operate with others for deliverance from the British, and struggle for it later in free India (*Cf.* Madani, *supra* pp. 195-96). He felt there was no weight in the difficulties they mentioned, when compared with the odds against which the Prophets had striven in order to establish the rule of God on earth : the movement depended not on external factors, but only on faith and determination. Freeing the country from foreign domination was not more urgent, since all government other than that of God was alike evil for Muslims. As he said in a speech on 9 May 1947: Muslims aimed not at changing the hands that run the system (*i.e.* replacing the English by the Indian, or the Hindu by the Muslim), but at changing the very system, and the principle on which it works.[46] He now thus disowned the gradualism which he had advocated earlier, in 1939.

Partition

In the same vein, in a dateless article Sayyad Mawdūdi expressed his indifference, as a Muslim, to the issue of India's partition and the establishment of a Muslim government in their majority areas. To rejoice in that there a Muslim rather than a Hindu would have absolute power was equivalent to "Muslim nationalism", which he believed was as accursed as "Hindu nationalism" (*Cf. supra* p. 214). The crucial question for him was whether the government of Pakistan would be based on the sovereignty of God or of man. In 1939 he wrote that the survival of the separate identity of Muslims as a secular nation (*qawm*) in India (as in Turkey and Iran), was no better than their absorption in a non-Muslim "nationhood." The alienation of Indian Muslims from the *'ulamā'* and their unprecedented trust in irreligious leaders ignorant of the faith, appeared to him to spell as much danger for Islām as the movement of geographical nationalism.[47]

Later however, Sayyad Mawdūdi completely changed his stand regarding Pakistan. Writing in the *Tarjumān* of July-Oct. 1944 he chided Muslims for overlooking their status as an ideological group, in which capacity the question of the freedom of their national (*qawmi*) homeland would have been insignificant for them : as a preacher of the Islāmic system even a lone Muslim could invite the world to his (*i.e.* the Islāmic) system of government, and if he struggled in the right manner, could even succeed in establishing it. But because they had acquired the status of a mere "nation", despite numbering crores they regarded the establishment of their government in a small region as their ultimate goal. However at the same time he also conceded that in their capacity as a "nation" their demand was justified, for every "nation" had a right to political and economic independence,[48] although earlier (in 1939) he had emphatically denied that they were a "nation" at all (*supra*, pp. 209-10). His attitude here is thus rather ambiguous.

In two statements of May and July 1947 Sayyad Mawdūdi stated that now that partition appeared inevitable, if the future government of Pakistan was Islāmic as had often been promised, his party the *Jamā'at-i Islāmi* would support it fully. If not, it would continue to strive to mould it on Islāmic principles ("by shaping public opinion in this direction"), as it was doing in the present system.[49] The strategy here outlined, of influencing public opinion, is comparable to his advocacy of more violent measures elsewhere (*infra*, pp. 235-38).

The Ideal Muslim State

Islāmic Revolution

In an article of December 1937 Sayyad Mawdūdi outlined the process of bringing about an Islāmic revolution in order to create a *dār-al Islām* like Madīnah. He believed that if Muslims could not find a free atmosphere outside India for its creation, they should establish such training camps in the country itself, where a purely Islāmic atmosphere may be created. For this the pattern of the Prophet's (Pbuh) method in Madīnah should be emulated *i.e.* four groups of people be entrusted with different functions. The first group of educated persons would undertake the task of developing Islāmic principles in each branch of knowledge, on modern lines (for details see *supra* pp. 217-18). The second group was to be trained as workers of Islām, with excellent character and morals, and organized as a strong revolutionary party, with a programme for building a new Islāmic social order. They would garner political strength by presenting their programme before the people, and ultimately take over the government machinery so that it was run on just principles.[50]

The third group, after spending some time in the training camps, would live elsewhere as true Muslims, influencing others and helping the second group in every way : materially, and actively, by preparing the ground for them in their area. The fourth group would comprise Muslims and non-Muslims who wished to stay temporarily in the camps as learners or observers. This was a rough outline of what he believed was an essential prelude to the Islāmic revolution. He further held that the success of the system depended on its approximating as closely as possible to the spirit of the exemplary Madīnah organization. However he was quick to clarify that this was not a reactionary movement, for it demanded neither external resemblance nor cultural retrogression : rather than opposing evolution and change, it aimed at diverting them to the furtherance of Islāmic, not evil ends.[51]

In a speech at Aligarh in September 1940 Sayyad Mawdūdi outlined a slightly different method for creating the Islāmic state : the first step was the genesis of a movement based on Islāmic principles, whose leaders and workers would be examples of these, and would mould the masses on the Islāmic pattern through a system of education and training. The truly "Muslim" products of this system, fortified with Islāmic ideology and spirit, would effectively challenge the present intellectual leadership, and build a system of thought and life based on Islāmic principles, exemplifying during their struggle the ideology which they claimed to represent. People would be attracted to the budding state as a guarantor of social justice and world peace; and it would be set up once the ground for it had been fully laid. The products of Islāmic education and training would provide the office-bearers for running it.[52] We recall that in 1935-36 Sayyad Mawdūdi had rejected Indian independence as a step towards the establishment of a Muslim nation-state (*supra* pp. 225-26). He now disowned even the latter, and held that a nationalistic movement (based on the desire for a national government for Muslims, or a reasonable share in a common government) could not serve as the first step towards the creation of an Islāmic state, due to its un-Islāmic leadership which sought only worldly advantages for its community. He therefore regarded as untenable the theory that once a Muslim national state was established it could be gradually transformed into an Islāmic state [although he would subscribe to it later, in 1947—*supra* p. 228]. He believed that change could not be effected from above by artificial means, but must work from below through the social fabric in order to be permanent and genuinely effective, specially in a democracy where power was vested in the people.[53]

Towards the end of 1944 Sayyad Mawdūdi outlined his final, and slightly different version of the process of the Islāmic revolution : those who accept true Islām and its demands and prove it by their actions should be organized as a party, which should try to ultimately absorb the whole community into itself through preaching and persuasion, and whose aim should be the establishment of the Islāmic system without any compromises and half-measures.[54]

Nationalism

In the speech of September 1940 Sayyad Mawdūdi emphasized that being exclusively ideological, the Islāmic state was distinguished by its complete freedom from all traces of nationalism. It was ruled by persons of different nationalities, whose acceptance of the principles on which the state was based, alone entitled them to have a voice in its affairs. He felt that since this was something novel in a world moving in the opposite direction, western-educated Muslims including those in India, could think only on the lines of a nationalistic state. Although they talked of forming an Islāmic state and used terms such as *ummat*, *millat*, and *amīr*, they regarded Muslims as a national group entitled to a separate existence in their own state, and followed the same method and strategy as adopted by other national groups. He was convinced that this could not serve as a starting-point for a state founded on spiritual rather than nationalistic principles, which alone could lead mankind to real peace in this world and the hereafter.[55] As we have observed, in 1944 while he criticized this attitude of Muslims, he also ambiguously justified their demand for a homeland, as a "nation" (*supra* p. 228).

Sovereignty of God

In mid-1939 Sayyad Mawdūdi made it clear that *dār-al Islām* was not merely a Muslim majority country, nor an un-Islāmic government run by Muslims. Rather, as he said in speeches in October 1939 and September 1940, in a Muslim state sovereignty must belong only to *Allāh*, all others being merely His subjects. Since He is the only law-giver with absolute rights of legislation, human beings must individually and collectively surrender all rights of overlordship, legislation, and authority over others : no person, class, or group, not even the entire population of the state as a whole could lay claim to sovereignty. Thus believers could not resort to totally independent legislation nor modify any God-given law, even if the desire for either be unanimous—this completely repudiated the concept of popular sovereignty on which western democracy was based.[56]

Sayyad Mawdūdi reasoned that it was only fitting that sovereignty should rest in God alone, since everything has been created by, and belongs to Him : He has retained the right of legislation not to deprive man of his natural freedom, but to safeguard it, and prevent him from going astray. He further believed that the basic cause of bad government was the lordship of man over man : those in power tended to become reckless and unbridled, since they were unmindful of accountability to, and fear of God.[57]

Besides the sovereignty of God, Sayyad Mawdūdi defined the other basic principle working behind the Islāmic polity as the vicegerency (*khilāfat*) of man. This implies that those running the government must recognize God as their sovereign, work as His deputy and trustee (*khalīfah*-24:55), and fulfil their responsibilities with the consciousness of accountability to God, and to all fellow Muslims (or caliphs) who had delegated their authority to those in power. Since the power to rule has been promised to the whole community (24:55), every believer is a caliph of God, and individually responsible to Him : this was the real foundation of democracy in Islām.[58] This belies Moin Shakir's[59] contention that the *amīr* who exercises power on God's behalf, is "responsible not to the people, but only to God."

The Islāmic polity was thus the "kingdom of God" or a "theocracy": not of a priestly class (as in Europe), but ruled by the whole Muslim community. It is thus a "theo-democracy" *i.e.* a divine democratic government in which Muslims have a limited popular sovereignty under the suzerainty of God. It is democratic in the sense that every Muslim who is capable and qualified to give a sound opinion on matters of Islāmic law, is entitled to interpret it when the need arises; and all administrative matters are settled by consensus of opinion among Muslims. It is a theocracy in the sense that where an explicit command of God or His Prophet (Pbuh) exists, none can alter it in the least. Since the Islāmic state is founded on divine law, its government was entitled to obedience only in its capacity as a political agency set up to enforce this law, and its commands would not be binding on the believers if it disregards divine law.[60]

Justification, Citizenship and Rulers

During the course of his sermons in the mosque of Dār-al Islām at Pathankot after he shifted there in 1938, Sayyad Mawdūdi deemed political power as being indispensable to Islāmic reforms. Henceforth he held that mere belief and preaching were inadequate : in order to abolish mischief and reform mankind, it was imperative to snatch power from wrongdoers, establish a government based on correct principles, and stop evils by force. He justified this seeking of power by a civilization which aimed at reforming humanity, so that it could fully enforce its programme : without such authority it was rendered helpless, and its leaders were even forced to make shameful compromises with the ruling civilization. He held that the Prophets too, since they had also been sent to establish a divinely ordained system of life, had all endeavoured to bring about political revolutions in their age.[61]

On the basis of verse 72 of *Sūrah al-Anfāl* Sayyad Mawdūdi inferred that the Islāmic state was territorial, its citizenship being limited to those who live within its bounds, or had migrated thereto.

Its relationship with other Muslims was merely one of Islāmic brotherhood : if they invoked its help against an enemy it was obligatory on the Islāmic state to protect them, but with due regard to its international commitments. If it was bound in a treaty or even an unrecorded understanding with the third "nation", it would have to first repudiate the agreement openly[62] (*Cf.* Madani, *supra* pp. 191-92).

In 1939 Sayyad Mawdūdi had expressed the opinion that since the objective of the Islāmic state was to establish its ideology, it should be run only by those who believed in it, without any geographical, racial, or linguistic bars (*Cf. supra* p. 230). Those who did not subscribe to its ideology were not entitled to have a hand in shaping its fundamental policy, although they could live freely within its bounds as non-Muslim citizens (*dhimmi*), practising their culture and entitled to protection as a minority. However by 1948 (forced perhaps by the exigencies of the situation in Pakistan, to which he had migrated after partition), he softened his stand in permitting the relaxation of this general principle in the case of a modern legislature, which he reasoned was considerably different from *shūrá* in its traditional sense. Non-Muslims could be allowed its membership provided the constitution ensured that it could not enact any law against the Qur'ān and *Sunnat*; the head of state would be a Muslim; and they could occupy general administrative, but not key posts—these measures would ensure that they could not influence the ideological policy of the state.[63]

In a speech in May 1947 Sayyad Mawdūdi reiterated the democratic nature of the Islāmic caliphate : the *amīr* or highest administrator, and the members of the *shūrá* should be elected; and the government should be run according to the opinion of the people, who should have the right of evaluation and criticism. He deduced from the Qur'ān and *Ḥadīth* that Muslims must obey God, the Prophet (Pbuh) and those in authority (*ulu'l amr*—the government, or those who were in charge of any of their affairs), who must themselves be Muslims, and obedient to God and the Prophet (Pbuh), the symbol of which (according to a *Ḥadīth*) was *ṣalāt*. If they discard it, it becomes permissible to strive to remove them; otherwise they must be obeyed whether or not one approves of their commands—unless it entails committing a sin, in which case obedience is forbidden[64] (*Cf. supra* pp. 231-32 and Āzād, *supra* pp. 135 and 138-39).

Jihād

In *Al-Jihād fi'l Islām* (which was serialized in a newspaper from 1926 to 1927 and published in 1930), Sayyad Mawdūdi attempted, on the basis of the Qur'ān, *Ḥadīth*, and the works of early Muslim scholars, to defend the Islāmic concept of *jihād* against the attacks of non-Muslims, particularly Europeans; and to refute their claims that Islām was a bloodthirsty religion which had no respect for human life, and encouraged its followers to adopt violent means. In *Risālah Dīnyāt*[65] also (which was written in 1932 but published in 1940), he offers a conventional view of *jihād* as the endeavour for the defence or promotion of the cause of Islām by any means, but technically applied to the fight against its enemies, undertaken solely for God's pleasure. As such it was a *farḍ-i kifāyah* or collective responsibility, but if an enemy invades a Muslim country it becomes obligatory on each of its inhabitants, and if they be incapable of repelling the attack, by degrees on all world Muslims (*Cf.* Āzād and Madani, *supra* pp. 141-42 and 175). In *Tajdīd-o Iḥyā'-i Dīn* (first published in 1940 and later translated as *A Short History of the Revivalist Movement in Islām*[66]), we get some inkling of his later views when he writes that it is obligatory on every Muslim to establish (if need be by *jihād*), the government needed to practically enforce Islām.

Sayyad Mawdūdi developed his peculiar concept of *jihād* in the course of his sermons at the mosque of Dār-al Islām, Pathankot (first published in 1940 as *Khuṭbāt* and later translated into English as *Fundamentals of Islām*[67]). He now defined *jihād* anew, as the effort to achieve the real objective of Islām *i.e.* abolishing the lordship over man of anyone other than God, and establishing His kingdom on the earth. However, a Muslim could not lay claim to governance unless he developed such purity of motives that his struggle was meant not for personal and national interests, but solely for God's pleasure and the reformation of His creation. Before staking his claim to government he must be trained to run it according to the law of God rather than his own desires, and not to fall into the errors of his predecessors. Thus before Muslims undertook this tremendous responsibility, Islām developed in them the strength to bear its burden, through its worship (*ṣalāt*, *ṣawm*, *zakāt* and *ḥajj*), which was not mere ritual but a purification and training of the soul for this pious struggle in the way of God. (He therefore believed that all worship devoid of the aim of *jihād* was futile, and would not bring the worshipper any closer to God.) When through worship Muslims become the most righteous of God's slaves on earth, Islām commands them to go forth to fight His rebels, and deprive them of all powers. He repeated these views in a pamphlet published in 1946.[68]

In the above two sources, and a speech that he delivered on Iqbāl Day (13 April 1939) at Lahore, Sayyad Mawdūdi elaborated that the significance of *jihād* in Islām arose from the fact that unlike other religions (*dīn*) it was not content with being accepted as the truth merely theoretically. Rather it wanted to wipe out all other rule and establish its own, so that all may benefit from its doctrine for the salvation of mankind. He however made it clear that the aim of Islāmic *jihād* was not to deprive any people of their belief, worship, social code, or way of life : while giving them full freedom in these matters, it wanted only to ensure that their principles should not rule. Since it could not be followed completely while living under any other system, it was not sufficient for Muslims to merely believe in Islām : wherever they lived, they must strive their utmost to establish it on earth, and this was *jihād*—the ultimate test of their faith. He even held that those who strove to establish, or were content to live under any system other than Islām were not true Muslims, and their worship was of no avail.[69]

It is therefore not surprising to see Sayyad Mawdūdi advance the theory that Islām was not a religion but a revolutionary doctrine which wants to rebuild the social order of the whole world according to its doctrine. Muslims were therefore not a "nation", but "an international revolutionary party" which Islām organizes to implement its programme. Whoever accepts its call becomes a member of this party (which is also the *jamā'at* or *ummat*) with equal rights, irrespective of his caste, race, or nationality (*Cf. supra* pp. 209-10). As soon as it comes into existence it commences *jihād* (which is also its *raison d'être*) for the attainment of its aim *i.e.* replacing the rule of un-Islāmic systems by that of God. *Jihād* which literally means "intense struggle" or "utmost endeavour", is that revolutionary struggle and extreme self-exertion which is undertaken to achieve this goal—whether by means of the power of speech, the pen, the sword, wealth, or physical exertion.[70]

Sayyad Mawdūdi thus made it quite clear that the religious

propagators of Islām were not preachers or missionaries but "God's soldiers", whose duty entailed abolishing all evil from the earth "by force", and establishing good instead. However, later in the same speech he described the function of the Muslim party as two pronged : on the one hand it would propagate its philosophy, inviting others to accept it; and on the other it would fight to replace un-Islāmic governments by an Islāmic one—if it had the power to do so. We recall that earlier in the same speech he had not allowed for any such concession, outrightly condemning as unbelievers, those Muslims who failed in this duty.[71]

Sayyad Mawdūdi felt that while the beginning must be made locally, the ultimate aim of the Muslim party should be a world-revolution, for Islām desired the deliverance of all mankind, not of any particular nationality. He believed that this was the policy on which the Prophet (Pbuh) and the Pious Caliphs had acted : first Arabia, and then neighbouring countries were brought under Islāmic rule. As for the question of whether *jihād* was defensive or offensive, at first he said that such categories, employed for the warfare of nation-states, did not apply to *jihād* since it was waged by an international party to invite all of mankind to its universal way. However later in the same speech he described it as both defensive and offensive—with regard to its own, and the other party's principles respectively.[72]

In the final part of *Siyāsi Kashmakash*[73] which he wrote soon after, Sayyad Mawdūdi spelt out the establishment of an ideological Islāmic state as the aim of *jihād.* This demanded that Islāmic principles be made the basis of a militant movement, and Muslims should rise as a *mujāhid* group to fulfil this aim. He also clarified that their belief that only Islām could lead to salvation was not due to their accident of birth as Muslims, but was based on its deep study, and comparison with other social theories. Having reached the conclusion that all other systems were imperfect in comparison to it, he felt it was their duty to strive to organize all collective life according to its principles, as would a believer in any other system such as democracy or communism : he saw no reason why it should be regarded as wrong of Muslims to do so. The speech and article just cited appear to be dominated by forceful overtones of violence. It is also worth marking that the purification of the soul, which he had earlier deemed to be an essential prerequisite for donning the mantle of *jihād*, is here not even touched upon.

The *Jamā'at*

In an article of Nov.-Dec. 1937 Sayyad Mawdūdi wrote that while describing the Islāmic *millat* as the *jamā'at*, the Prophet (Pbuh) is reported to have said that God's hand is over it; he who breaks away from it in the least shall be deemed to have forsaken Islām; and he who tries to sow dissension in it should be killed (*Cf.* Āzād, *supra* pp. 135-36). However in 1939 he clarified that *"jamā'at"* in the above mentioned *Ḥadīth* refers only to the organization formed not with worldly motives, but purely for God's pleasure, and the service of Islām. He therefore criticized those who quoted commands in the Qur'ān and *Ḥadīth* about fidelity to the *"jamā'at"*, in order to plead for loyalty to un-Islāmic nationalist organizations and political parties. He also contended that the *sawād-i a'zam* which the Prophet (Pbuh) had asked Muslims to abide by, signified not merely any Muslim majority but that which is on the Islāmic path, and will never agree on evil.[74]

In a speech in December 1946 Sayyad Mawdūdi explained that since only a small part of Islām pertains to private life, it cannot be fully realized at the individual level alone: it was necessary to launch a collective effort to fulfil the twin duties of calling mankind to Islām (*da'wat*), and establishing it fully (*iqāmat*). Organized corporate life had therefore been made mandatory, life without the *jamā'at* being ignorance, and secession from it equivalent to secession from Islām. Being convinced that Muslims could fulfil the requirements of Islām only through corporate life (*jamā'at*) and collective struggle (*jihād*), he inferred from a *Ḥadīth* that an organizational discipline must be established whose members would, in obedience to their leader, take up *hijrat* or *jihād* as the situation demanded.[75] His views here are comparable to those of Āzād (*supra* pp. 136-37).

Sayyad Mawdūdi therefore placed three alternatives before Muslims : joining the Jamā'at-i Islāmi [which he had founded in August 1941]; or any other organization; or forming a party devoted to the ideal of fully establishing Islām; for he did not claim that only his party was on the right path (*Cf. supra* p. 227, when in 1944 he had dismissed all other Muslim organizations as being misguided). He in fact admitted that no single *al-jamā'at* comprising the whole *ummat* existed at present, to which every Muslim was bound to give his allegiance, and nor could it be created at the outset. It was inevitable that more than one party, organization, or group should emerge in the initial stages of the Islāmic movement, working for the same ideal according to their own methods and plans. He however hoped that their unity of purpose would inevitably unite them in the future.[76]

The Jamā'at-i Islāmi

In a speech in May 1947 Sayyad Mawdūdi described the aim of the Jamā'at as the organization, first in India and later wherever it found an opportunity, of a society true to Islāmic principles. [The mellowed stand here is comparable to his earlier views, when he had held it obligatory on every Muslim—individually and as a group, to strive to establish the truly Islāmic society—by force if necessary [*supra* pp. 235-36]. Since it regarded any collective organization based on secularism, democracy, and nationalism as evil and corrupt (even if those running it were Muslim in name), it would arouse the people to strive to displace it, wherever it existed. In the speech in December the previous year he had described the working of the Jamā'at thus : it places Islām first before its members and then before all Muslims, inviting them to become living examples of it as individuals, and as a society. (For this purpose it trains its members to explain Islām in a reasoned and convincing manner, through speech and writing.) This organized and truly Islāmic society would, through its incessant striving, eventually overthrow all godless systems, and replace them with the just system of Islām.[77]

Notes and References

All references in this chapter unless otherwise specified, are to the works of Sayyad Abu'l A'lá Mawdūdi.

1. A monthly started by him in 1932 as an organ of his religious views, and dedicated to the cause of Islāmic renaissance.
2. *Mas'alah-i Qawmiyyat* (Delhi, 1962) pp. 27, 34-35 and 48.
3. *Tafhīmāt,* 2 vols. (Delhi, 1967-68) vol. I, pp. 156-58, 161, 163-66 and 172.
4. *Ibid.*, pp. 174-75 and 179-180.
5. *Mas'alah-i Qawmiyyat,* pp. 30, 32, 37, 43 and 48; *Jamā'at-i Islāmi ki Da'wat* (Delhi, 1972) pp. 15-16.
6. *Mas'alah-i Qawmiyyat*, pp. 30-31 and 49-50.
7. *Nationalism and India* (trans.) (Malihabad, 1948) pp. 9-11, 16-25 and 29-31.
8. *Jamā'at-i Islāmi ki Da'wat,* pp. 19-20.

9. Quoted by Moin Shakir, *Khilafat to Partition* (New Delhi, 1970) p. 253.
10. *Nationalism and India*, pp. 34-37.
11. Khurshīd Aḥmad, ed., *Tehrik-i Āzādi-i Hind awr Musalmān* (Lahore, 1964) pp. 196 and 199; *Nationalism and India*, pp. 40 and 47.
12. *Nationalism and India*, pp. 41 and 43-45.
13. *Ibid.*, pp. 46-51.
14. *Ibid.*, pp. 8, 37 and 41; *Musalmān Awr Mawjūdah Siyāsi Kashmakash* (Delhi, 1962) vol. III, pp. 168-69.
15. *Mas'alah,* pp. 74-76 and 78.
16. *Ibid.*, pp. 81-83 and 87-91.
17. Aḥmad, *Tehrīk-i Āzādi*, pp. 436-38.
18. *Tafhīmāt* II, pp. 381, 389-390 and 396-97.
19. *Ibid.*, pp. 399-401; *Nationalism and India*, pp. 52-56 and 58-59.
20. Aḥmad, *Tehrīk-i Āzādi,* pp. 226-27 and 229.
21. *Musalmān Awr Mawjūdah Siyāsi Kashmakash* (Pathankot, n.d.) vol. I, p. 71.
22. *Nishān-i Rāh* (Pathankot, n.d.) p. 27; *Tanqīhāt* (Pathankot, n.d.) pp. 126 and 212.
23. *Tanqīhāt*, pp. 126, 201, 205, 207 and 213; *Naya Nizām-i Ta'līm* (Pathankot, n.d.) pp. 25-26.
24. *Tanqīhāt*, pp. 206-07, 213 and 219; *Naya Nizām-i Ta'līm,* pp. 25-28; *Nishān-i Rāh*, pp. 43-44.
25. *Tanqīhāt*, pp. 127, 210, 213-14, 216 and 219; *Naya Nizām-i Ta'līm,* p. 31.
26. *Tanqīhāt*, pp. 118-19, 121 and 125-27.
27. *Ibid.*, pp. 127-28, 207-08 and 217.
28. *Ibid.*, p. 209.
29. *Siyāsi Kashmakash* I, pp. 24-26; *Rāh-i 'Amal* (Haydarabād Dakkan, 1946) pp. 35-37.
30. *Siyāsi Kashmakash* I, pp. 35-37 and 44-45.
31. *Ibid.*, pp. 43-44, 51, 76 and 78-79.
32. *Ibid.*, p. 73; Aḥmad, *Tehrīk-i Āzādi,* pp. 182, 465-66, 468 and 471.
33. *Siyāsi Kashmakash* I, pp. 30, 33 and 39.
34. *Ibid.*, pp. 4-5, 30-31 and 72.
35. Aḥmad, *Tehrīk-i Āzādi*, pp. 183-86, 190-91 and 300-01.
36. *Ibid.*, pp. 237-38; *Siyāsi Kashmakash* I, pp. 37-38.
37. *Siyāsi Kashmakash* I, pp. 71-73; Aḥmad, *Tehrīk-i Āzādi*, pp. 220-21 and 245-46.
38. Aḥmad, *Tehrīk-i Āzādi*, pp. 468-69 and 473.
39. *Ibid.*, pp. 416-17 and 449.
40. *Ibid.*, pp. 263-65, 268 and 466.
41. *Ibid.*, pp. 288 and 297; *Siyāsi Kashmakash* I, p. 89.
42. Ahmad, *Tehrīk-i Āzādi*, pp. 299-301.

43. *Ibid.*, pp. 475-482; *Siyāsi Kashmakash* I, pp. 41-42, 86 and 90-91.
44. *Ibid.*, pp. 4-9.
45. *Rāh-i 'Amal,* pp. 17-23, 25-26 and 37-38.
46. *Ibid.*, pp. 26-30; *Jamā'at-i Islāmi ki Da'wat*, p. 6.
47. *Rāh-i 'Amal,* pp. 16-17; *Siyāsi Kashmakash* III, pp. 9-10.
48. *Rasā'il-o Masā'il,* 4 vols. (Delhi, 1970-71) vol. I, pp. 339-340.
49. *Ibid.*, pp. 341-42; *Jamā'at Islāmi ki Da'wat*, p. 29.
50. *Nishān-i Rāh,* pp. 42-44.
51. *Ibid.*, pp. 44-48.
52. *The Process of Islāmic Revolution* (Lahore, 1979) pp. 17-19.
53. *Ibid.*, pp. 20, 22, 24-25 and 27.
54. *Rasā'il-o Masā'il,* pp. 334-35.
55. *Islāmic Revolution*, pp. 8-11.
56. *Ibid*, p. 13; *Siyāsi Kashmakash* III, p. 15; Khurshid Ahmad, (trans.) *The Islamic Law and Constitution* (Lahore, 1977) pp. 130-32.
57. Ahmad, *Islamic Law*, pp. 133-34; *Fundamentals of Islam* (Lahore, 1978), pp. 247-48; *Ḥaqīqat-i Jihād* (Lahore, 1946) p. 12.
58. Ahmad, *Islamic Law,* p. 132 and 141-43; *Fundamentals of Islam,* pp. 248-49.
59. *Op. cit.*, p. 250.
60. Ahmad, *Islamic Law,* pp. 131-33.
61. *Ibid.*, p. 159; *Fundamentals of Islam*, pp. 243-46; *Ḥaqīqat-i Jihād*, pp. 6 and 11; al-Ash'ari, trans. *A Short History of the Revivalist Movement in Islam* (Lahore, 1979), pp. 23-25.
62. Ahmad, *Islamic Law*, pp. 177-79.
63. Ahmad, *Islamic Law*, pp. 139-140.
64. *Ibid.*, pp. 171-72; *Jamā'at-i Islāmi ki Da'wat*, p. 23.
65. Abdul Ghani, (trans), *Towards Understanding Islam* (Pathankot, 1944) pp. 77-79.
66. *Ibid.,* p. 25.
67. *Ibid.,* pp. 243, 250 and 253.
68. *Ḥaqīqat-i Jihād*, pp. 5-6, 16-18 and 21.
69. *Ibid.*, p. 32; *Fundamentals of Islam*, p. 249; *Tafhīmāt* I, pp. 92-93, 105-06 and 111-112.
70. *Tafhīmāt* I, pp. 91-93 and 103-04.
71. *Ibid.*, pp. 104-05 and 109.
72. *Ibid.*, pp. 108-112.
73. *Ibid.,* pp. 19-20, 37 and 57.
74. *Siyāsi Kashmakash* III, pp. 91-93; *Mas'alah-i Qawmiyyat*, p. 35.
75. Khurram Murad, (trans.) *Witnesses Unto Mankind* (London, 1986) pp. 46-48.
76. *Ibid.,* pp. 48-49.
77. *Ibid.*, pp. 45 and 50-51; *Jamā'at-i Islāmi ki Da'wat*, pp. 4-5 and 18.

Chapter 8

CONCLUSION

Sir Sayyad Aḥmad Khān's political stance to a large extent stemmed from his conviction that: British rule was here to stay for none else could govern India; it was a folly to challenge its authority since it had proved itself invincible; and its permanence would be beneficial for Indians, and particularly Muslims. In 1858 he urged a rebellious Muslim aristocrat to support the government rather than fighting it, so that it would promote him in return; and this was the logic which he applied to its relationship with the Muslim community, wherein originates his staunch loyalism. He tried to demonstrate the religious sanctions for this attitude, ruling out *jihād* or rebellion against the government as being un-Islāmic. As for the Qur'ānic verses commanding Muslims to fight all unbelievers until all mischief was abolished, he did not hesitate to say that they had only contemporary and local, rather than universal application.

We notice a fluctuating pattern in Sir Sayyad's views regarding Hindu-Muslim relations from the earliest. Although he perceived the antagonism between the two major communities even in 1858, as a government servant he himself displayed no trace of prejudice. Due to his impartial and devoted services, he won the trust and affection of the majority community as well. On a personal level too, he believed in serving not only his co-religionists but also compatriots, and began to set up various academic and political organizations in which the Hindus also participated actively.

In 1867 even while he asserted the geographical basis of nationhood, and that Muslims had become an inalienable part of the native Indian population; Sir Sayyad believed that like Europe India was not a single nation, but comprised numerous similar nations. The Urdu-Hindi conflict arose in the same year. Although he is said to have been so pained by the events that he despaired of the two communities ever working together as a nation, the very next year he set up an organization to send members of both groups abroad for study. In 1870, even while he repeated that the issue would greatly damage Hindu-Muslim relations, he admitted that it would be in Muslim interests to keep these healthy; and expressed his desire for the welfare of all Indians irrespective of faith.

During the same period, even while he welcomed the employment of Muslim teachers in government schools, and "Hindustani" as the medium of instruction; the revival of Arabic and Persian and the office of the *qāḍi*; and the introduction of religious education—not from communal motives but only in order to popularize education among Muslims; Sir Sayyad also displayed a streak of chauvinism in rejoicing at the populousness of Muslims (as compared to Hindus) in eastern Bengal. Yet this is also the period when he not only encouraged Muslims to develop true friendship with all irrespective of faith, but also justified this on religious grounds. Yet the inherent dualism in his mind between "country" and "community" comes to the fore when in 1875 he adopted a motto for his newspaper that encouraged love for the latter rather than the former.

Yet Sir Sayyad's efforts for the joint emancipation of Hindus and Muslims continued. He however did not hesitate to defend Urdu from another attack by the former in 1882, describing it as the product of their interaction, rather than the language of any one group. While reminding Hindus that like the Muslims they were also originally foreign settlers in India which had now become the native country of both, he again repeated that one's faith should not deter one from good relations with all fellow humans. In 1883 he founded an organization to help Muslims to go abroad for study, but assured the Hindus that he was not motivated by partisanship or lack of sympathy for them, but only the fact that Muslims faced greater hurdles in this respect.

This is also the period when Sir Sayyad opposed the introduction of pure representation in India on the grounds that it was not a nation, but a continent with not only rigid religious and caste differences, but also varying degrees of education and progress. He felt that in such a situation representative institutions would only aggravate differences and the conflict of interests between various segments of the population. This is also the first time that he expressed the fear that the stronger community would completely dominate the weaker. These and similar arguments would later be extensively employed by those opposed to Indian nationalism.

Yet it is surprising that only a year later, in his speeches of early 1884 Sir Sayyad did not hesitate to describe both India and Europe as single nations despite their religious and racial diversity, reaffirming the territorial (as opposed to religious) basis of nationality. He appealed for concord among all Indians, who were one nation, for the welfare of their common country, and particularly for Hindu-Muslim unity. He repeatedly described them as a single nation, while emphasizing the social and cultural bonds between them. By defining a "Hindu" as a native of Hindustan rather than the member of a religious group, he even proved that far from being aliens, Muslims were also "Hindus." He believed at this stage that their children should be brought up and educated together as brothers, and clarified that by setting up a college for Muslims he did not intend to set them apart from the Hindus. The latter also appreciated his efforts for all his fellow-countrymen—both as an educationist and a member of the Legislative Council.

Yet even in January 1884 itself, Sir Sayyad undermined the territorial basis of nationhood by saying that Islām had abolished it to create a new national bond that was spiritual; and since Islām was the basis of their identity, Muslims must remain true to it. But he added that their compatriots of all faiths were also their brothers—in social and cultural matters, and Islām preached good neighbourliness towards all. Even while he defined his nation as the *ummat* of the Prophet (Pbuh), which he loved and desired to serve, he explained that his efforts for its educational upliftment were meant to contribute towards the progress of India as a whole. Yet despite these pronouncements he did not hesitate to express his conviction that neither community separately, nor both together, could rule India.

A marked change can be detected in Sir Sayyad's attitude in an undated article, wherein he expressed the desire to make Muslims a nation, whereas in early 1884 he had used the same phrase for both communities together. Thus he now held that merely education was not sufficient, and a spirit of nationality must be created among Muslims through collective education in their own national institutions. He also now believed in the need to teach them Arabic and Persian (which he described as the languages of Muslims), and to impart elementary, if not advanced religious education—not as earlier, to popularize education, but in order to strengthen their national consciousness.

The Indian National Congress was formed in 1885, and Sir Sayyad came out against it openly in December 1887. He now reverted to the view that the different Indian peoples had not so far intermingled to form a single nation, and nor were they equally matched. He reiterated his earlier opposition to the implementation of pure representation, and felt that due to their backwardness and fewer numbers, Muslims particularly were unfit to compete with others. He therefore advised them to concentrate only on trade and education, and abstain from the political agitation of the Congress. He also feared that the strong and vindictive arm of the government would fall most heavily on them. His reaction was obviously conditioned by his experiences of 1857: he continued to believe that since Indians could not harm the government in the least but would only injure themselves by a confrontation, it was wiser to secure benefits by winning its trust through loyalty. He felt that the activities of the Congress would spark off a power struggle between the various Indian communities; and that through it the Hindus hoped to politically subjugate, and even annihilate the Muslim community.

Yet soon after his stiff opposition to political co-operation between the two communities, he reaffirmed his earlier desire for religious amity and social unity.

In March 1888, Sir Sayyad suggested that since the Hindus were joining hands against the Muslims, the latter should unite with the British and strive to make their rule permanent, rather than becoming subjects of the Hindus by joining the Congress. He repeated that in order to ensure peace in India, the English should remain for ever, since it was unthinkable that the two communities could share power equally—one would have to subdue the other in order to ensure peace. He objected to the Congress on the grounds that it regarded India as one nation, whereas the conflict of interests among its different groups precluded such a possibility even in the future. He therefore denied that there could ever be a truly national Congress benefitting all alike.

By now Sir Sayyad could not only state categorically that Muslims should study and live together, but also that they should not study with others, in order that the desirable national feelings be generated among them. He also believed that in order to remain a part of their nation, Muslim students should remain true to Islāmic values, and not be led astray by western ways. In December 1893 and 1894 he again perceived a threat to Muslim nationhood from western education, as well as from Muslims being educated among a non-Muslim majority. In order to strengthen it he reiterated the need for separate, collective, residential, religious, education, and the teaching of Arabic, Persian, and Islāmic history.

In September 1893 Sir Sayyad repeated that India was not a country but a continent incorporating great variety, whereas representation without religious, national, and social homogeneity would only produce conflict. His drawing attention to the lack of political unity ever since the fall of the Mughal empire strengthened his earlier hypothesis that India's major communities could not rule it independently of the British, who had bestowed administrative unity on it.

In 1897 while he continued to hold that the Congress was harmful not only for Muslims but for all Indians; as before Sir Sayyad expressed his desire for social intimacy unimpeded by religious and political differences. He repeated that Hindus and Muslims were not only compatriots but also brothers, and that there should be no estrangement between them, for Muslims not only had Aryan blood, but were also "Hindu" by virtue of being natives of Hindustan.

Sir Sayyad opposed the pro-Turkish tendencies of Indian Muslims in 1897, as being in conflict with their duty to remain loyal subjects of their British rulers. He completely undermined the right of the Turkish Sultāns to the universal Islāmic caliphate (which he held had ended thirty years after the demise of the Prophet [Pbuh]), and their authority over Indian Muslims. He also rejected the possibility of a world-wide Muslim state with a single caliph as its head. Having earlier employed religious arguments to buttress his case for loyalism, he now held that religion must be kept apart from politics. Accordingly he reasoned that it was unjustified to give wholly political wars a religious colouring, and to defy the government even if its policy was against Muslim states. In 1898 for the last time he opposed the efforts of Hindus against Urdu, which he defended virtually from his death-bed.

Many Muslim thinkers such as Sayyad Sulaymān Nadwi[1], Ṭufayl Ahmad Manglori[2], Ḥusayn Aḥmad Madani[3], and Sayyad

Abid Hussain[4] have attributed, what they perceived as a sudden and radical change in Sir Sayyad's views, to the influence of the British principal of the M.A.O. College, Theodore Beck. However there is no evidence to substantiate this view. We have tried to show that there was no such one-time shift in his stand, and that the fluctuating pattern of his thought is in evidence throughout. All we can say is that while in the early period he alternated between Indian and Muslim nationhood, his later commitment to the latter was final and complete.

Sir Sayyad was not concerned with theorizing about Muslim identity in India, his sole aim being the socio-economic, educational, and cultural rehabilitation of his community; and all his efforts were geared towards this end. Accordingly, he supported British rule in India, Hindu-Muslim unity, and the united Indian nationhood which stemmed from the latter, because he felt it was conducive to the attainment of these ends. Yet even in the early period he was astute enough to perceive the inherent antagonism between the different Indian communities. Even before the formation of the Congress he felt that Muslims could not compete with the Hindus in politics, and later opposed it due to the threat that it posed to the permanence of British rule. It was perhaps for him also a symbol of the resurgent Hindu nationalism which he had felt rearing its head during the Urdu-Hindi issue, and perceived as a threat to Muslim progress and security.

Therefore all attempts at categorizing Sir Sayyad's views are bound to fail. However, since both strains are present in his thought, later votaries of both the "nationalist" and "separatist" schools picked on the aspect which suited their purpose, carried it to its logical conclusion, and claimed him as their own.

Shibli Nu'māni was a young contemporary of Sir Sayyad. Although he betrays the latter's influence in the early period, he later charted his own independent course.

From 1877 onwards Shibli frequently displayed sympathy for Turkey and its Sultāns. However Sayyad Sulaymān Nadwi's calling him a confirmed pan-Islāmist is unacceptable, particularly when in 1898 he denied the Turkish claim to the Islāmic caliphate, even while upholding the latter's sanctity and validity. In 1911-12 too he quashed the pan-Islāmic sentiments of Indian Muslims by falsifying the misplaced hopes they had pinned on other Muslim countries for their help and deliverance. The sentimental nature of his attachment is evident from the fact that it was mostly expressed in poetry rather than prose. Here it would also do well to recall H.A.R. Gibb's differentiation between "Islāmic universalism" and "pan-Islāmism" as religious and political ideals respectively (*Modern Trends in Islām*, 1945, pp.111-12). Shibli may be said to have believed in the former rather than the latter.

In 1887 Shibli agreed with Sir Sayyad that a feeling of nationhood should be nurtured among Muslim youth. But he did not dwell on this aspect later—except once in 1893, when unlike his mentor who was very mindful of social distinctions, Shibli believed that these must be eliminated among Muslim students in order to truly enforce their feeling of nationhood.

Although there is not much explicit political content in Shibli's thought, there is an unmistakable political insight underlying all his views. For instance in 1886 he emphasized the need for western education among Muslims, not only for the sake of government employment, but also to make them politically active, and able to communicate with the government. From this early date he had begun to envisage the lofty role he would later outline for the *'ulamā'*—they would serve as not only religious, but also political guides for the community, while also interacting freely with the government as equals. In 1893 while he upheld the need for traditional education alongside the modern stream in order to keep alive Muslim nationhood, he felt that its prevalent form was profitless, for its products were politically unaware. Being themselves alienated from the mainstream of national life, they were unconcerned about the low Muslim representation not only in government jobs, but in all kinds of organizations. In 1904 he felt that present-day religious scholars must learn English besides being generally well-informed, so as to successfully combat the challenge posed by modern western philosophy to Islām.

From 1907 onwards Shibli repeatedly asserted that Muslim nationhood was based not on race or region, but on religion, which was therefore the axis of the community, and the very means of its revival and progress. He therefore wanted to replace (Sir Sayyad's) "nation" by "religion" or "Islām" as the central concern of Muslims, in order to ensure religious commitment in all their future efforts. The next year he tried to show that since India under the British was a *dār-al Islām*, it was the religious duty of Muslims to remain loyal to their government. Considering the general trend of the age, this was perhaps not as much of an aberration from his political philosophy as it may seem.

From 1908 onwards Shibli was troubled by the threat which he perceived to Islām from modern science; the atheism of Europe; its misrepresentation of Islām; and the religious ignorance of rural and western-educated Muslims, which made them vulnerable to the activities of Christian and Hindu missionaries, and had led to the reconversion of a large number of Muslim Rājpūts. He saw the last as not only a religious, but also a political issue, for it would affect the numerical strength of Muslims, which was the basis for securing political rights.

In view of these dangers, between 1910 and 1912 Shibli suggested various steps for the defence and spread of Islām (such as religious education for rural and western-educated Muslims; the appointment of Muslim teachers in government primary schools; and teaching of English, Sanskrit and Bhāshā to religious scholars), which would however be undertaken in a spirit of reconciliation rather than confrontation towards other religious groups. He established a special department for this purpose at the Nadwah-al 'Ulamā', which he envisaged as the institution that would implement his special scheme of education, and thus produce a class of *'ulamā'* true to the lofty ideal and multi-faceted role he foresaw for them. Attacking reformers (like Sir Sayyad) who, he felt, by wiping out traditional education had ransomed the very identity of Muslims only to produce a service class, he upheld its relevance for the performance of purely religious functions by the *'ulamā'*, who had always been an important and influential part of the Muslim community. He felt further that by mastering European languages and research they could be made competent to fulfil modern religious needs, which included the genesis of a modern *'ilm-al kalām*, and the preaching of Islām in foreign lands. In 1910 he repeated that since Muslim nationhood was based on religion, religious education was necessary in order to preserve it, and to ward off the dangers posed to Islām.

Shibli's attitude to the Urdu question was also very practical. As the Secretary of the *Anjuman-i Taraqqi-i Urdu*, in 1903 he tried to show that Hindus were also closely associated with its work, and it appreciated their efforts. The next year, with the help of detailed historical and literary evidence he refuted allegations that the religious bigory of Muslims had prevented them from learning Hindi despite years of close contact with the

Hindus, and those who showed interest in it were ostracized by the community. He proved that not only the common folk, but Muslim rulers too had given ample evidence of their interest in it, and in fact in all other aspects of Hindu culture too. Between 1910 and 1912 he suggested that elementary religious books for rural Muslims should be written in Hindi, since it was easier to learn. In 1912 he opposed the Vernacular Scheme of the Allahabad government because he felt that it would create a third language, whereas the need of the hour was to develop both Urdu and Hindi independently. Describing the former as the language universally used by both educated Hindus and Muslims, he was sharply critical of those who were unfair enough to accuse the Hindus of trying to wipe it out. He felt on the other hand that they had done more for its progress and development than the Muslims themselves.

In 1911-12 Shibli illustrated the cordiality of Hindu-Muslim relations in a historical perspective. Wisely defining politics as the rights of subjects over the government, or to participate in governance, he made the significant observation that with respect to it, the status of Muslims as subjects of the British held precedence over their religious identity. He tried to jolt them out of the mould of Sir Sayyad's outdated political philosophy, which he felt had led to the numbing of their political consciousness, and their ability to strive for legitimate freedom and rights; whereas he greatly admired the political insight, courage, and sacrificial spirit of the Hindus.

Although Shibli fully supported the Congress and appreciated its efforts towards self-government through administrative reforms; he felt that rather than joining it in imitation of the Hindus, Muslims should chart their independent political course. Since their needs, although common, were also different, they needed a separate political stage. He however wholly disagreed with the aims and methods of the Muslim League due to its attitude of confrontation and conflict with the Hindus, rather than demanding rights from the government. He therefore urged it to refrain from divisive and narrow group politics, and to join hands with the Congress for the achievement of common and broad goals, for true politics was characterized by universality and wideness of aims. Astutely describing politics as the most potent sentiment in the world, equal in power to religion, he realized the importance of political training, education, and information—both for leaders and the masses.

Shibli wholly disagreed with the stand of Sir Sayyad and his followers : that the Hindus had been mistaken in forming the Congress which had created a rift between them and the Hindus, and that unity between them was impossible since they could not share a political stage. He believed on the other hand that they should form a joint stage for common issues. He also disagreed with them on the point that participation in the political activities of the Hindus would lead to the loss of their identity. Finally he reminded Muslims that they should not unite with the Hindus because their international allies had been weakened (who anyway could not help them against their neighbours), but because such unity had, and would always remain desirable.

Shibli was not plagued by the fear and insecurity that characterized Sir Sayyad. We sense in him a new confidence and courage, and the awareness that Muslims had no reason to fear the Hindus—rather both should unite politically, and demand their common rights from the government. (This aspect of his thought was enlarged upon by later thinkers like Mawlānas Āzād and Madani.) He thus believed in political co-operation despite religious differences, his attitude to the latter also being free of any bitterness or hostility. Whereas Sir Sayyad had presented different religious and social arguments in favour of the case for Hindu-Muslim co-operation, for Shibli it was as if a self-evident truth which need not be justified laboriously and elaborately. Although he described the basis of Muslim nationhood as Islām, he was silent on the vexatious question of whether India was a single, or comprised numerous nations. His political insight is also commendable.

Muḥammad Iqbāl had formulated the basic premises of his political thought very early. In the period 1909-11 we find him giving expression to nearly all the ideas which he would elaborate on in great detail later.

In this period we find him dwelling at some length on the problem of education, which he believed (as Sir Sayyad and Shibli had done), would play a key role in preserving Muslim nationhood. He felt that this required intimately acquainting the community with its past, so as to create in it national pride and self-respect. The present western-oriented system of education on the other hand threatened their very identity by completely alienating Muslims from their tradition and history. Like the two thinkers before him, he too believed in the need and importance of religious education in order to preserve Muslim solidarity, which depended on Islām. Later however this issue did not engage his interest much.

From 1909 onwards Iqbāl defined Islām or identity of belief (rather than territory, language etc.) as the basis of Muslim nationhood. Interestingly enough, we find him justifying Muslim fanaticism for religion as a survival instinct which every group possesses towards the ground of its being—only that in the case of other nations it took the form of patriotism, and was directed towards their country. Similarly, in 1934 he reasoned that since for Muslims Islām was not only a faith but also the object of patriotism, toleration was for them equivalent to suicide. He therefore defended what others felt was intolerance among Muslims, as a defensive and vital instinct, stemming from their perceived threat to the survival of the community.

Iqbāl's positing of a purely ideational basis for Muslim nationhood drove him to a haunting insecurity—he felt that due to its abstract foundations the Muslim nation was more prone to disintegration. Herein lies his obsession with the problem of survival, which even in 1910 made him wary of indiscriminate cultural assimilation, and led him to advocate the importance of conservation in preserving communal identity. In 1928-29 he felt that Muslim society was rendered weak not only by its non-territorial, but also its non-racial character, since it was composed of different, even repellant races. He therefore reasoned that in such a society reform must be carried out within proper limits, for change might prove to be a disintegrating factor. Accordingly, even while he asserted the importance of *ijtihād* as the instrument of evolution in Islāmic law, he warned that it must be tempered with conservatism in order to preserve the past, which constituted the identity of the community. In 1938, striking an uncompromising posture, he would take a more static view of divine law while affirming its incompatibility with nationalism.

Since Muslim nationhood was beyond race and territory, even in 1910 Iqbāl saw it as attempting to create an ever-expanding, and ultimately world-wide multi-national state, which might yet incorporate individual sovereign states. In 1921, since he felt that territorial and racial organizations were only temporary phases of collective life, he appealed to mankind to abandon their false idols of race and nationality, and unite through Islām, which would win them over through example and persuasion. In

1928-29 he again upheld the Islāmic aim of the final combination of humanity, and the belief that not nationalism but only religious renewal could lead it to salvation. Rejecting the relevance of the caliphate for the present age, he now defined the ideal Islāmic political order as a league of independent nations in which boundaries would exist only for facility of reference. Within each state the principle of *ijmā'* would serve as the basis for the Islāmic republican system, according to which the authority of the caliph and the power of *ijtihād* would be transferred to an elected legislative assembly.

In 1930 Iqbāl reiterated the power of religion in individual and collective life. In 1931 and 1933, while he categorically rejected the viability of political pan-Islāmism in the sense of the unification of Muslims into a political state, he would interpret it rather as a humanitarian Islāmic ideal which aimed at unifying nations, and even religions, by destroying racial and other differences between men. He believed that Asia should assimilate Islāmic ideals by thinking in terms of mankind, not race. In 1935 he described the League of Nations he had spoken of earlier as only the second-best form that Muslim political solidarity could take. He now defined its ideal form as a world-state; whereas the least desirable form was that of independent states, whose relations were determined by purely economic and political considerations. In 1938 he repeated that Islām was the only social order which could ensure peace by uniting mankind. However it is interesting that while he regarded this human brotherhood as being above race, nationality, colour, and language, he did not include religion here. Since he now repudiated missionary effort, it is not clear exactly how Islām was to influence others.

From 1910 onwards Iqbāl held that the idea of nationality was antithetical to Islām. In 1928-29 he repeated that according to the Qur'ān racial divisions were meant for identification only, whereas as a non-territorial social movement Islām had achieved complete equality among its heterogeneous adherents. He opposed modern Muslim nationalism as a manifestation of racialism, which was against Islām's humanistic outlook, and would ultimately replace its universal ethics by narrow national ones.

Iqbāl's attitude towards Muslim nationalism becomes ambiguous in 1930, perhaps because this was the year when he began campaigning in favour of territorial Muslim nationalism in India. He now described Muslim nationalism as helping to realize the

Islāmic ideal of unifying mankind by beginning with the People of the Book. Yet he also opposed it as threatening Islām's humanizing work by confining the Muslim outlook to race and country. He feared that it would make religion a private affair of the individual, and divorced from his temporal and national life, as it had in Europe; whereas since the religious and ethical ideal of Islām was an inalienable part of its social and political order, rejection of one would imply that of the other too. In 1931 he explained that he had turned against nationalism because it was opposed to Islāmic unity.

In 1935 Iqbāl finally reconciled himself to nationalism in Muslim countries, for he felt that there it did not conflict with Islām. He however held that in countries like India, where Muslims were in a minority, nationalism would threaten the loss of their identity by its merger into the dominant nationality. He again spoke of the conflict such territorial nationalism would create between religious and political loyalty. Making their faith a purely personal affair, it would compel them to follow social, legal, and political systems other than those of Islām. The geographical basis of such nationalism would thus displace Islām as the principle of their solidarity.

In 1938 Iqbāl's attitude again betrays some ambiguity when he described nationalism in Muslim countries as a ploy by western nations to shatter the religious unity of Muslims and further their own imperialistic ambitions. In the Indian context he explained that it was nationalism as a political, (rather than purely geographical concept) which conflicted with Islām, which as the *dīn-i qayyim* could not accept any other principle of human solidarity. Even while he realized that this would generate political controversy in India by suggesting that Muslims could not unite with others for national ends, he felt that there could be no compromise on divine law, which was eternal and unchanging. He reasoned further that political nationalism was incompatible not only with Islām, but with religion itself, and would create rampant irreligiously in India, as it had in Europe.

Iqbāl had been an ardent nationalist, until his visit to Europe in 1905 led to his complete disillusionment with the ideology. Consequently, his rejection of a common Indian nationhood as a practically unviable ideal dates back to 1909. In 1910 he held that India was composed of discordant political units which England had conquered, but not unified. By 1927 (even while repudiating united nationalism as an unattainable ideal in India), he had begun to give expression to the mutual hostility and suspicion which he sensed between its communities, perceiving each to be aiming at the other's domination and even destruction, and its own selfish aggrandizement. (In this, and his consequent opposition to the implementation of the principle of pure competition in India, he seems to be closely following Sir Sayyad.) By 1930 he had come to believe (again like Sir Sayyad), that India was not a single nation but a continent, the differences between whose various indigenous nations were not only territorial, but also racial, linguistic, and religious; and who were moreover not willing to sink their individuality in a larger whole. In 1930-31 he again followed Sir Sayyad's reasoning : that due to the presence of different communal groups with conflicting interests, democracy could not succeed in India, and would only lead to civil war. Like Sir Sayyad he perceived a Hindu conspiracy to subjugate all other communities including the Muslims. In 1931-32 he again expressed his conviction about the disparity between India's cultural units, which he felt could therefore never have a single national point of view.

Whereas Iqbāl had earlier been in favour of obliterating religious differences, by 1909 he had come to believe that Hindus and Muslims should preserve their separate national identity. He would later, in 1930, call this the positive aspect of communalism *i.e.* affording cultural autonomy to each group, without ill will towards others. He now believed that rather than forcing nationalism and artificial unity upon the different Indian communities, they should be allowed to develop according to their own culture and tradition; whereas the dishonest patriotism of the nationalists was not willing to concede this right to others. Accordingly he recommended the creation of communal provinces as the only way to build a harmonious nation without compromising diversity. Interestingly enough, in 1933 he described this as only an intermediate stage in the evolutionary political process. In 1935 he felt that the nationalists resented Muslim political and religious solidarity because they wanted to build a nation by suppressing India's different cultural entities. He believed that whereas this would lead to bitterness and conflict, only interaction could produce true and enduring unity.

Even in 1910 Iqbāl had formed some idea about the existence of a "Muslim nationality in India." Interestingly enough he called Awrangzeb its founder, due to his political perception that the

Muslim rulers of India must consolidate their strength rather than relying on the goodwill of the majority. In 1930 he elaborated that by virtue of being not only a religious group but also a distinct, homogeneous, cultural, and political entity, Indian Muslims were a nation (in the modern sense of the word), and therefore wanted to develop independently as such. (Interestingly enough, he would not credit Hindus with being a nation, due to their social inequality and consequent lack of homogeneity.) In 1932 he clarified that since Islām was the basis of Muslim nationhood, their patriotism (or loyalty) was directed towards it (and the culture and historical tradition associated with it), rather than towards their country.

Accordingly, it was to preserve and further develop this very cultural identity of Muslims within the Indian body politic, and to protect them from non-Muslim domination that Iqbāl proposed the creation of a Muslim state (or states) within an Indian federation in 1930. He felt that this would ensure peace by creating an internal balance of power; whereas for Muslims free development was not possible under the unitary government through which Hindus were trying to impose their permanent communal dominance. He clarified that there would be no religious rule in the Muslim state, and it would protect its minorities.

Although Muslim thinkers may have spoken of Indian or even world-wide Muslim nationhood, they were for the most part concerned about the welfare of the Muslims of their home-state—for Sir Sayyad this was Delhi and U.P., and for Iqbāl north-west India, particularly Panjab. Besides the fact that his scheme of a Muslim state would benefit only its population, he even advised its majority Muslims, and those of Bengal, to ignore the Muslims of the minority provinces for the time being, even while he urged the Muslim League to concentrate on politically arousing the Muslims of the north-west. This callousness towards some of his co-religionists is incomprehensible, and speaks of a degree of parochialism.

Muḥammad 'Ali Jinnāh began his political career as an ardent nationalist. While in 1915 he had appealed to all Indians to work unitedly for progress, in 1916 he credited the national movement (and therefore indirectly British rule), with having triggered the evolution of a common Indian nationality, which had generated national self-consciousness and feelings of territorial patriotism among Indians. Yet he was not blind to the racial, cultural, and religious diversity in India (which he therefore called a "continent"), and the difficulties which it posed in the way of nation-building. Even at this early date we perceive a tension in his thought between nationalist and communal loyalty—he clearly differentiated the latter from sectarianism and separatism (although he himself once used the term "communal bigots" derogatively). While he frequently appealed not only for goodwill but also the "union" of the two major communities, he also justified the anxiety of Muslims to protect their communal identity through separate political organizations and safeguards. Even while he urged them to work for national unity rather than only self-interest, he reasoned that minorities should have a sense of security before they could develop a national viewpoint, and for this the majority should win their trust.

While he continued to appeal for political unity as indispensable for self-government, reiterated his commitment to nationalism, and denied that he had become a leader of communal strife; in 1926-27 Jinnāh again appealed for separate electorates (although he personally did not believe in them), for the sake of promoting a sense of security among Muslims. We perceive perhaps some cynicism, and a hardening of posture in his declaration that communalism was an undeniable reality in India, and could not be wished away. While he continued to hold that friendship was the only way for the two major Indian communities to rise to the nationhood to which they were aspiring (which in turn would bring them closer to responsible government), from 1928 onwards he would repeatedly express his conviction that the problem of minorities should be faced squarely. He reasoned that since religious majorities tended to be tyrannical, the desire of the minorities for safeguards was understandable, and should be granted in order to win their support, for without it there could be no stability.

While he continued to support the "union" of the two communities in the struggle for freedom, in 1935 Jinnāh repeated that the question of minorities (whom he described as a separate entity in the state, differing in religion, language, race, or culture), should be solved as a political issue. In 1936 he made a final bid to balance his nationalistic and communal sentiments. While he continued to affirm his desire for unity (as the only means to self-government) and India's welfare, he felt it was natural for Muslims to protect their future position as a minority, and it was wrong to brand this as communalism (which he had earlier accepted, while rejecting sectarianism). He urged them to prove their patriotism even as they organized themselves politically, and accordingly defined the object of the Muslim League as the protection of the political, religious, cultural, and other rights of Muslims.

We feel that the unity which Jinnāh so ardently championed was perhaps only a skin-deep political co-operation of two different entities, whose sole aim was the achievement of self-government; for he does not seem to have dwelt on cultural or human bonds between the two communities. Perhaps this is the reason why he was later able to repudiate it so easily.

The experience of Congress rule in several provinces after the elections of 1937 appears to have completely altered Jinnāh's political perceptions. He now described the League as struggling not only for Muslims, but to secure all minorities (including non-Brahman Hindus) from caste-rule. He now ruled out the possibility of even a settlement between the two communities, rejecting "justice" and "goodwill" in politics, and replacing these by "power" and "fear."

Jinnāh also completely turned against the Congress, accusing its provincial governments of cultural, religious, and political repression against Muslims, and of foisting Hindu culture on them. He now charged it of alienating them from the mid-1920s itself by following a pro-Hindu policy, while they masqueraded as nationalists. He therefore called it a Hindu body which falsely claimed to represent all Indians. He would also highlight caste-differences within the Hindus, and believed that the Brahman-dominated Congress was as inimical to the interests of the lower castes as to non-Hindus. He felt that it was insisting on complete democracy so as to maintain its permanent dominance, and crush all other communities and cultures. He therefore equated its *swarāj* with Hindu *rāj*, which he described as a Hindu government based on ancient Hindu religion and culture.

Jinnāh was particularly hostile to Gandhi, whom he accused of not only introducing religion into politics, but also of making the Congress an instrument for his mission of reviving Hinduism, and sabotaging all efforts for unity after 1925. As for the Muslims in the Congress, he felt that they were betraying a defeatist mentality by urging their co-religionists to unconditionally surrender to the Hindus. His bitter anti-Congress stand appears to have mitigated his anti-Britishness, and he seems now to have slackened in his opposition to foreign rule. In 1938, while he denied the Congress charge that the League supported imperialism, he also asserted its right to adopt any political manoeuvre and allies (including the British) to further its political ends.

By 1939 like Iqbāl, Jinnāh too held that instead of chasing the noble but impossible ideal of becoming one nation, Indians should accept that their country was a subcontinent of totally different nationalities, races, religions, cultures, and languages; the social, political, and economic differences between whom were too real to be brushed aside. He also shared with Sir Sayyad and Iqbāl the view that for this very reason western democracy which was based on the concept of a single, homogeneous people was unfit for India, and would produce division rather than unity. He now concurred with them on the point that a parliamentary system would imply a permanent hegemony of the majority, whereas in 1917 he had refuted it vigorously. Although he had earlier held religion to be a private affair, he now believed that since in India it governed all aspects of life including politics, Indians were deeply divided on religious lines. He held that in the past too, India had never been politically united, and that the present artificial unity had been created and sustained by British administration, and would be dissipated if it was withdrawn.

Jinnāh particularly emphasized the differences between India's two principal communities, and now denied any ground for union, or even co-operation between them, due to their conflicting ideology and goals. He described them as two distinct nations representing separate civilizations. He believed that such basic differences could never be smoothened out to pave the way for the evolution of a common nationality; and that this was borne out by their past history, which had failed to forge unity despite centuries of close contact.

In December 1938 Jinnāh wanted Muslims to develop a national consciousness and individuality like the Hindus. However, from January 1940 onwards he asserted that they were in fact a separate nation rather than a minority, and wanted to preserve their political identity as such. He reasoned that the early Muslims had brought their own civilization to India, and further developed it here; local converts too had developed as a group separate from the parent community; and this had contributed to the distinct national traits of present-day Muslims. Although in order to undermine the caste-based nationalism of the Jāts in Panjab he asserted that Muslim nationhood was above caste, in 1944 he chose not to address himself to the question of how territorial nationalism affected world-wide Muslim nationhood. While from 1937 onwards he repeatedly expressed sympathy for other Muslim peoples particularly the Arabs, in 1947 he repudiated pan-Islāmism as a political theory, while continuing to uphold friendship and co-operation between eastern [rather than Muslim] nations.

Like Iqbāl, Jinnāh too reasoned that Muslims would not tolerate being shifted from British to Hindu subjection. Rather, as a nation they demanded their separate homeland so that they could independently develop their political and cultural life according to their own ideals. He followed Iqbāl's view that the acceptance of a united India with a central government would mean complete extinction for them and Islām in the subcontinent. He reasoned that the Muslim demand did not amount to secession, since India had always been divided by nature into Hindu and Muslim parts (yet he vigorously opposed a division of Panjab and Bengal). He optimistically stated that partition would end the rivalry between the two communities and the desire of each for supremacy, conveniently ignoring the fact that the question of majority and minority would persist in each country. Like Iqbāl he appears callous about the fate of India's minority Muslims. Besides summarily dismissing the sacrifice that partition would demand from them, his arguments to prove that they would be no better off in an undivided India, are unconvincing. His proposal of reciprocal agreements for safeguarding the interests of each minority is also not feasible, since it implies extra-territorial responsibility of a sovereign state.

Jinnāh's stand regarding the future system of government in Pakistan appears ambiguous and even evasive. While on the one hand he tried to allay the fears of its prospective minorities by assuring them that it would be a democratic, secular, republic, occasionally he also vaguely hinted at its "Muslim" character, apparently in a bid to pander to popular sentiment. His frequent references to Islām and its ideology also appear to be meant to serve the same purpose, for they are not supported by the general trend of his thought. His complete brushing aside of all difference of opinion among Muslims regarding the desirability of partition is also unacceptable. Finally, he desired to instil into the people of

Pakistan the kind of territorial nationalism and loyalty to the state which is above religion, caste, and creed, and which he had thoroughly repudiated in India. He now not only reverted to the view that religion was a personal matter, but by calling for its gradual obliteration in political life, undermined the very basis on which he had demanded the creation of a seperate state.

In the final analysis we may say that Jinnāh was an astute politician rather than a profound thinker—there is not much intellectual content in his thought. It is therefore not surprising that unlike Iqbāl he did not theorize on the problem of Muslim nationhood in India—for him it was primarily a political problem. His indebtedness to Iqbāl regarding the philosophical aspect of the issue (which he did not develop any further), is quite obvious. Indeed he appears more eloquent, impressive, and convincing as a nationalist, than later as a communal leader, and his radical reversal of roles is not easy to comprehend. In the end he himself appears to have been doubtful about the wisdom of the momentous step he had taken.

At the beginning of his career, in 1903 to be precise, *Mawlāna Abu'l Kalām Āzād* disapproved of the cultural exchange between the two major Indian communities, which he was to later ardently uphold. In fact he then believed that Muslims must shed the Hindu ways and customs which they had imbibed over the centuries, and return to their original Arab and Iranian culture.

Āzād's belief that Islām calls upon Muslims to strive for freedom and parliamentary government by non-violent means, dates back to 1912. Shibli's influence over him in this period is very marked. He was very critical of Sir Sayyad's loyalism, his decrying of all political effort, and of the Muslim League's confrontationist attitude towards the Hindus rather than the government, all of which tended to weaken India's political struggle for self-government. Although he admired the efforts of the Hindus in this direction, at this stage he believed in following not them, but the Qur'ān and *Sunnat*, in all political matters.

Between 1912 and 1914 Āzād repudiated the value of secular territorial nationalism for Muslims, and believed instead in their adherence to a world-wide Islāmic nationhood. This served as the launching-pad for his Turkish sympathies. Bitterly critical of Sir Sayyad's attitude to the caliphate, Āzād dismissed his educational movement as a local Muslim effort which far from benefitting the Muslim world community, had made Indian Muslims indifferent to its fate. Accordingly he repeatedly urged them to nurture sympathetic links with their brethren world-wide, and particularly Turkey, which he called the centre of the Islāmic world.

During this period and again in 1920, Āzād perceived European Christians as the enemies of Islām, who were trying to destroy its religious and political unity by attacking its nerve-centre—the caliphate. While he continued to uphold the idea of a world-wide, united Muslim nationhood, he now also developed the concept of "collectivism" in order to support his views, and exalted the caliph or *imām* as the centre of this collective life. Accordingly, while he believed that there should be one government of Muslims on the whole earth with a single caliph, one language, and one nationality; he also upheld the need for a single *imām* or *amīr* for all India's Muslims, the latter apparently being subordinate to the former, although he did not elaborate the point. Whereas in 1912 he had opposed all personal power, Āzād now advocated unquestioning obedience to the caliph irrespective of his qualities. He tried his best to instil obedience and sympathy for the Turkish Sultān among Indian Muslims, and to arouse anti-British feelings by recounting its injustices towards the Islāmic caliphate. Accordingly he urged them to adopt non-co-operation against the government so long as it did not fulfil the joint demands of *khilāfat* and *swarāj*. In contrast he presented the Hindus as a community which should be befriended since it had never been aggressive towards Islām and Muslims.

Towards the end of 1921 *khilāfat* and *swarāj* not only presented themselves to Āzād as the twin aims of Indian Muslims, but the latter appears to be gradually acquiring precedence. While he repeatedly appealed for Hindu-Muslim unity, he also made it clear that this was not merely a strategic or political unity, but a religious duty for the latter. (His claim that he had realized this even twenty years back and made it the aim of *al-Hilāl*, is not borne out by his earlier writings—we shall repeatedly find him making such claims.) He in fact believed that their faith called upon Muslims not only to nurture friendship with the Hindus, but to form a single nation with them—for the same reason for which the Prophet (Pbuh) had done so with the Medinan Jews—to combate the threat posed to Islām. At the same time he also urged them to remain faithful to their Islāmic nationhood (whose basis was the

Sharī'at), by fulfilling their duties to the caliphate, and organizing themselves under an *amīr* in India. Whereas in 1921 he felt that being a secular political organization the Congress could not influence Muslims, in 1922 he would entrust the *khilāfat* issue wholly to it, ruling out any independent agreement of the Muslims with the government, and urging them to completely trust and follow its leader Gandhiji, who he believed was right on every count. He was prepared to drop *khilāfat* demands if *swarāj* was granted, but not *vice versa*. He now claimed that it was *al-Hilāl* which had persuaded Muslims to unite fearlessly with the Hindus. Whereas he had earlier advocated non-violence as a religious principle, he now held that Islām recommended a violent struggle against foreign aggressors, but Muslims were compelled to adopt non-violence on grounds of expediency.

In 1923 Āzād again took the credit for urging Muslims to trust the Hindus and participate in the Congress, which he felt was the only party India needed, due to its non-sectarianism and championing of united Indian nationhood. Hindu-Muslim unity was thus an end in itself rather than merely a means to freedom, which was unacceptable to him sans the former. He saw Indian nationalism as being strengthened by joint endeavour despite the many obstacles of religion and race, chief among which he regarded as the Hindu-Muslim question in 1924. He urged Indians to rid themselves of divisiveness in order to develop true patriotism and nationalism, and to realize that the country belongs to them all. He differed from Shibli and Mawlāna Ḥusayn Aḥmad in believing that for the sake of freedom Indians must defer all sectarian activities: since these could not be kept apart from political unity, they were sure to damage their prospects for freedom. For the same reason, in 1934 he would restrain Muslims from trying to reply to the attacks of the Arya Samaj, while also trying to persuade them not to interpret these as indications of general Hindu aggressiveness towards them.

Āzād's attitude towards the protection of Muslim rights fluctuates frequently. While in 1925 he believed in demanding a fair deal for them from the Hindus without souring the relations of both; in 1937 he not only held that it was wrong of them to demand assurances about the future, but also claimed to have thought thus since 1912. In February 1940 he held that Muslims had a right to struggle for safeguards, whereas in March he said that since the days of *al-Hilāl* he had repudiated the need for these, even while he stated as President of the Congress that it was in favour of providing safeguards to the minorities. In 1942 he claimed that his views had been unchanged, and that since 1904 he had believed that Muslims should strive for independence rather than obstructing it by demanding safeguards. From 1940 onwards he held that India's democratic and loosely federal structure would insure Muslims and other minorities against domination by the majority. Expressing great confidence in the ability and will of the Congress to protect Muslim interests, he appears to be urging the community to follow it unquestioningly.

Although in 1904 Āzād was disturbed by the move among Bengali Muslims to reject Urdu in favour of their mother tongue, by 1937 he appears to have turned against imposing an artificial uniformity over India's diverse regional languages, although he continued to believe throughout that only Urdu deserved to be called its national language. Later as Education Minister he would feel the need for every Indian to learn both Urdu and Devanāgri scripts, while he continued to uphold education in the mother tongue rather than in English. He was also opposed to communal universities, and believed that if religious education was imparted in schools, it should be of a kind as to nurture tolerance rather than narrow-mindedness.

In 1940 Āzād described Indian nationhood as being the synthesis of the various culture-currents which had made India their home. He particularly glorified the joint Hindu-Muslim culture which had developed over the centuries, and completely repudiated the cultural revivalism he had espoused in 1903, for their joint nationality was now an irrevocable reality for him. Asserting his equal and unflinching claim to both his Islāmism and Indianism (he interestingly described the latter as having been forced upon him by circumstances), he declared that there was no conflict between religion and nationality. He blamed the British for perpetrating the falsehood that rather than being a united nation India was divided along communal lines, in order to consolidate their own position. In October 1945 he finally freed nationality from the religious basis in terms of which he had defined it earlier, by admitting, albeit guardedly, that nationality does not change with religion.

Āzād was of course strongly opposed to partition, which he

felt was not only impractical and harmful for India, but would also prove detrimental to its Muslim minority by rendering them smaller, scattered, and therefore weaker, in what he interestingly described as a Hindu *rāj*. For him partition was equivalent to cowardice and defeatism, and he therefore urged the Muslims to get rid of their fear-complex. When it finally appeared inevitable he could only hope that it would be short-lived, for he was convinced that the two peoples were one at heart.

Although Āzād began as a believer in Islāmic universalism, his later commitment to Indian nationalism was complete and unflinching. The shift however does not appear abrupt due to his early sympathies with the political struggle of the Hindus, although he did not then believe in following them. 1920, which was the high-water mark of his pan-Islāmic convictions, also saw him leaning towards the Hindus as an ally against the British, and marks the beginning of his involvement in the national movement. By 1921 he had come to believe in the need for united Indian nationhood as a religious duty in order to protect Islām, even while he continued to uphold the latter's universal nationhood. By 1922 his shift towards the former became marked, even while he expressed complete loyalty for Gandhi and the Congress. His commitment towards united Indian nationhood would become more intense with the passage of time, and he repeatedly urged both communities to refrain from doing anything to damage it. In fact he seems to be suggesting a policy of complete surrender for the Muslims, with no guarantees for the protection of their political, religious, and cultural rights, except the goodwill of the Congress. In 1940 he would ultimately altogether deny the religious basis of nationality.

Mawlāna Ḥusayn Aḥmad Madani not only followed Āzād in asserting the validity of the Islāmic caliphate, but also exceeded him in glorifying the Turkish Sultāns as its repositories, and in urging Indian Muslims to rise in its defence. Although he did not believe in political pan-Islāmism, his Islāmic universalism was one of the many facets of his anti-British stand. He thus highlighted Britain's enmity for the caliphate in the larger perspective of Christian hostility towards Islām. On another plane he emphasized not only the religious, but also the political, economic, and other losses accruing not only to Muslims, but to all Indians, from British rule, which thus helped to forge an implicit bond between them. He also explicitly called upon them to unite for the overthrow of the tyrannical foreign government, and to establish *swarāj*—even while keeping intact their religious freedom. This would serve as the basis of his later version of nationalism. Whereas even in 1921 he felt that it was the religious duty of Muslims to struggle against the British, from 1942 onwards he would equate this struggle with *jihād*.

In 1931 Sayyad Ḥusayn Aḥmad first suggested what would become his constant refrain later—that political strategy should be ruled by prevailing circumstances—and cited the *Sunnat* to support this view. On this basis he reasoned that Muslims should join hands with the smaller enemy—the Hindus—to combat the greater *i.e.* the British. In this regard he differed from Āzād who was more pro-Hindu, and for whom unity with them was not merely a political strategy. However, on a few occasions Mawlāna Madani too appealed for good relations with them on grounds other than those of expediency, citing social and religious reasons in favour of it. Unlike Āzād who in the early period often suggested *hijrat* as one of the alternatives open to Muslims, Mawlāna Ḥusayn Aḥmad Madani tried to bring home to them the reality that they could not leave India en masse, and must therefore create amity through tolerance. Another reason which he cited in favour of this was that as a missionary religion Islām needed to attract others towards itself rather than repel them through hostility. He therefore greatly admired Akbar's Hindu policy, and was in favour of its being followed.

From 1938 onwards these different trends in Mawlāna Madani's thought converged in his theory of united nationhood, which he developed in great detail, and it appears, primarily in response to Iqbāl's invective against it. It was for him a means of achieving unity among Indians (through their only common territorial bond, and despite their numerous differences), as a part of the strategy to combat the British, who were their common enemy. By differentiating between *millat* and *qawm*, he tried to set apart the religious and secular or territorial identity of Indian Muslims. Although these were overlapping, he held that their demands were not conflicting. Unlike Āzād whose commitment to it was more unquestioning, Mawlāna Ḥusayan Aḥmad clarified that Indian nationalism was not opposed to religion since it signified only unity for joint action, each constituent group being free in all religious and cultural matters. Defending it against Iqbāl's attacks, he reasoned that if Muslims were firm in preserving their faith, there would be no danger to it, nor of their being absorbed into the majority. He thus held that Islām was flexible enough to permit such a relationship with non-Muslims for strategic purposes, so far as its principles did not suffer.

Although he conceded that Europe had destroyed world-wide Islāmic unity by perpetrating geographical nationalism in the Muslim world, Mawlāna Madani held that in the present the two did not pose any conflict for Indian Muslims, who could participate equally in both. Whereas in 1938 he seemed to be asserting the precedence of the former, and affirmed that it was the duty of all world Muslims to help an oppressed brother, later he would pose the condition that this must not be in violation of any agreement with non-Muslims.

Sayyad Ḥusayn Aḥmad upheld the secular and nationalistic credentials of the Congress, and believed that Muslims should participate in it—because it was fighting for freedom, and only so long as it did so. Unlike Āzād whose loyalty to it was unflinching, he held that they should not hesitate to criticize those of its proposals which were opposed to their interests, and to act independently on religious issues. In 1945 he reasoned that there was nothing objectionable in Hindu-Muslim unity for freedom, due to the close bonds between the two communities. Again unlike Āzād he reasoned that although Hindus were enemies of Islām by virtue of being unbelievers, the British were the greater enemy, who had promoted them and set them up against Muslims, and had sowed hatred between the two communities as part of their policy of divide and rule. Juxtaposing present Hindu-Muslim hostility with their centuries-old concord, he attributed it to British machinations rather than any genuine religious differences. He therefore felt that those Muslim leaders who were opposed to united Indian nationhood were in fact beguiled by British tactics, and were helping to further its interests.

Unlike Sayyad Mawdūdi, Mawlāna Madani did not think it necessary to replace British rule by Islāmic. Again taking recourse to the politics of expediency, he believed that since the latter was desirable but unattainable in the present circumstances, Muslims should continue striving for it, while opting for the "lesser evil" of an Indian government with safeguards for them. In fact the goal of an Islāmic government appeared elusive to him not only in India, but elsewhere too. He thus advocated realism and gradualism in politics.

From 1945 onwards Sayyad Ḥusayn Aḥmad was very critical of the Muslim League for its pro-British and anti-Hindu stance, and for obstructing freedom rather than struggling for it. Accepting the need for co-operation between it and the Jamī'at-al 'Ulamā'-i Hind, he however blamed it for the failure of all efforts in this direction. He felt Pakistan was a brain-child of the British, conceived to continue its hold over India. He denied any connection between the demand for it, and the falsely alleged atrocities of the provincial Congress governments, since the former pre-dated the latter. He felt that at a time when nations were coming closer together, it was absurd to demand division on the basis of culture and race—interestingly he excluded religion—the chief ground of the demand.

Mawlāna Madani therefore urged Muslims to unite with the Hindus rather than pressing for a course of action (on the basis of their anti-Hindu feelings), which would only prove detrimental for them. He pointed out that a future Pakistan would incorporate as many conflicting groups and interests as its parent state. He also opposed it on the ground that it would limit Muslim missionary activity by spreading hatred against non-Muslims. While he ruled out the possibility of the establishment of an Islāmic government in Pakistan due to the presence of a strong minority, he felt that the contradictory claims of League leaders in this connection were meant to mislead Muslims and win their sympathy.

As late as in March 1947, Sayyad Ḥusayn Aḥmad adopted the stand that Muslims were participating in the struggle for freedom only on condition of the protection of their political, religious, and cultural rights. Yet he also held that it was more urgent for them to join hands with others for freedom—rights could be demanded later. He favoured a gradual approach towards the goal of the Islāmic state, progressing from the initial stage of a democratic, secular state, whose loosely federal structure would afford the Muslim element an opportunity for the gradual 'Islāmization' of its religion, culture, and polity through missionary work, for only Islām could ensure true peace and security.

Prabha Dixit[5] believes that the ideology of the pan-Islāmic movement provided the Muslim League with a statement of Muslim nationalism. However it is significant that the chief ideologues of the latter—Iqbāl and Jinnāh—were not only uninfluenced by pan-Islāmism, but completely repudiated its relevance. She similarly holds that it emphasized the distinct political identity of Muslims, highlighted their need for an independent centre, and rejected the territorial concept of nationhood advocated by the Congress. Yet among the thinkers we have studied so far, the two most ardent pan-Islāmists—Āzād and Madani—also turned out to be most committed to Indian nationalism.

With reference to these two leaders particularly, it is misleading to say that "for the *khilāfat* leaders, the freedom of India was not an end, but an instrument for freeing the enslaved Islāmic states of Asia and Africa"—at most the last can only be described as an added incentive. It is also questionable as to how far "the abolition of the *khilāfat* . . . forced Indian Muslims to shift the emphasis from their "international brotherhood" to their "solidarity" in India. Rajat Ray[6] is apparently closer to truth in his belief that for Āzād pan-Islāmism and nationalism became integral parts of the "same religious-political experience." He also believes that Āzād's conviction that the two were not contradictory but identical, "was based on his Middle-Eastern experience."

Sayyad Abu'l A'lá Mawdūdi laid great emphasis on dress, language, and script, as elements of nationality. He therefore urged Muslims to maintain distinctiveness in these, and to abstain from imitation of other nations in order to preserve their national identity. His early views regarding nationhood correspond closely to those of Iqbāl. He highlighted world-wide Islāmic nationhood and its claims on Muslims, while completely undermining territorial nationalism. Whereas at one point he would admit some degree of patriotism (which must however be forsaken if it conflicted with religion), elsewhere he held that since Muslim nationhood was incompatible with other nationalities of race, country, and language, Muslims must sever all bonds of land and blood. While he believed that they should be friendly towards non-Muslims, he ruled out the possibility of the two ever becoming a single nation.

Sayyad Mawdūdi undermined the treaty of Madīnah as only a military alliance which lasted for barely two years. He felt that undue importance was being laid on the word *ummat*, which he defined as Mawlāna Madani had done *qawm*—as one or more groups bound by time, place, religion, or common aims. Like Iqbāl, he too held that the modern concept of nationalism which the

Congress wished to realize in India was opposed to Islāmic principles, and was very different from the Islāmic concept espoused by Mawlāna Madani. He also agreed with Iqbāl that it would ultimately subordinate religion to nationality, as differences would be progressively eliminated to achieve homogeneity—although Mawlāna Madani's nationalism (which he was mistakenly ascribing to the Congress also), might not envisage this. He was opposed to Muslim participation in the Congress for yet another reason : since the legislature which it aimed to establish would have the power to revoke or amend the *Sharī'at*, it would give the majority the power to influence all aspects of Muslim life.

While Sayyad Mawdūdi's attitude to the freedom movement appears ambiguous, in the final analysis we may say that he was against Muslim participation in it, for he perceived the system which it sought to establish, as a greater evil than British rule. He felt that the nationalists wanted to wipe out all national differences within India, whereas he believed in preserving religious identity. At one point he said that Muslims should be excused from participation in the freedom movement until they could influence India's political development and defend their interests as Muslims. He believed that they should struggle for a freedom which would empower Islām in India, and make it a *dār-al Islām*, or at least like one, so that Muslims would have an influential enough share in governance to organize themselves on Islāmic lines. He also suggested the establishment of autonomous minority states within India in order to preserve the identity of Muslims, or else they would in effect only be transferred from British to Hindu subjugation.

In 1936 Sayyad Mawdūdi was critical of the Aligarh University for injuring religion by making Muslims slaves of western culture. He felt that it had failed to preserve Muslim identity and Islāmic culture, whereas it should have been a practical manifestation of these. He also believed in making Arabic compulsory as the language of Islāmic culture, and the means of direct access to Islāmic sources. This was also the period when he outlined his scheme of Islāmic education according to which, rather than artificially grafting religious and secular education, they should be wholly integrated, with the religious viewpoint guiding even secular sciences. For this he felt that the facts of knowledge must be compiled afresh in the Islāmic intuitional mould, by weeding out the western viewpoint from these.

While Sayyad Mawdūdi shared Āzād's belief in the sanctity of the Islāmic *jamā'at*, he held that it signified not any Muslim majority or party, but only that which was true to Islām, and formed for its service. In 1937 he first outlined the process of an Islāmic revolution to create a *dār-al Islām* by establishing training camps in which there would be a division of functions between different groups. The core group would be a revolutionary party whose members would be trained to develop excellent Islāmic character. They would garner political strength by influencing the masses, and ultimately take over the government machinery to build a new Islāmic order.

Until 1932 Sayyad Mawdūdi had ascribed to the conventional view of *jihād* as the endeavour for the defence or promotion of Islām. However it is from 1938 onwards that he appears to have developed his novel concept of *jihād* as the attempt to establish Islāmic rule, under which sovereignty should belong only to God. He reasoned that since Islām could not be truly and uncompromisingly followed under any other system, it was not content with being accepted only theoretically, and desired political power and rule. He therefore believed that only belief and preaching were not sufficient—in order to abolish evil and reform mankind Muslims must snatch government from wrongdoers, establish it on Islāmic principles, and stop evils by force. The violent overtones are balanced by Sayyad Mawdūdi's emphasis on the spiritual emancipation of the Muslim, which alone qualified him to undertake this struggle with pure and unselfish motives, and was to be attained through worship.

However Sayyad Mawdūdi's discourse on *jihād* in 1939 bears strong overtones of violence, while being silent on the moral training and uprightness which he had earlier emphasized. He now defended it from the viewpoint of the *mujāhid*—since he had concluded (on the basis of study rather than merely birth), that only Islām could lead to salvation, it was the *mujāhid's* duty to organize all collective life according to its principles.

In 1938 Sayyad Mawdūdi held that where fundamental differences of religion, race, and language existed, democracy would mean the perpetual tyranny of the majority. He rejected fundamental rights as a means of protecting the religion, culture, language and script of the minority, since it ruled out only the use of force, whereas the majority could create conditions to bring about their gradual extinction. (Yet in the same period he had also once said that Muslim culture was not equivalent to external manifestations such as dress and language, but the Qur'ānic mode of life and thought, and Muslims were concerned with preserving the latter rather than the former.) Whereas in 1935-36 he had held that the two major Indian communities could co-operate on common issues, he now believed that the fundamental differences between them (which were exploited but not created by the British), precluded unity. He now held that Muslims were an independent nation.

However by 1939 Sayyad Mawdūdi had come to believe that Muslims were not a nation but an international revolutionary party with the aim that its principles should rule the world. Despite his repudiation of "Muslim nationalism", his thought is very close to Iqbāl's Islāmic universalism, which is not surprising, since as we have seen, the latter tended to conflict with the former. Like Iqbāl he held that India possessed unity of political, but not cultural nationality, which was born from identity of religion, thought, and culture; and even ruled out its creation in the future due to deep-rooted differences and mutual antagonism. Again echoing Iqbāl, he asserted the need for federal principles—that the individuality of each group, the right to its preservation, and its sovereign control over its "subjects" be recognized, while the idea of joint action for common interests again became acceptable to him.

However Sayyad Mawdūdi clearly distanced himself from Muslim nationalists, who he felt were concerned not with the revival of Islām, but of the Muslim nation—even if it was outside Islāmic bounds. Whereas Iqbāl had ultimately reconciled Muslim nationalism with Islām, he held that they were incompatible. He therefore believed that the survival of the separate identity of Muslims as a secular nation was no better than their absorption into non-Muslim nationhood. Accordingly he believed that merely a Muslim majority country or an un-Islāmic government run by Muslims was not equivalent to *dār-al Islām.*

Sayyad Mawdūdi defined an Islāmic state as a divine democratic government, in which Muslims would have limited popular sovereignty under the suzerainty of God, so that His and the Prophet's (Pbuh) explicit commands could not be altered. He reasoned on the basis of the Qur'ān (8:72) that the Islāmic state is territorial, and should help other Muslims only if this did not conflict with its other commitments.

Earlier Sayyad Mawdūdi had held that it was obligatory on every Muslim to strive to establish such a government (needed to practically enforce Islām), if need be by *jihād*. However in 1940 and 1944 he outlined the process of the creation of an Islāmic state as an intellectual, at first an elite, and later a mass movement, based on education and training—he is now silent on the use of force. He felt that a nationalistic Muslim movement or state could not serve as the first step for its creation, since the latter must be free from all traces of nationalism. He did not agree with the likes of Mawlāna Madani that since divine government was unattainable in the present, Muslims should co-operate with others for deliverance from the British, and strive for it later in free India; for he felt that the Islāmic movement depended on faith and determination, rather than external factors.

In 1944 Sayyad Mawdūdi's stand regarding the Indian political situation again betrays ambiguity. While he declared that Muslims did not desire a national homeland since they were not a nation but a world-wide ideological group, he also held that in their capacity as a nation, their demand for political and economic independence was justified. In 1946 Sayyad Mawdūdi again emphasized collective organization and effort, for Islām could not be fully realized at the individual level alone. While he conceded that no single *al-jamā'at* comprising the whole *ummat* existed at present (to which every Muslim owed allegiance), he reasoned that this was inevitable in the initial stages of the movement, and hoped that since all the parties were working for the same ideal, they would ultimately unite in future.

Sayyad Mawdūdi had formed the Jamā'at-i Islāmi in 1941, its aim being the creation of a truly Islāmic society (through preaching, persuasion, and example), which would ultimately overthrow all godless systems, and replace them with the Islāmic—through incessant striving. In 1947 he would speak of influencing public opinion in order to create a mass movement to displace any system (including that in future Pakistan), based on secularism, democracy, and nationalism, even if it was run by Muslims. He now however appears to have accepted the idea of Pakistan as a Muslim, territorial, national state, reverting to his original view that Islām does not object to nationality and patriotism if these are free of prejudice, and within their natural limits. He also promised full support to the government of Pakistan if it would be Islāmic, and if not, believed that it could be moulded on these lines in future, whereas he had earlier denied this possibility.

We observe that religious authority was invoked by all Muslim thinkers, and the Qur'ān and *Ḥadīth* profusely quoted, often even to support two conflicting views, by means of varying interpretations and inferences. The concept of Islām serving as the basis of Muslim nationhood is also common to all the thinkers, but whereas for Sir Sayyad and Shibli it does not go beyond that, for Iqbāl it is the central idea, around which he weaves his views of Muslim nationhood. For Āzād and Mawlāna Madani it does not contradict in any way with a parallel Indian nationhood. Sayyad Mawdūdi's stand is fluctuating—whereas he ascribes to the idea initially, later he would deny that Muslims were a nation at all, and would ultimately try to reconcile both views. It is also worth remarking that all the thinkers were preoccupied (to a greater or lesser extent), with the problem of education, and its intimate relation to the question of Muslim nationhood, which is not surprising, since education has much to do with identity and self-perception.

An interesting point that emerges from this study is the ambiguity surrounding the word *qawm*. We have tried in the introduction, to define its English counterpart "nation", which is by no means an easy task. However the Urdu *qawm* proves to be more problematic, due to its extremely loose usage, and the fact that it connotes more than one form of the word "nation." We have already discussed in the First Chapter, the ambiguity surrounding Sir Sayyad's usage of the word. It became somewhat more well-defined later, but that did not altogether eliminate its complex character. The deliberate retention of the single English word "nation" for all its shades of meanings is meant (besides ensuring uniformity), to throw light on this very ambiguity.

Notes and References

1. *Hayāt-i Shibli* (n.p., n.d.) p. 296 *ff.*
2. *Musalmānoṇ ka Rawshan Mustaqbil* (Delhi, 1944) pp. 288-329.
3. *Muslim Līg Kya Hay*? (Delhi, 1945) pp. 29-31 and 33.
4. *The Destiny of Indian Muslims* (Bombay, 1965) p. 35.
5. "Political Objectives of the Khilāfat Movement", *Communal and Pan-Islāmic Trends in Colonial India*, ed. Mushirul Hasan (New Delhi, 1981) pp. 55 and 59.
6. "Revolutionaries, Pan-Islāmists and Bolsheviks: Mawlāna Abu'l Kalām Āzād and the Political Underworld in Calcutta, 1905-1925", *Ibid.*, pp. 59-60.

BIBLIOGRAPHY

PRIMARY SOURCES

English

Āzād, Abu'l Kalām. "Presidential Address to the Ramgarh Congress, March 1940." *Congress Presidential Addresses.* Ed. A.M. Zaidi. n.p., 1989, vol. V (1940-85).

_____, *Mawlana Azad: Selected Speeches and Statements.* Ed. P.N. Chopra. New Delhi, 1990.

Iqbāl, Muḥammad. *The Reconstruction of Religious Thought in Islam.* London, 1934.

_____, *Letters and Writings of Iqbal*, Ed. Bashir Aḥmad Dar, Karachi, 1967.

_____, *Letters of Iqbal*, Ed. Bashir Aḥmad Dar, Lahore, 1978.

_____, *Stray Reflections: A Notebook of Allama Iqbal.* Ed. Javid Iqbal, Lahore, 1961.

_____, *Speeches, Writings, and Statements of Iqbal.* Ed. Latif Aḥmad Sherwani, Lahore, 1977.

_____, *Speeches and Statements of Iqbal.* Ed. Shamloo, Lahore, 1944.

_____, *Iqbal: His Political Ideas at Crossroads: A Commentary on Unpublished Letters to Prof. Thompson, with Photographic Reproductions of the Original Letters*, Ed. S. Hasan Aḥmad, Aligarh, 1979.

_____, *Thoughts and Reflections of Iqbal*, Ed. Syed Abdul Vahid, Lahore, 1973.

Jinnāh, Muḥammad 'Ali. *Gandhi-Jinnah Talks : Text of Correspondence and Other Relevant Matters (July-Oct. 1944)*, New Delhi, 1944.

_____ , *Muhammad Ali Jinnah: An Ambassador of Unity: His Speeches and Writings (1912-17),* Madras, n.d.

_____ , *Quaid-i Azam Speaks: His Vision of Pakistan*, Karachi, 1991.

_____ , *Quaid-i Azam's Presidential Addresses, All India Muslim League (1937-1943)*, Delhi, 1945.

_____ , *Writings of the Quaid-i Azam*, Ed. Ahmad Saeed, Lahore, 1976.

_____ , *Quaid-i Azam Muhammad Ali Jinnah (Speeches, Statements, Writings, Letters, etc.)*, Ed. Mohd. Hanif Shahid, Lahore, 1976.

_____ , *Quaid-i Azam Muhammad Ali Jinnah: Speeches in the Legislative Council of India (1924-30)*, Ed. M. Rafique Afzal, Lahore, 1976.

_____ , *Selected Speeches and Statements of the Quaid-i Azam, Muhammad Ali Jinnah (1911-34 and 1947-48)*, Ed. M. Rafique Afzal, Lahore, 1973.

_____ , *Sayings of the Quaid-i Azam Muhammad Ali Jinnah*, Ed. Rizwan Aḥmad, Karachi, 1976.

_____ , *Quaid-i Azam Muhammad Ali Jinnah's Speeches in the Indian Legislative Assembly (1935-47),* Ed. Waheed Ahmad, Karachi, 1991.

_____ , *Quaid-i Azam Muhammad Ali Jinnah: The Nation's Voice Towards Consolidation: Speeches and Statements (March 1935-March 1940)*, Ed. Waheed Ahmad, Karachi, 1992.

Khān, Sayyad Aḥmad, *Political Profile of Sir Sayyid Ahmad Khan: A Documentary Record,* Ed. Hafeez Malik. Islāmabad, 1982.

_____ , *Writings and Speeches of Sir Syed Ahmad Khan*, Ed. Shan Mohammad, Bombay, 1972.

Mawdūdi, Sayyad Abu'l A'lá, *Fundamentals of Islam*, Trans., Lahore, 1978.

_____ , *Nationalism and India*, Trans., Malihabad, 1948.

_____ , *The Process of Islamic Revolution,* Trans., Lahore, 1979.

_____ , *Towards Understanding Islam*, Trans., Pathankot, 1944.

_____ , *A Short History of the Revivalist Movement in Islam*, Trans., Al-Ashari. Lahore, 1979.

_____ , *Witnesses Unto Mankind*, Trans., Khurram Murad, London, 1986.

_____ , *The Islamic Law and Constitution*, Trans., Khurshid Ahmad, Lahore, 1977.

Urdu

Āzād, Abu'l Kalām, *Mas'alah-i Khilāfat,* New Delhi, 1987.

_____, *Pagyhāmāt-i Āzād*, Bijnawr, n.d.

_____, *Maḍāmīn Lisān-al Ṣidq*, Ed. 'Abd-al Qawi Dasnawi, Lucknow, 1967.

_____, *Mawlāna Abu'l Kalām Āzād ki Taqrīren,* Ed. Anwar 'Ārif, Delhi, 1988.

_____, *Mukālimāt-i Abu'l Kalām Āzād,* Ed. 'Aqīl Aḥmad Ja'fri, Hydarābād, 1944.

_____, *Ā'īnah-i Abu'l Kalām Āzād*, Ed. Aṭīq Ṣiddiqi, Delhi, 1976.

_____, *Ṣubh-i Ummīd*, Ed. Ḥāfiz Fayyāz Aḥmad, New Delhi, 1959, Vol. I.

_____, *Khuṭbāt-i Āzād*, Ed. Malik Ram, New Delhi, 1974.

_____, *Bayān Mawlāna Abu'l Kalām Āzād,* Ed. Mushtāq Aḥmad, Meerut, n.d.

_____, *Majmū'ah Maḍāmīn Mawlāna Abu'l Kalām Āzād*, Ed. Mushtāq Aḥmad, Meerut, n.d. Vol. VI.

_____, *Tāzah Maḍāmīn Abu'l Kalām Āzād,* Ed. Mushtāq Aḥmad, Meerut, n.d.

Iqbāl, Muḥammad, *Maḍāmin-i Iqbāl*, Ed. *Taṣdīq Ḥusayn Tāj*, Hydarābād Dakkan, 1941.

Khān, Sayyad Aḥmad, *Khuṭbāt-i Sir Sayyad*, Ed. Muḥammad. Ismā'īl Pānīpati. 2 vols., Lahore, 1972-73.

_____, *Maktubāt-i Sir Sayyad*, Ed. Muḥammad. Ismā'īl Pānīpati, 2 vols., Lahore, 1976 and 1985.

_____, *Maqālāt-i Sir Sayyad*, Ed. Muḥammad. Ismā'īl Pānīpati, 16 vols., Lahore, 1941-65.

Madani, Sayyad Ḥusayn Aḥmad, *Khuṭbah-i Ṣadārat, Jamī'at-al 'Ulamā'-i Hind ka Sālānah Ijlās, Saharanpur,* Delhi, 1945.

_____, *Muslim Līg Kya Hay*? Delhi, 1945.

_____, *Muttaḥidah Qawmiyyat awr Islām*, New Delhi, n.d.

_____, *Pākīstān Kya Hay*? 2 vols, Delhi, 1946.

_____, *Taqrīr Jalsah Syohārah*, n.p., n.d.

_____, *Nazaryah-i Qawmiyyat par Mawlāna Ḥusayn Aḥmad Madani awr Iqbāl ki 'Ālimānah Khaṭ-o Kitābat*., Lahore, n.d.

_____, *Maktūbāt-i Shaykh-al Islām*, Ed. Najm-al Dīn Iṣlāḥi., 3 vols., Deoband, 1371 A.H.

Mawdūdi, Sayyad Abu'l A'lá. *Ḥaqīqat-i Jihād*, Lahore, 1946.

_____, *Jamā'at-i Islāmi ki Da'wat,* Delhi, 1972.

_____, *Mas'alah-i Qawmiyyat*, Delhi, 1962.

_____, *Musalmān awr Mawjūdah Siyāsi Kashmakash*, vol. I, Pathankot, n.d. vol. III, Delhi, 1962.

_____ , *Naya Nizām-i Ta'līm*, Pathānkot, n.d.
_____ , *Nishān-i Rāh,* Pathankot, n.d.
_____ , *Rāh-i 'Amal*, Haydarābād Dakkan, 1946.
_____ , *Rasā'il-o Masā'il*, 4 vols., Delhi, 1970-71.
_____ , *Tafhīmāt*, 2 vols., Delhi, 1967-68.
_____ , *Tanqīhāt*, Pathānkot, n.d.
_____ , *Tehrīk-i Āzādi-i Hind awr Musalmān,* Ed. Khurshīd Aḥmad, Lahore, 1964, vol. I.
Nu'māni, Shibli, *Safarnāmah-i Rūm-o Miṣr-o Shām*, A'zamgarh, 1340 A.H.,
_____ , *Bāqiyyāt-i Shibli,* Ed. Mushtāq Ḥusayn, Lahore, 1965.
_____ , *Maqālāt-i Shibli*, Ed. Mas'ud 'Ali Nadwi and Sayyad Sulaymān Nadwi, 8 vols., A'zamgarh, 1932-65.
_____ , *Khuṭbāt-i Shibli*, Ed. Sayyad Sulaymān Nadwi, A'zamgarh, 1965.

SECONDARY SOURCES

English

Ahmad, Aziz, *Islamic Modernism in India and Pakistan (1857-1964)*, London, 1967.
Faruqi, Ziya-ul Hasan, *The Deoband School and the Demand for Pakistan*, Bombay, 1963.
Gangadharan, K.K. Ed. *Indian National Consciousness: Growth and Development*, New Delhi, 1972.
Hasan, Mushirul, Ed. *Communal and Pan-Islamic Trends in Colonial India*, New Delhi, 1981.
Hussain, S. Abid, *The Destiny of Indian Muslims,* Bombay, 1965.
Malik, Hafeez, *Muslim Nationalism in India and Pakistan*, Washington, 1963.
Murad, Mehr Afroz, *Intellectual Modernism of Shibli Numani: An Exposition of His Religious and Socio-Political Ideas,* Lahore, 1976.
Renan, Ernest, "What is a Nation?" *Modern Political Thought: The Great Issues*, Ed. William Ebenstein, New Delhi, 1974.
Shakir, Moin, *Khilafat to Partition: A Survey of Major Political Trends Among Indian Muslims During 1919-47,* New Delhi, 1970.
Smith, Wilfred Cantwell, *Modern Islam in India: A Social Survey*, Lahore, 1969.

Urdu

Ḥali, Alṭāf Ḥusayn, *Ḥayāt-i Jāwīd,* Kanpur, 1901.
Muḥammad Ismā'īl Pānīpati, Ed., *Sayyad Aḥmad Khān Kā Safarnāmah-i Panjāb*, Delhi, 1979.
Nadwi, Sayyad Sulaymān, *Ḥayāt-i Shibli*, n.p., n.d.
Ṣābri, Ḥabīb-al Raḥmān Khān, *Miftāḥ-al Taqwīm*, New Delhi, 1961.

INDEX

W

Z